MOVEMENT FOR DEMOCRACY IN MYANMAR

Movement for Democracy in Myanmar

Langpoklakpam Suraj Singh

AKANSHA PUBLISHING HOUSE
NEW DELHI-110 002 (INDIA)

AKANSHA PUBLISHING HOUSE
4649B/21, Ansari Road
Daryaganj, New Delhi - 110 002
Phones: 011-23263193, 9811582579
Email: ektabooks@yahoo.com

Movement for Democracy in Myanmar

First Published, 2006

ISBN 81-8370-045-4

[The responsibility for the facts stated, conclusions reached etc. is entirely that of the Author. The Publisher bears no responsibility for them, whatsoever.]

PRINTED IN INDIA

Published by M.P. Misra for Akansha Publishing House, New Delhi-110059 and Printed at Tarun Offset Press, Delhi.

Contents

Professor and Associate Dean
Faculty of Political Science,
Thammasat University
Bangkok 10200, Thailand

Foreword

Dr. Langpoklakpam Suraj Singh's book manifests the scholarly consciousness in its conceptualization and methodology and theory-building. Drawing on the work of other foreign scholars, he delves into the perceptions, norms, and experiences of knowledgeable Myanmar informants to get their view of the Movement for Democracy in Myanmar during 1988-1997 as well as the latest developments on the issue in the new millennium.

As a researcher and teacher of Political Science, I find his work very helpful indeed especially in my experiences on Southeast Asia. This book will also contribute to scholars on Southeast Asia, particularly on Myanmar.

I am privileged to be Dr. Suraj Singh's guide in this study and to have the opportunity of writing this foreword to truly significant, original contribution to knowledge and understanding on Movement for Democracy in Myanmar. Based on primary and secondary data from various sources, this study exemplifies what a serious scholar can accomplish with imagination and discipline and no little "blood, sweat, and tears".

September 29, 2005 **Professor Sida Sonsri**

Preface

The present work is an attempt to examine and evaluate the movement for democracy in Myanmar in the context of the rapidly increasing trend of democratisation in the world. Initially in its thesis form the study primarily covers the period from 1988-1997. However, in this volume I have taken the study further up to the early part of 2005 updating and revising it thus.

In 1988, Myanmar witnessed, for the first time in its history, one of the largest mass uprisings for restoration of democracy. It was a culmination of long years of neglect under authoritarian rule. Faulty policies of the military rulers, based on their perverted version of socialism, ultimately brought Myanmar down to the level of begging from being one of the richest countries in South East Asia which even peace loving Myanmarese could no longer bear.

The post-independence history of Myanmar, with the exception of the era of parliamentary democracy from 1948-1958, and 1960-1962, is a history of authoritarianism. Soon after its independence in January 1948 it adopted a parliamentary form of democracy following the ideals of its founder father, *Bogyoke* Aung San. However, democracy could not survive long. Growing political crisis, deteriorating economic condition, increasing ethnic and communist insurgency, intra-party conflict within the ruling Anti-Fascist People's Freedom League (AFPFL), hesitant attitude towards development programmes, inability to ensure people's security, weak stand against the Shan's demand for more autonomy, state religion issue once more forced authoritarian rule to take roots in the country with the army seizing political power in 1962. An interim body called the Revolutionary Council (RC) was formed for carrying out administration.

No doubt, the Myanmarese military was able to establish its own credibility in the eyes of the masses with the successful caretaker role it had played from 1958-1960. The Revolutionary Council (RC) under General Ne Win projected themselves as the most disciplined patriots equipped with moral qualities and efficient administration that the civilian leaders dispossessed. Moreover, the fact that Ne Win being one of the "Thirty Comrades" who struggled for Independence under the able leadership of Gen. Aung San gave more credibility to the junta. He justified the seizing of power on the ground of (i) safeguarding the unity of the country; (ii) establishing of socialism; and (iii) preserving the culture and tradition. The RC, upon taking over power, started with a strong nationalistic ideology which was anti-communist and anti-foreign elements. And, at the same time, it was to lead the country along a line known as "Burmese Way to Socialism". With the adoption of the above ideal the new military government started for a sweeping change in the socio-political and economic set up of the country. A large number of formal institutions, starting from court to parliament, were either abolished or dismissed. It remained in its historic political isolation in 1964, practically cutting itself off from the rest of the world. It ceased to be a member of the British Commonwealth and the Non-Aligned Movement (NAM). At home, these military leaders ruled the country by decrees, eliminated systematically all opposition, jailed elected and popular leaders and forced others to go into exile. It established the Burma Socialist Programme Party (BSPP), the only legal political party allowed to function. Newly drafted constitution of 1974 inaugurated a constitutional dictatorship with the BSPP as the only ruling party and the country's name was changed from 'Union of Burma' to 'Socialist Republic of the Union of Burma'.

Outside the government, the military rulers used repressive measures against university students, Buddhist monks and opposition leaders who were critical of the military government. A hard line approach in the form of heavy military campaigns was also carried out against ethnic rebels and leftist undergrounds.

In the economic field, the military government under Gen. Ne Win, was unable to cope with the situation. Poor experience of the military in the management of economic affairs resulted in utter failure. In the initial stage of his rule it seemed that the Myanmarese economy was moving in the right direction. Dismissal of all foreign businessmen and all foreign investment, nationalisation of commercial and business sectors were seen as positive steps towards rapid economic development. However, despite all these steps, the economy was, is no way, taking the country towards its desired goal. Domestic products were far short of target, bureaucratic corruption was widespread, black marketeering flourished, unemployment and under employment became rampant. Smuggling became widespread. Inflation became uncontrollable. Foreign debt rose. The result was the continuation of economic stagnation. Myanmar, previously an important rice exporting country became a rice-rationed country. In 1987, the United Nations declared Myanmar as the Least Developed Country (LDC) in the world.

Under the circumstances, slightest provocation seemed to spark off a movement. Withdrawal of high currency notes from circulation under its demonetisations of 1985 and 1987, rice shortage acted as catalytic agent. Widespread resentment and discontent on the part of the common masses brought them to the streets with a tendency of revolt. In short the root cause of the present democracy movement in Myanmar, to a great extent, could be traced to the dictatorial and arbitrary rule of Gen. Ne Win and his perverted and ill-conceived socialist based economic goals and policies.

From March 1988 onwards, a series of students' demonstrations took place. And ultimately it resulted in the epoch making '8-8-88 Uprising' demanding an end to dictatorship. It was a turning point in the history of Myanmar. Thousands and thousands of people from all walks of life came out to the streets of towns and cities demanding the end of

Ne Win's rule. The army reacted fiercely to subdue the movement. In another move, the BSPP, in order to contain the widespread demonstrations, declared in September 1988: (i) to hold free elections within three months, (ii) to dissociate armed forces, police and bureaucrats from the BSPP. Immediately after the announcement a new junta under the leadership of Gen. Saw Maung, a Ne Win protégé, seized power on 18 September 1988. He formed a 9-Member State Law and Order Restoration Council (SLORC), banned demonstrations, imposed dusk to dawn curfew and massacred not less than 1000 demonstrators, mostly students.

SLORC announced to hold a multi-party democratic election and allowed for the first time since 1962 to form political parties. Many political parties and leaders emerged. The most prominent one is Aung San Suu Kyi, the daughter of Gen. Aung San, and her party, the National League for Democracy (NLD). Former Prime Minister U Nu formed his League for Democracy and Peace. The BSPP changed its name and registered it as the National Unity Party (NUP).

The promised election was held on 27 May 1990. To the surprise of many it was purely a free and fair election as the junta was overconfident of its victory. But contrary to the expectation of the junta, the pro-democracy groups swept the polls with the NLD alone capturing 392 seats out of 485. The NUP and its allies got only 10 seats thereby the Myanmarese giving a clear-cut mandate for the NLD.

In spite of the landslide victory and repeated international pressure for democratic transformation and peaceful transfer of power the military government (changed from SLORC to SPDC in 1997), even after more than 15 years, is still not yet ready to hand over power to the duly elected civilians. In the pretext of safeguarding the unity and integrity of the country it went on postponing the issue of transferring power to the elected people. Instead, the SPDC regime resorts to a systematic arrest and harassment of the elected persons specially belonging to the NLD led by Aung San Suu Kyi and treat them with brutality. No doubt, there was the fear on the part of the military leaders of vindictiveness once the power changed hands.

The delay in handing over power to the civilians, large-scale cases of human rights violation by the SPDC invited international condemnation. Subsequently, Japan, UK, US, Canada, Australia and EU imposed economic sanctions and restrictions against the SPDC. Efforts have also been going on the part of the UN to pressurise the junta to bring about an amicable settlement of the ongoing issue. However, the policy of 'Constructive Engagement' followed by the Association of South East Asian Nations (ASEAN) by taking Myanmar in its fold in 1997; India, establishing a more vigorous trade and diplomatic relationship with Myanmar; and China's strong support towards the country had greatly enhanced the legitimacy of the regime but weakening the movement for Democracy. More tragic part is that no nation came forward to recognise the National Coalition Government of the Union of Burma (NCGUB), the Government in exile, formed by some of the duly elected representatives.

Notwithstanding all the shortcomings, movement for democracy draws support from the general masses including the students and ethnic rebels in and around Myanmar projecting Aung San Suu Kyi, the Nobel Laureate (1991) as their undisputed leader. Myanmarese living outside the country are lobbying mostly the western powers to exert pressure on the SPDC to honour the results of the elections held earlier. Suu Kyi demands transfer of political power to the duly elected civilians.

The present work is an attempt to examine various aspects relevant to the movement for democracy in Myanmar and its prospects. Chapter I briefly discusses the historical background in which political leadership and ideology are discussed for a better understanding of the role played by the political leaders in the process of nation building in the post independence era. Chapter II deals with the economic initiatives undertaken by the Revolutionary Council headed by Ne Win and see how far these initiatives and fallouts are responsible for the mass uprising of 1988. In the following chapter political aspects are examined. While doing so an attempt is made to see how far political aspects became so intimately associated with the country's economy and government's performance. Various political aspects also are taken into consideration for an objective assessment. Special attention is focussed on the remaining four chapters to highlight the movement proper and the issues so closely associated with it. Lastly, the concluding part sums up the various stages of the movement; and finally comes to the possible outcome of the movement.

The work primarily covers the period from 1988 to 1997 although it does refer to the important developments which have taken place subsequently. Further, sequence and events related with the movement has been updated till the beginning of 2005.The year 1988 is significant for launching the movement in a mass scale unprecedented in the history of Myanmar; while 1997 is important as Myanmar was admitted into the ASEAN as its member thereby confirming the legitimacy of the military rule in disregard of popular demand and electoral results as well as protection from the condemnation and pressure of the international community for its violation of human rights.

In examining and evaluating the movement the name of the country herein my work I have used both 'Burma' and 'Myanmar' wherever it is necessary and convenient. I also took the liberty of using both the old as well new name of places in the country invariably wherever necessary.

Langpoklakpam Suraj Singh

Acknowledgements

This work is the outcome of my Ph.D. thesis submitted to Manipur University, Manipur (India). The subject being a dynamic one I took my studies further and had added one more material to the work on the recent developments and events associated with the movement for democracy in Myanmar. Thus the effort is to take the work to its most current stage.

In the preparation of this work I was greatly assisted by many people in different ways in providing me suggestions, information, rare source materials or helped me locate other sources and personal contacts coupled with guidance and moral support.

At the very outset I am especially indebted to my supervisor and guide Dr Konsam Ibo Singh, Ph.D. (JNU), Associate Professor, Department of Political Science, Manipur University. Without his constant help, sensible intellectual guidance and untiring encouragement it would not have been possible for me to complete the work. My sincere thanks also go to my teachers Prof. Ksh. Bimola Devi, Dr. S. Rajen Singh Head of Department, Dr. Mrs. Ratna Tikoo, Dr. G. I. Sharma, Dr. S. Mangi Singh and Dr. L. Rajen Singh in the Department of Political Science, Manipur University, for their encouragement and valuable suggestions.

I would like to express my sincere appreciation and humble gratitude to Ajaan Sida Sonsri, Associate Professor and Director for Special Training Programme, International Relations, Faculty of Political Science, Thammasat University, Bangkok, who was my guide and guardian during my one month stay in Thailand in January-February 2001. It was under her guidance that I could gain best possible benefit of my visit to the country.

I am also deeply grateful to many scholars, student activists, social workers, leaders of Myanmarese insurgent groups and friends for their unconditional help and cooperation during my stay in Thailand. Many of them have spared time for me despite having tight schedule and personal risk. I would like to thank Pornpimon Trichot, Assistant Director, Institute of Asian Studies, Chulalongkorn University, Bangkok; Aye Saung, Chairman, People's Liberation Front (PLF), Chiangmai; Kyaw Hla, Chairman, Muslim Liberation Organisation of Burma (MLOB), Chiangmai; Saw Barnabas (formerly of KNU), Saw Wingate and Dr Aung Tun of National Health and Education Committee (NHEC), Chiangmai; Aung Thu Nyein, Vice-Chairman of Democratic Party for a New Society (DPNS), Chiangmai; Kduensai Jaiyen of Shan Herald Agency News (SHAN), Chiangmai; and members of Students and Youth Committee of Burma (SYCB), Chiangmai. My friend Hla Htay of ABSDF was my companion in the journey to Chiangmai and it was he who made initial arrangement for my contact with other important Burmese groups there. For all these and more I am grateful to him. I am also indebted to Yee Htun (NHEC), Soe Khaing (ABSDF) and Aung Naing (formerly ABSDF and presently of Network for Democracy and Development) for arranging overall contacts and making my visit to Chiangmai a success.

Among the Burmese friends I am most indebted to Ko Thein of ABSDF – Western Burma (Manipur) through whom it was possible for me to establish a vast networking with all those involved in the Myanmarese democracy movement and also the opportunity to understand it from a very close quarter. It was through his enduring cooperation and help that I could access to lot of source material. It will be failing on my part if I do not mention the contributions of Ko Gyi of FTUB's, Imphal office, Moe Zoe and (late) Ko Tin Win of ABSDF's Imphal office, and Ko Osho.

I am also thankful to Aung San Myint (FTUB, Bangkok), Dr Than Khe (Executive, ABSDF) and Dr Aung Kyaw Oo (Executive, ABSDF) for extending their invaluable help both in India and Thailand. I would like to thank Dr Tint Swe (MP), U Bo Thaung (MP), U Mya Win (MP), Ramjeet Verma (NLD-LA), Dr Zaw Win Aung (FTUB), Kyaw Than (Vice-President, ABSL) for giving a detailed insight into the movement. My thanks also go to Cassey of ABSDF's Bangkok office, Ko Zin Naing of ABSDF's Delhi office and Ko Nyo of Radio Free Asia. I am also thankful to Om of Metro Guest House, Bangkok, for assisting me during my stay in Thailand.

I record my humble gratitude for Indian Council of Social Science Research, New Delhi, in general and it's Assistant Director in the same office, Jessy George, in particular for making my field trip to Thailand possible. My thanks also goes to Dr.Partho Ghosh, one of the Directors of ICSSR, for the same. The field trip grant greatly helped in enhancing the quality of my research work at a time when it became really difficult to get source materials on Myanmar. Thailand, being one of the most important hub of the Myanmarese democracy movement helped me immensely.

In getting important and rare source materials I have to depend lots on sources and friends in different parts of the world for which I remain always indebted to them. To mention a few I am deeply grateful to Faith Doherty, Executive Director of South East Asian Information Network, Thailand, for sending me important research materials in the initial stage of my research; and Donna Guest, Researcher (Southeast Asia) of Amnesty International, for sending me publications on Myanmar.

I would also like to express my thanks to the library staff of the of the Faculty of Political Science, Thammasat University, the staff of Jawaharlal Nehru University Library (New Delhi) and the library staff of Manipur University. Thanks also to K.Subhas Singh, Stenographer, Department of Political Science, Manipur University, and Laishram Ibochoubi Singh, Assistant in the Examination Department of the same university, for assisting me on matters relating to official work and timely communication of any information related with me. I would be failing on my part if I do not mention the help of Joykumar Singh, Stenographer at the office of Dean of Students Welfare, for typing many of my early drafts, Lokeshwor Singh of Modern Press for penultimate drafts, and Ayekpam Rajmani Luwang, Jr. Stenographer, Department of Mathematics, for the final draft of my work.

My thanks also go to K. Indramani Singh, Lecturer of D.M.College(Arts), who is my colleague as well as a sort of elder brother, for his help and cooperation. I am also thankful to Dr. Laishram Suresh for his helpful suggestions in the initial stage of my work.

Regarding my personal friends, it would be individious to single out individuals, nevertheless I thanks Vikas Jain and Khoiba for their wholehearted cooperation whenever necessary. I would also like to express my special and heartfelt gratitude to Suraj for his unwavering friendship. It is not always possible to mention all my well wishers who had helped me in one stage or the other, but they, I believe, know of my gratitude.

Above all, I dedicate my whole work to my parents and my family members for all their sacrifices - especially my father, who instil in me the intellectual and psychological strength, and my mother, who gave me the meaning of life with her intense love and care. Words are not sufficient to express for what they did for me. Besides, my brothers and sisters - Indugiri, Lakhikanta, Mira, Shakhensana and Laxmi - had all stood by me with their love and affection. And my wife, Padma, had continuously given me psychological support and constant inspiration - a significant force in the final stage of my work. All of them had patiently endured with me during my long hours of research and their constant encouragement helps at times when the mind became tedious and the body became fatigue.

Lastly my special thanks and appreciation to Mr. M.P. Mishra, Akansha Publishing House, for the zeal shown in bringing out the book, that too at a very short period.

And in the end I bow my head to the Supreme One in the universe, the Almighty, for making me what I am today.

Langpoklakpam Suraj Singh

Abbreviations and Acronyms

AASYC	:	All Arakanese Students and Youth Congress.
ABFSU	:	All Burma Federation of Student Union.
ABMU	:	All Burma Muslim Union.
ABSDA	:	All Burma Students' Democratic Association.
ABSDF	:	All Burma Students' Democratic Front.
ABSL	:	All Burma Students' League.
ABSU	:	All Burma Students' Union.
ABYLH	:	All Burma Youth League Headquarter.
ABYMU	:	All Burma Young Monk's Union.
ADB/ASDB	:	Asian Development Bank.
ADNSC	:	Anti-Military Dictatorship National Solidarity Committee.
AFPFL	:	Anti-Fascist People's Freedom League.
ALP	:	Arakan Liberation Party.
ARF	:	ASEAN Regional Forum.
ASEAN	:	Association of South East Asian Nations.
BBC	:	British Broadcasting Corporation.
BDA	:	Burma Defence Army.
BIA	:	Burma Independence Army.
BIMSTEC	:	Bangladesh, India, Myanmar, Sri Lanka, Thailand Economic Cooperation.

BRO	:	Border Road Organisation.
BSPP	:	Burma Socialist Programme Party.
BUDP	:	Burma United Democratic Party.
BWPP	:	Burma Workers' and Peasants' Party.
BWS	:	Burmese Way to Socialism.
CNVP	:	Chin National Vanguard Party.
CPA	:	Communist Party of Arakan.
CPB	:	Communist Party of Burma.
CRDB	:	Committee for Restoration of Democracy in Burma.
CRPP	:	Committee Representing People's Parliament.
DAB	:	Democratic Alliance of Burma.
DAC	:	Development Assistance Committee of the OECD.
DDSI	:	Directorate of Defence Services Intelligence.
DFB	:	Democratic Front of Burma.
DKBO	:	Democratic Kayin Buddhist Organisation.
DPNS	:	Democratic Party for a New Society.
EEC	:	European Economic Community.
EGYMA	:	Evergreen Young Men's Association.
EU	:	European Union.
FDI	:	Foreign Direct Investment.
FEER	:	Far Eastern Economic Review.
FTUB	:	Federation of Trade Unions - Burma.
GDP	:	Gross Domestic Product.
GOSDA	:	Graduates and Old Students Democratic Association.
GSP	:	Generalized System of Preference.

IBRD	:	International Bank for Reconstruction and Development.
ICFTU	:	International Confederation of Free Trade Union.
IDA	:	International Development Association.
ILO	:	International Labour Organisation.
IMF	:	International Monetary Fund.
KDA	:	Kachin Democratic Army.
KIA	:	Kachin Independence Army.
KIO	:	Kachin Independence Organisation.
KNDO	:	Karen National Defence Organisation.
KNLP	:	Karen New Land Party.
KNPLF	:	Karenni Nationalities People's Liberation Front.
KNPP	:	Karenni National progressive Party.
KNU	:	Karen National Union.
KNUP	:	Karen National United Party.
LDA	:	League for Democratic Alliance.
LDC	:	Least Developed Country.
LDF	:	Lahu Democratic Front.
LDP	:	League for Democracy and Peace.
LNUP	:	Lahu National United Party.
MEIC	:	Myanmar Export and Import Corporation.
MFN	:	Most Favoured Nation.
MIS	:	Military Intelligence Services.
MLOB	:	Muslim Liberation Organisation of Burma.
MNDAA	:	Myanmar National Democratic Alliance Army.
MPU	:	Member of Parliamentary Union.

MTA	:	Mong Tai Army.
NAM	:	Non - Aligned Movement.
NCGUB	:	National Coalition Government of the Union of Burma.
NCUB	:	National Council of Union of Burma.
NDA	:	National Democratic Alliance.
NDF	:	National Democratic Front.
NDUF	:	National Democratic United Front.
NHEC	:	National Health and Education Council.
NLD	:	National League for Democracy.
NLDJ	:	National League for Democracy and Justice.
NLD-LA	:	National League for Democracy-Liberated Area.
NMSP	:	New Mon State Party.
NPF	:	National Politics Front.
NSCN (IM)	:	National Socialist Council of Nagalim (Issac-Muivah).
NSCN (K)	:	National Socialist Council of Nagalim (Khaplang).
NUF	:	National Unity Front.
NUP	:	National Unity Party.
ODA	:	Official Development Assistance.
OECD	:	Organization for Economic Co-operation and Development.
OPEC	:	Organisation of Petroleum Exporting Countries.
OSI	:	Open Society Institute.
PDP	:	Parliamentary Democracy Party.
PLA	:	Patriotic Liberation Army.
PLP	:	Patriotic League for Peace.

PNA	:	Pao National Army.
PNO	:	Pao National Organisation.
PPLO	:	PaO People's Liberation Organisation
PPP	:	People's Progressive Party.
PRA	:	People's Revolutionary Army.
PSDP	:	People's Students Democratic Party.
PSLA	:	Palaung State Liberation Army.
PSLF	:	Palaung State Liberation Front.
PSLP	:	Paluang State Liberation Party.
PVO	:	People's Volunteer Organisation.
RC	:	Revolutionary Council.
RIT	:	Rangoon Institute of Technology.
Rmb	:	Renminbi (Chinese currency).
RPF	:	Revolutionary People's Front.
RUSU	:	Rangoon University Students' Union.
SAIN	:	Southeast Asian Information Network.
SCME	:	System of Correlation Between Man and His Environment.
SDU	:	Shan Democratic Union.
SEE	:	State Economic Enterprise.
SF	:	Swiss Franc.
SHAN	:	Shan Herald Agency for News.
SLORC	:	State Law and Order Restoration Council.
SPDC	:	State Peace and Development Council.
SRPD	:	Students' Revolutionary Party for Democracy.
SSA	:	Shan State Army.
SSIA	:	Shan State Independence Army.
SSNLPLO	:	Shan State National People's Liberation Organization.

SSPP	:	Shan State Progress Party.
SYCB	:	Students and Youths Committee of Burma.
UBMAFPFL	:	Union of Burma Main Anti Fascists People Freedom League.
ULFA	:	United Liberation Front of Assam.
UN	:	United Nations
UNCHR	:	United Nations Commission on Human Rights.
UNDP	:	United Nationals Development Programme.
UNDP	:	United Nations Development Programme.
UNHCR	:	United Nations High Commissioner for Refugees.
UNHRC	:	United Nations Human Rights Commission
UNICEF	:	United Nations Children's Fund.
UNLF	:	United National Liberation Front.
UNTA	:	United Nations Regular Programme of Technical Assistance.
USDA	:	Union Solidarity and Development Association.
UWSA	:	United Wa State Army.
VOA	:	Voice of America.
WFP	:	World Food Programme.
WNO	:	Wa National Organization.

Glossary

Adipati	:	Head of state.
Baht	:	Thai currency.
Bogyoke	:	Army officer or General.
Daw	:	Courtesy title given to Burmese ladies.
Dhamma	:	Buddhist law and teaching.
Dobhama Asiayone	:	'We Burmans Association'.
Ko	:	Literally mean 'elder brother', respectful term of address as between equals.
Kyat	:	Burmese currency.
Lanzin	:	Burmese name for BSPP, mean 'new light'.
Lon Htein	:	Riot police.
Ma	:	Burmese form of address to a young female.
Min Ko Naing	:	Mean 'Conqueror of kings'.
Naing or Ngan	:	Mean State.
Ngapi	:	Paste of fermented fish.
Pyidaungsu	:	Union party.
Pyidawtha	:	'Welfare State' or (literally) 'pleasant country'.
Pyithu Hluttaw	:	National Assembly.
Sangha	:	'Assembly of monks' or 'order of monks'.

Saw	:	Respectful term of address to a Karen elder.
Sayadaw	:	Head monk of a Buddhist monastery.
Shwe	:	Gold or Golden.
Sinyetha	:	Poor man's party.
Tatmadaw	:	The Armed Forces of Burma.
Thakins	:	Masters.
Thanaka	:	A traditional cosmetic use as face cream
U	:	Literally mean 'uncle', respectful term of address to a gentleman.
Vinaya	:	Code of conduct for the monastic order.
Yahanpyo	:	Young Monks Association.

List of Tables

1

Introduction

Liberal democracy or democratisation is the new order of the present age. It is steadily gaining ground around the globe. The world today is coming rapidly under the influence of a new 'wave of democracy'- the emphasis being more on the Third World countries. Transition from authoritarian to democratic forms of governance has been going on in countries of Asia, Africa, Latin America and former communist countries of Europe. This wave of change had engulfed many of the previous military and autocratic regimes. Many of the rigid regimes of Eastern Europe have given way to their people's aspiration for a change, former military dictators prescribed new versions of democratisation, party conferences in Africa gently depose their dictators, and non-government bodies have become the new ray of hope for a democratic awakening in the world. Myanmar remains an exception.

Burma, now called Myanmar by the junta, is the largest of all the countries of mainland Southeast Asia. It has an area of 676,553 sq.km having a population of 48.4 million. Burmans or Bamars constitute around 68 per cent of the entire population and inhabits in the plains of the country. There are a number of ethnic minorities which surrounds the fertile plains. Among the ethnic minorities Shans, Karens, Rakhines, Kachins, Mons, Chins, Kayahs, Pa-Os, Lahus are prominent. The Shans constitute around 9 per cent, the Karens 7 per cent, the Rakhines 4 per cent, the Mons and

Kachins1 per cent each while the others constitute less than 1 per cent each. There are a number of Indians, Chinese, and Pakistanis. Chinese constitute around 3 per cent, the Indians around 2 per cent. Buddhist constitute around 84 per cent, Christians around 4 per cent of which 3 per cent are Baptists and 1 per cent is Roman Catholics, while Muslims are around 4 per cent and others 3 per cent.

In the 1930s Myanmarese political life was largely dominated by the '*Thakin* Movement'. The *Thakin* Movement primarily aimed at developing a ' master mentality' instead of 'slave mentality' as social stratification was prevalent in the Myanmarese society in which British colonisers were regarded as 'masters'. Therefore, the young leaders addressed themselves as *Thakins* as a form of respect. Some of the prominent *Thakins* were Aung San, U Nu, etc.

In 1935 *Thakins* Maung (later U Nu) and Aung San became the President and Secretary of the Rangoon University Students' Union respectively. Both of them were expelled from the University for publishing an article. Though they were readmitted after an agitation, they had already established themselves as future politicians. In 1936 two of the *Thakins* got elected to the legislature. However, they were not guided by a single political ideology. No doubt, they were greatly influenced by Fabian Socialism and Marxism. Unlike others they were mostly secular, non-communal in their application. Aung San was a product of this approach having a broader outlook who mostly thought of the entire nation including the minorities instead of only for the *Burmans* or *Bamars*. Immediately before the outbreak of the Second World War Aung San became the General Secretary of a newly formed alliance known as the 'Freedom Block' which was formed by the main faction of the *Dohbama Asiayone*, led by Ko Daw Hmaing and *Sinyetha* led by Dr Ba Maw. The young *Dohbama* members who joined the party became the radical younger generation members. In 1940 when the Japanese accepted the proposal of Dr Ba Maw for military training the legendary 30 comrades led by Aung San left for Tokyo between March and July 1941. Indeed, the plan was prepared by Aung

San. The group was supposed to receive military training and instruction on how to cooperate with invading Japanese forces. Included among them was that post office clerk Shu Maung (Ne Win).

During the course of the Second World War Aung San and others established Burma Independence Army (BIA). Contrary to the British policy of recruitment of minorities into the Myanmarese army, mainly the Chins, Kachins and Karens, Aung San recruited Burmans more. The BIA also targeted the Indians whom they saw as an ally of the British colonialism, hated the Karens, as would be fifth columnist. In August 1942 Dr Ba Maw became the *adipati* (equivalent of German fuehrer). Aung San was made the War Minister and the Commander of the 4000 strong Burma Defence Army (BDA), the successor of BIA. With Japanese help they declared Myanmar as an independent country though their government was regarded as a puppet. Burma National Army (BNA), new name of the BDA, the Communist Party of Burma (CPB) and Peoples' Revolutionary Army (PRA), a new under ground front, the Anti-Fascist Organisation was formed but was again renamed the Anti-Fascist People's Freedom League (AFPFL) in August 1945. The new front was led by the Commander- in - Chief Aung San but the CPB also was behind the organisation.

When the tide of the war was not in favour of the Japanese the AFPFL turned against Japan and established contact with the Allied Powers. It was during this time that Aung San distanced himself from the CPB. In July 1946 the power within the AFPFL compelled *Thakin* Than Tun to resign as General Secretary of the party. The AFPFL and some remnants of the PRA and his own personal army numbering about ten thousand was reorganised into the Peoples' Volunteer Organisation (PVO). The British government made an offer to Aung San about the transfer of power to the AFPFL in September 1946. He accepted the British offer on behalf of the party. He also accepted the position of the Governor's Executive Council, with himself appointed Counsellor for Defence and Deputy Chairman or *de facto* Prime Minister. The CPB strongly denounced his move and finally broke with AFPFL. The AFPFL remained the only one properly organised party to deal with the British government. Though denounced by the CPB Aung San took the pangs of touring most of the ethnic minority inhabited areas to win them over. He allowed the terms of the minorities to be incorporated in the constitution. While the drafting of the country's new constitution was going on Aung San, along with his six ministers were assassinated. U Nu became the leader of the AFPFL and subsequently the first Prime Minister of Independent Myanmar.

After about thirty years of struggle Myanmar got its independence on 4 January 1948, six months after the assassination of Bogyoke Aung San – the Maker of Modern Myanmar. A new government under U Nu was installed .U Nu was one of the original thirty comrades and the chosen leader of Aung San. Theoretically, he opted for a parliamentary democracy with a federal structure. However, independence brought delicate problems and crises. Communist revolt, PVO insurrections, secessionist tendency on the part of the Karens and the Shans, and above all intra-party rivalry within the ruling Anti-Fascist People's Freedom League (AFPFL) were serious problems. Keeping the country united became the foremost task before U Nu.

Soon after independence the country plunged into endemic insurgencies and civil war as already mentioned. The communists were the first to revolt. They went into open revolt just three months after independence, which greatly undermined the legitimacy of the U Nu government. On 29 July 1948, four months after this insurrection, the 'White Band' People's Voluntary Organisation (PVO) under Po Kun and La Yung also revolted, which was followed two weeks later by mutinies of Union Military Police and First and Third Burma Rifles[1]. The story did not end here. Instead, it was, in a way, just the beginning. Those minority groups who were dissatisfied with the constitutional arrangement worked out in the 1947 constitution jumped into the melee. By the end of August and beginning of September 1948, the Karen also rose into rebellion. The first year of independence thus witnessed a series of political turmoil. Premier U Nu tried his best for saving the country from disintegration. Formulae for unity were advanced with more frequency rather than on the basis of rationality[2]. However, each effort seemed futile.

In January, Karen National Defence Organization (KNDO) went against the government, aided by some deserters of the government's own Karen military and police units[3]. These units occupied Bassein and Prome in Lower Irrawaddy, the city of Insein only fifteen miles from Rangoon and Toungoo in the Sittang valley where they collaborated with the communists though marginally[4]. Geographically with the exception of Rangoon, by far the most important part, all was in the hands of rebels[5]. In the early 1950s, the Shans formed ad-hoc alliances and fought against the government[6]. And, in the midst of these crises, there was the strike of the Ministerial Services Union of the civil servants in February 1949 protesting against the imposed salary cut. The cut was mainly to supplement the source of government revenue caused by the non-payment of taxes from rebel occupied areas. In fact, the strike during the period of rebellion nearly paralysed the working of the U Nu government. There were fightings, lootings, destruction of villages, burning of schools and places of worship and great loss of lives throughout the country[7]. The fiercest and bloodiest clash was with the Karens[8]. Complete anarchy prevailed in the political life. The insurrectionary activities spread rapidly throughout the country. Combined with the dissension and division which had started showing within the AFPFL, U Nu government was on the verge of collapse. However, taking advantage of the disunity and lack of coordination among the insurrection groups, U Nu with the help of the army chief, General Ne Win, was able to bring it under control by 1952. His government officially banned the Communist Party of Burma (CPB) in 1953. However, intra-fighting in the party continued with no solution in sight.

Now, the ongoing intra-party conflict within his ruling AFPFL became the most serious crisis threatening the survival of U Nu's government. Initially it was ideology based but later on it turned out to be personality based, an essential feature of Myanmar political life. At the very outset of independence some socialists within the party made a bid for power. However, they retreated to the background when they failed.

The continuing intra-party conflict was even worse than the armed insurrections and rebellions as it grew from within. In the early stage of independence, particularly in the provisional government period which lasted until 1952[9], the ruling AFPFL had no real opposition. Even in the first election of 1951-52, opposition in the form of Burma Workers' and Peasants' Party (BWPP) could not pose much challenge to AFPFL. The scenario however changed during the Second General Election of April 1956. The U Nu Government was gradually losing its popularity because of its failure to curb the severe insurrectionary problem and improve its deteriorating economic condition. The voters were not satisfied with the working of the government. Consequently in this election the ruling party could not maintain its absolute dominance. The internal bickering going on for a long time within the AFPFL also made it weaker while BWPP led combined opposition, the National Unity Front (NUF), had emerged as a formidable force. Though AFPFL won the election the real picture was dismal. Unity was lacking within the impressive 155 members AFPFL majority government. Whereas the opposition NUF alone registered two third of the votes obtained by the AFPFL candidates, the combined opposition amounted to forty six percent of the total[10]. This, in fact, was the sign of breaking down in the internal set up of the party's monolithic structure. Whatever U Nu had decided for a *Pyidawtha* (Welfare state) country also became meaningless in the light of the increasing arrogance and high handedness of his party leaders.

Here, in this phase, the ironical as well as the tragic part of the story was that even after two elections and lot of changes and experiences in the government many of the party leaders in the ruling AFPFL were not ready to look beyond their narrow horizon of self interest, hedonistic nature and personal ego. They were not ready to admit their mistakes and rectify them. Instead, mud slinging and criticism of each other continued. In June 1956, Premier U Nu even stepped down from office for nine months leaving the reins of the government in the hands of U Ba Swe, the Deputy Prime Minister. This was done with the sole purpose of removing corruption from the party and to re-establish harmony among rival leaders, but without success[11]. Further, to resolve this internal crisis and differences a peace convention in the form of Third All Burma Congress of the AFPFL was initiated. The Congress which was held in the Peace Pagoda site in January 1958 was attended by about two thousand delegates[12]. However, nothing concrete came out from the side of this Congress. U Nu left everything as it was. In the meantime the political crisis in the U Nu government became more critical. The differences within the AFPFL became so intense that it ultimately led to the split of the party into two rival factions in May, the same year. To some extent the rivalry between U Nu and Kyaw Nyein, was also responsible for the split. The two factions which came out of the split were the U Nu - Thakin Tin led 'Clean Faction' and the U Ba Swe - U Kyaw Nyein led 'Stable Faction'. Ironically ideology played little or no role in the split, as all of them were committed to the same vague socialist goals[13]. Issues revolved mainly around personalities and cliques, the usual situation in Myanmarese politics[14]. In fact, leaders personalised power which in turn surpassed the prevailing pseudo - political institutions of the country. The split was to come one time or another since quarrels among party members had been going on for a long time - since the time of independence.

The split in the AFPFL did not occur suddenly. It was the culmination of a long process of complex politics encompassing various causal factors. But the most serious and the ultimate ones were personal antagonism, structural defects and the changing political climate[15]. However, political crisis did not end with the split. Rather, the political situation became more complex and confusing. After the split a special parliament session was duly called to decide which faction would rule. "In a test of political strength for the control of parliament Nu - Tin group got 127 votes against119 of the Swe - Nyein leadership"[16], in the 250-seat lower house. But in order to survive the no-confidence test Nu - Tin group had to accept the support of NUF, the leftist opposition group, and the minorities. The resulting unstable political situation led to widespread unrest and confusion[17]. Once again leftist groups like the PVO, and communist under Than Tun became active. They started blackmailing the government indirectly for negotiating for the demands. Ethnic Karens and Shans also once again revived their earlier demand for greater autonomy or even secessions. The production of the economy had slowed down. The situation of the country had thus become too difficult for Premier U Nu to control. The political situation in the country was such as to create the most serious threat to the integrity and security of the state[18]. Consequently, on 26 September 1958, four months after the special parliament session, U Nu was compelled to resign in favour of a "caretaker government", led by General Ne Win[19].

General Ne Win was installed by the parliament as the new Prime Minister of the caretaker government on 28 October 1958. He ruled the country for eighteen months during which he proved that armed forces could run the country more efficiently than the civilians. His brief rule attached much more importance to territorial integrity and strong measures against the insurgents. Number of insurgent related incidents came down drastically. He made progress in cleaning up the cities and the bureaucracy. He successfully conducted the Third General Election in February – March 1960. General Ne Win proved himself that the armed forces stood for nation's unity, efficiency, cleanliness etc. The impressions so created during his brief rule were most profitably used in the later years.

U Nu's 'Clean-AFPFL' won an absolute majority of 157 out of 250 seats held in the Lower House or Chamber of Deputies[20]. On the other hand the result of election brought the dismal performance of the 'Stable-AFPFL'. It was reduced to a minority party securing only a total of 42 seats[21]. The NUF, the main opposition in the previous election, was also wiped out. It secured only 4 seats though it held 48 seats previously[22] as a result of the election of 1956. And, on 1 April 1960, with the convening of a new parliament session, General Ne Win surrendered his power to U Nu as the head of the majority party in the parliament. Thus, once again a civilian democratic government was restored; U Nu again came to power.

Here, it may not be out of place to mention that during the election campaign U Nu declared that he stood for democracy and promised to work against fascism and also assured to declare Buddhism as the state religion if he became Prime Minister. He further hinted the formation of separate Mon and Arakanese States which invited problems especially from the Shans.

After elections U Nu changed the name of his party to *Pyidaungsu* or Union Party; and assured the people of bringing the spirit of parliamentary democracy and communal harmony in the country. However, after his election victory the questions of Buddhism as state religion and autonomy of Mon, Arakanese became serious political issues with no solution in sight.

The state religion issue became so controversial especially to the minorities e.g. the Kachins. It was one of the causes for launching the Kachin Independence Organization (KIO). The Kachins who were Christians became critical of government's policy. The question of giving autonomy status to the Mons and the Arakanese opened a 'Pandora's Box' setting a chain reaction as the Shans could have exercised their right to secede. In short, in the words of Brigadier General Aung Gyi, Minister of Trade Development, Industry and Supplies, was that the question of religion and federalism was the delicate question which prompted a military takeover.

U Nu , no doubt, made sincere attempts to bring the discontented ethnic leaders together. He wanted to reduce the strain in the relationship between the union government and the states pertaining to issues like secession, greater autonomy and ethnic minority rights. This being the most serious problem threatening the integrity of the nation U Nu was very much conscious about it. In order to pacify and reconcile the centrifugal forces and to promote harmony among the citizens, both majority and minority, a Federal Seminar was held in February and March 1962. Most of the leaders from different groups participated. All these leaders, both from "the proper as well as from the states", were invited to express their views and help in finding out alternatives and solutions to the problem. Meanwhile, on the contrary, the nation's armed force under Gen. Ne Win was not happy with this new development. It considered the process as a compromising attitude on the part of the parliamentary government. He was of the view that the said measures would lead to further disintegration and division of the country. Besides, the army had tasted political power and overnight acquired a grossly exaggerated view of its own capabilities[23]. It was too much overconfident of its administrative capacity experienced during the short span of caretaker period. This illusion of its ultra ability to run administration, combined with the lust for power compelled the army to stage a coup. The pretext was of avoiding a grave danger of the disintegration of the country. And indeed, a coup was staged on 2 March 1962, when the Federal Seminar of U Nu was still going on. Many of the political as well as ethnic leaders were arrested and jailed. With it, came the end of U Nu's utopia of a *Pyidawtha* or welfare state; and also an end to Myanmarese experimentation with parliamentary democracy.

The study of the aforesaid political developments clearly shows that a number of serious issues threatened the practice of democracy during U Nu's rule. However, the period from1948 to 1958 there was practice of parliamentary democracy in Myanmar. Freedom of speech, press and assembly was widely respected. Judiciary was independent.

Politics was dominated by the AFPFL which received wide and popular support because of its historical role in the struggle for independence. This trend continued even during the period from 1960 to 62.

The above discussion also points out that political factors were largely responsible for the failure of parliamentary democracy. However, it is to be noted that economic factors played no lesser role for the failure of U Nu's rule and parliamentary democracy. A brief discussion will highlight its relevance.

As prevailed in many countries, the leaders of freedom movements were influenced by certain political ideologies. Socialist and Marxist teachings largely influenced these leaders; and Myanmarese political leaders were not exceptions. Aung San, U Nu and Ne Win, all were influenced by these ideologies. Therefore, it is not surprising that U Nu and Ne Win tried to apply some of the Socialist and Marxist principles in the formulation of policies. Briefly speaking, land reform, nationalisation and socialist industrial plan became the keystone of government's economic policy. U Nu and other AFPFL leaders worked hard to build a socialist welfare state. No doubt, nationalism also provided an impetus. However, nationalisation was mainly directed against both Western and Indian owned firms. Regarding land reforms, the Land Nationalisation Act of October 1948 transferred absentee land holdings to the government to redistribute to individual cultivators. Though the Ministry of Land Nationalisation was created progress of land distribution was very slow.

Nationalisation did not spare even the transportation and industrial sectors of the economy. In 1948, the Bombay-Burma Trading Corporation, a reputed firm, lost its teak concession and saw mills. In 1954, oil companies became sector for joint ventures with the government holding one-third interest. However, the process of nationalisation was slowed down to attract foreign investment. In 1952, U Nu had announced an ambitious eight-year plan for development drawn up with the assistance of United States and UN advisors. A target Gross Domestic Product of kyat 7 billion equivalent of 1.5 billion US dollars was set for 1959. Industry, mining, electrification, transportation, communication and irrigation were supposed to receive big investment, not less than 1 billion kyat. The welfare state programme *Pyidawtha* was to be financed through export, principally rice, and without taking any foreign loan. However, the end of the Korean War in1953 brought about a collapse in international rice prices; which affected Myanmarese rice more seriously. And in 1955 the 8-year *Pyidawtha* development plan was scrapped and a modest 5-year plan was proposed. It was during this time that Myanmar started increasingly dependent on foreign investment such as (1) Japanese War reparations, (2) PL-480 grants of United States, (3) long term loans from the World Bank and the United States, and (4) gifts from the Socialist countries including former USSR.

Despite all these attempts Myanmarese economy could not recover even to reach the pre war level. Rice export was 64 per cent, petroleum and tea export were 42 per cent and 39 per cent respectively. Just before the military coup of 1962 many of the socialist oriented earlier economic plans were dropped and instead, the development of the economy through private sector was encouraged. These measures were strongly opposed by the military officers committed to socialist ideas.[24]

These deteriorating economic conditions including failure to control spiralling prices, hesitant attitude towards trade combined with inability to safeguard its national security, 'weak stand' against the demands of the Shan minority for setting up of a federal government instead of a unitary government became armed forces' justification of its takeover.

NOTES

1. Frank N. Trager, *Burma - From Kingdom to Republic : A Historical and Political Analysis* (New York: Praeger, 1966), p.102.
2. Ibid, p. 108.
3. Ibid, p. 106.

4. John F. Cady, *The United States and Burma* (Cambridge, Mass: Harvard University Press, 1976), p. 200.
5. F.S.V. Donnison, *Burma* (New York: Praeger, 1970), p. 134.
6. Mary P. Callahan, "Building an army: The early years of the Tatmadaw". *Burma Debate* (Washington D.C.), vol.4, no.3, July/August 1997, p. 8.
7. n. 5, p. 144.
8. Ibid.
9. The provisional Government period lasted from independence to 1952 - till the first general election was held. It was not an elected government.
10. n. 4, p. 215.
11. Josef Silverstein, *Burma: Military Rule and Politics of Stagnation* (Ithaca, N. Y.: Cornell University Press, 1977), pp. 27-28.
12. n.4, p.218.
13. David I. Steinberg, *Burma's Road Towards Development : Growth and Ideology Under Military Rule* (Boulder: West View Press, 1981), p.15.
14. Ibid.
15. n.11, p.64.
16. Maung Muang Gyi, *The Burmese Political Values : The Socio-Political Roots of Authoritarianism* (New York : Praeger, 1983), p.120.
17. n.11, p.28.
18. D.R. Sardesai, *Southeast Asia: Past and Present* (New Delhi: Vikas Pub. House, 1983), p.343.
19. U Nu later on considered it as the first coup of the post independence era.
20. n.11 p.71.
21. Ibid.
22. Ibid.
23. n.16, p.121.
24. Frederica M. Bunge (ed.), *Burma: A Country Study* (Washington D.C.: American University, 1983), pp.51-52.

2

Myanmar's Economic Policy Before 1988 Initiatives and Fallouts

In the previous chapter it is seen under what circumstances General Ne Win seized political power in Myanmar overthrowing, in a military coup, U Nu's civilian government which practiced parliamentary democracy. In this connection various factors responsible for U Nu's failure had been highlighted. At the same time it is also seen how the armed forces also justified for the seizure of political power especially by General Ne Win who spearheaded the coup. Then, who is this man? What is his background?

Before the coup, General Ne Win was considered as an able military commander, saviour of the nation, and a revered leader of the Myanmarese people. Originally named as Shu Maung (means apple of one's eye) he left his native place for Rangoon only to become a doctor but ordained otherwise to become a military leader and a public figure of the country. General Ne Win was one of the founder members of the Burmese Independence Army (BIA) that had played an important role in the struggle for Myanmarese independence. He was also one of the Thirty Comrades or *Thakins* which spearheaded the freedom struggle of the country. As part of 'Thirty Comrades' he went to Japan in the beginning of 1941 for a six-month military training. After returning to Myanmar it was he along with Aung San who gave direction to the BIA in their fight against the imperialist forces. In fact, while *Bogyoke* Aung San was the political head of the whole freedom struggle it was Gen. Ne Win who directed the operations in the military front. With the gaining of Myanmarese Independence on 4 January 1948 he became its first Commander-in-Chief. He was a minister for a short time in U Nu's cabinet and also had tenure as the Prime Minister of the Caretaker Military Government of 1958-60, whose administrative efficiency was praised by a large section of the public. Thus, in the pre-coup period General Ne Win was able to create for himself the image of a perfect public leader in the minds of the general public which, in turn, also enhanced the credibility of the Myanmarese army.

Soon after coming to power the junta formed an interim military body known as the Revolutionary Council (RC) for carrying out the administration of the country. It was composed of General Ne Win and sixteen other senior army officers[1]. General Ne Win justified the coup for (i) safeguarding the unity of the country; (ii) establishment of socialism; and (iii) preserving the culture and tradition. Initially the people were told that its main purpose was solely to preserve the Union and restore order and harmony in the society, and that it could last only for a short period[2]. However, it was not to be so.

2.1. Economic Initiatives of the Government

Now, the attention of the Revolutionary Council was focused on its economy. It brought many drastic changes. A new doctrine called "The Burmese Way to Socialism" was introduced. Mass nationalisation was the first policy measure taken up by the Revolutionary Council of General Ne Win under his doctrine of 'Burmese Way to Socialism'. Under a new law called "Law to Protect the Construction of the Socialist Economy" (1963) he carried out a rapid economic programme. In the beginning his nationalisation covered mainly the secondary and tertiary sectors of the economy where as the primary sector was mainly left out for the private individuals. Large industries, banks, insurance, foreign trade, domestic wholesale trade, and ninety per cent of the retail trade were nationalised in the first year of the start of the programme itself. The whole banking system of the country was nationalised on 23 February 1963[3]. Fourteen foreign banks in Yangon, two branches of foreign banks in the districts, ten private national banks and five branches of private national banks were nationalised[4]. And the entire system was put under 'Union Bank of Burma' which was acting as the Central Bank[5].

Apart from the nationalisation of banks, the RC continued to nationalise industries. All major industries were also nationalised on 1 June 1963 under the "New Enterprise Nationalisation Law" (February 1963) and private industries were forbidden to set up new factories[6]. The nationalisation of basic industries was followed in August 1963 by the nationalisation of consumer industries such as department stores, warehouses, and wholesale shops[7]. As regard to the nationalisation of medicine industries, it was done mainly in the late 60s and early 70s. Above these, the RC government also brought under its control all those business units where disputes were in progress, under the new "Trade Disputes Amending Law, 1963".

These domestic changes affected Indian and Chinese businessmen to maximum extent. As mentioned above, these Indians and Chinese, who were the main actors of the Myanmar's economy in the first decade of independence, were expelled and their properties were largely confiscated.[8]. Even out of the two groups the more seriously affected one were the Indians who controlled 60 per cent of the country's trade and commerce at that time[9]. Banks, insurance companies and assets of British owned trading companies were also not spared. And thus after mid 60s all the processes of production, distribution, procurement, import and export of goods became the sole monopolies of the state.

Here, what one needs to understand is that the whole process of nationalisation drive was legalised by two duly enacted laws (mentioned above) of the same government - 'the Enterprise Nationalisation Law' and 'The Socialist Economy Protection Law'. However, the mass nationalisation started with the sole objective of creating a self reliant economy created a set back for the country. As a result of the priority given to the building of a modern industrial sector, agriculture was neglected. The industrial sector also failed to perform well, despite the priority it received in terms of investment. The inability of Myanmarese people to cope with the precarious situation after the expulsion of foreigners created shortages in the area of trained manpower. Above this, the inefficiency of the public distribution system in the supply of consumer goods compelled to develop lucrative black market economy parallel to the already existing inefficient economy of General Ne Win. The State Trading Corporations established to look after the nationalised sector could not carry out its assigned duties properly. It even failed in the satisfactory distribution of commodities. Ultimately it was the people who bore the brunt of the crises resulting in their resentment.

Another peculiarity of General Ne Win's whole economic policy was his neglect, from the very beginning, of the primary sector – the main foundation of the entire economy. In spite of his having the knowledge of the importance of the primary sector he completely left it out in private hands. His policy of mass nationalisation, while confining mostly in industries and trade, had forgotten many vital links of the economy. Agriculture, the most important occupation in the primary sector, and also the mainstay of Myanmarese economy, was more or less left to the private sector. Hardly 15 per cent of the total government expenditure was allocated to it[10].

In the mid 60s the economic crisis of the country became visible. Foreign exchange reserves of the country dwindled sharply. While the Ne Win government carried on with its drastic cuts on imports. All budget allocations of foreign reserves to various ministries were slashed down to about fifty per cent. Even the Ministry of Defence was not spared. There was also a drastic reduction of consumer goods. Consequently, there was lack of varieties and competitiveness in the market. In fact, uniformity created in the market by the military government of General Ne Win bred contempt. There was no choice at all on the part of the consumers.

Besides, the rapid decline in private sector trade of consumer and retail items due to government's effort of creating a self-reliant economy instead created a set back for the country. As a result of interference, and the consequent increase in hoarding and black market, an atmosphere of artificial scarcity of essential consumer items existed.

The policy of neutralism opted by General Ne Win in the international front, side by side to his mass nationalisation in the domestic level, did not make it much easier for the already deteriorating Myanmar's economy. This policy was an outcome of the Burmese Way to Socialism. From 1964 onwards, General Ne Win suddenly revert the country to its historic isolation, practically shutting itself off from the rest of the world[11]. The movement of anything foreign, whether person, goods, aid or communication were strictly censored by the government. The international community was at first intrigued by this tendency but they gradually lost interest[12]. However, this policy of isolation in the international arena followed by the country under General Ne Win's rule proved really defective for the country's economy. It resulted in a nearly total cut off of any trade relation of Myanmar with the outside world. This projected a poor image for the country in the conduct of foreign relations, especially in terms of trade and commerce. The result was a sudden decline in every sector of foreign trade which had its adverse effect on the domestic economy. The ratio of foreign trade to G.D.P. was 40 per cent in 1950, during U Nu's rule, fell to 26 per cent between 1960 and 1970, and further to 13 per cent between 1970 and 1977, one of the lowest among developing economies[13]. We can also observe this decline in the foreign trade in the form of export and import as a proportion to the country's GDP. In 1960 the import was 10 per cent of the GDP which had declined to 2 per cent in 1981, whereas export declined from 20 per cent to 9 per cent in the same period[14]. The balance of trade was severely affected. The surplus in the balance of payment which was evident in 1960-61 declined and soon by the beginning of 1970s deficit became a feature of foreign trade.

While illustrating the decline in the export items one

good example is the export of rice for which Myanmar was well known to the outside world. It was its first major item of export which was in great demand. Even the export of this item, the main component of the Myanmarese economy, declined from the mid 60s. (See Table 1). The average drop in rice export was about 2, 55,000 tons every year[15].

Table 1
Rice Exports by Tons

Year	*Tons (million)*
Pre-war	3.1
1947	1.3
1950	1.4
1955	1.9
1961	1.6
1962	1.7
1964	1.4
1966	1.1
1968	0.3
1970	0.7
1972	0.6
1974	0.2
1975	0.3
1976	0.7
1977	0.7
1978	0.4
1979	0.6
1980	0.7
1981	0.7
1982	0.7
1983	0.8

(Contd...)

1984	0.7
1985	0.5
1986	0.6
1987	0.5

Source : The United States Department of Agriculture. Cited in David I. Steinberg, "Neither Silver Nor Gold", in Josef Silverstein (ed.), *Independent Burma at 40 Years* (Ithaca : Cornell University Press, 1989), p.47.

This decline in the availability of rice for export may be attributed to factors like insecurity in the fields, lack of mobility of labour in the peak period, relatively high labour costs, less efficient organisation of labour, and less incentive for farmers to grow more[16]. In fact, the country ceased to be an important rice exporting country, rather there were even shortage of rice in some regions which compelled the government to resort to rationing, an incident unheard of in the history of Myanmar. In the context of foreign assistance also, in the first decade of General Ne Win's rule (1962-72), the country on an average received only about US $ 28 million per year[17]. That too, was utilised in infrastructural set up rather than to direct productive projects, resulting in one factor for the stagnant economy. This assistance was mainly supplied by the United Nations agencies.

On the other hand, after about five years of the launching of General Ne Win's socialist oriented economic programmes, it became quite evident that the programmes were not moving in the desired direction. Productivity was not upto the desired level in almost all the sectors of production. Besides, upto January 1966, 426 items[18] including necessary and minutiae of the retail trade were under government control which was to be entirely sold in People's Shops. This also led to dissent as well as black-marketeering and hoarding of essential consumer items. The year 1967 also proved to be a disastrous one for General Ne Win and his Revolutionary Council government. The multitude of events such as shortage of rice and other consumer items, riots by workers in August, increasing black-marketeering and smuggling etc, shook the very foundation of the government. In a way the 'Burmese Way to Socialism' was losing influence. And by the end of the 60s the government, too, realised that its economic policies were not working up to the people's expectation on the one hand and was also failing in reaching its projected goal on the other. It even admitted the failures. As a remedial move, the economic measures were slightly liberalised, allowing 34 out of the 426 controlled consumer goods item to be sold in open market[19]. Nonetheless, there was no improvement in the general situation as the prices of decontrolled essential items continued to be 400 per cent to 500 per cent higher than the pre control levels[20]. However, what need to be understood here is that the slight liberalisation or change in the policy had no impact on the whole economy as well as the people and that it was just the beginning of a series of mistakes committed by the whimsical natured General Ne Win and his team of marionettes.

The first decade of military rule had been one of extreme economic deprivation as socialisation paralysed the old economic system[21]. The widespread effort of the RC for Burmanisation of the economy through suppression of the free market mechanism and rapid socialisation of all the means of production failed terribly. It could not lead the country towards a point of rapid development and progress, as hoped by the junta leaders including General Ne Win himself.

In the early part of 70s Ne Win really became seriously concerned about his policies and programmes as economic growth remained very dull. Ne Win was compelled to review his entire policy when it failed to bring any progress even after ten years of implementation. In view of this many economic reforms were approved at the first Burmese Socialist Programme Party Congress in 1971.

In September 1972, the meeting of the Fourth BSPP's Committee adopted a document for economic reforms popularly known as '20 - Years Plan'. It aimed at developing the primary sector, a sector neglected in the first decade, with a view to import substitution. This involved priority for the production and export of primary products; the decentralisation of management and greater use of commercial incentives, efficiency within state enterprises, and enhanced role for the private sector; and most significantly, a new willingness to seek and accept external assistance in an effort to gain access to both capital and technology[22]. Thus in the beginning of the 70s his policy shifted towards gradual economic liberalisation, contrary to the slight liberalisation carried out in the late 60s. There were changes in objectives, priorities and implementation of economic policies though his doctrine 'Burmese Way to Socialism' still remains the basic guidelines.

Ne Win brought certain changes in the administrative and judicial structure of the country also. In fact, the early 1970s reflected the Ne Win government's move towards constitutionalism and gradual economic liberalism after about a decade of imposition of tight authoritarian regime over the politico-economic system of the country[23]. It gave emphasis on setting up of new enterprises capable of producing the best results in the quickest possible time[24]. As mentioned above, it also marked, in the economic history of Myanmar, the beginning of a "Long Term 20-Year Plan" divided into five 4-Year Plan. The plan which started in 1973/74 was to extend up to 1993/94, if it continued without any interruption. The ultimate goal was, by the end of the plan, Myanmar was to achieve the status of an industrialised socialist economy[25].

Ne Win's new economic policy attracted foreign loans and assistance, also as result abandonment of its isolationist policy. Now economic necessity intimidated the Ne Win government to join the World Bank in 1972 and the Asian Development Bank (ADB) in 1973. In fact, since 1974, the country had been moving towards a new liberalized economic policy and became more receptive of international aid[26]. However, in spite all these, the suspicious and overcautious nature of its leadership on anything foreign still remained, to a large extent.

The initiation of the ambitious 20-Year Plan (1973/74-1993/94) had arisen following the imperatives to attract foreign capital, aid and technical assistance without which the desired goals could not be achieved. Thus, Myanmar's foray in the multinational institutions like World Bank and ADB proved beneficial in attracting large- scale financial and technical assistance, under the direction of Ne Win.

As Myanmar was potentially rich in resources, various countries of Asia and Europe did not hesitate to invest in the country. They wanted to benefit from this richness. Many countries[27] and organisations[28] started sending their assistance in the form of foreign loans and aid into Myanmar. In case of bilateral assistance Japan topped the list of donors with 69.7 per cent of the total aid in the period 1974-1976 and 58.24 per cent in 1984-86[29]. In actual value, the foreign assistance of Japan to Myanmar was US $ 44.0 million in 1974 which rose to US $ 225.8 million in 1986[30]. Federal Republic of Germany was in second position during the said period (1974-86). Meanwhile in case of multilateral foreign aid International Development Association (IDA), a subsidiary of the World Bank , topped the list with 57.7 per cent in 1974-76 which slightly dropped to 49.1 per cent during 1984- 86[31]. There was slight increase on the part of the ADB. In terms of value, the contribution of IDA was US $ 1.9 million in 1974 which rose to US $ 43.8 million in 1986[32]. (See tables 2 to 4).

In connection with the above Official Development Assistance (ODA) received by the country from foreign sources it is necessary to point out that it was inclusive of grants. Most of these loans included a certain degree of grants. In the case of some foreign assistance the degree of grant was 100 per cent or almost 100 per cent. For instance, between 1983 and 1986 assistance received by Myanmar from countries like Australia, Austria, Belgium, Canada, New Zealand, Norway, U.K., U.S.A. , etc were 100 per cent grants[33]. Whatever may be the case the technical grant received from bilateral as well as multilateral source in 1976-78 were 24.1 per cent and 89.8 per cent respectively of the total foreign assistance[34]. In 1984-86 there were 28.3 per cent and 77.0 per cent respectively[35]. In actual value, in a period

Table 2
Bilateral and Multilateral Foreign Loans and Aid of Burma: Net Receipt

(Million of U.S. dollars)

Year	*Bilateral*			*Multi-lateral*	*Total (Bil. & Multi:)*	*Percentage*		
	DAC Countries	*OPEC Countries*	*Total*			*Bila-lateral*	*Multi-lateral*	*Total*
1974	60.2	-	60.2	5.2	65.4	92.0	8.0	100.0
1975	22.2	-	22.2	26.6	48.8	45.5	54.5	100.0
1976	42.5	-	42.5	30.6	73.1	58.1	41.9	100.0
1977	58.8	-	58.8	47.3	106.1	55.4	44.6	100.0
1978	237.7	-	237.7	120.0	358.1	66.4	33.6	100.0
1979	413.2	-	413.2	104.8	518.1	79.7	20.1	99.8
1980	324.6	-	324.6	78.1	402.7	80.6	19.4	100.0
1981	248.0	-	248.0	80.0	328.0	75.6	24.4	100.0
1982	310.8	-	310.8	111.2	421.9	73.7	26.3	100.0
1983	211.3	-	211.3	86.2	297.5	71.0	29.0	100.0
1984	200.0	-	200.0	125.9	325.8	61.4	38.6	100.0
1985	254.5	-	254.5	102.3	356.7	71.3	28.7	100.0
1986	306.1	-	306.1	107.7	413.8	74.0	26.0	100.0

Source : (1) OPEC, Geographical Distribution of Financial Flows to Developing Countries, Paris, Various annual issues from 1976 to 1988.

(2) Calculated percentage figures are also shown.

Given in Khin Maung Nyunt, *Foreign Loans and Aid in the Economic Development to Burma: 1974/75 to 1985/86*, (Bangkok : Institute of Asian Studies - Chulalongkorn University, 1990), p.25.

Table 3
Bilateral Foreign Loans and Aid of Burma: Net Receipts

(Millions of U.S. dollars)

	1974	1975	1976	1977	1978	1979	1980	1981	1982	1983	1984	1985	1986
1. DAC COUNTRIES	60.2	22.2	42.4	58.8	237.7	413.2	324.6	248.0	310.8	211.3	200.0	254.5	306.1
Australia	4.0	3.0	2.8	2.1	6.7	11.0	19.3	5.7	13.7	5.4	6.9	6.7	7.0
Austria	-	-	-	-	-	-	44.0	-	- 1.7	-	- 3.0	- 2.9	0.1
Belgium	- 0.4	-0.4	- 0.3	- 0.3	-	-	3.8	10.9	-	- 2.0	1.8	- 0.6	- 2.0
Canada	1.3	0.5	1.8	6.2	2.7	4.4	3.7	2.6	1.9	1.9	1.5	2.3	1.1
Denmark	-	-	0.2	0.1	5.6	9.9	11.7	5.6	0.9	0.7	3.0	4.7	2.8
Finland	-	-	-	-	-	-	-	-	-	2.4	1.1	1.4	4.1
France	8.3	0.2	- 0.9	8.2	- 1.0	14.7	1.8	18.0	18.2	13.1	-2.4	5.2	8.2
FRG(Germany)	2.5	- 1.3	7.3	12.3	16.3	91.5	- 13.7	45.6	71.6	76.3	29.7	64.0	17.2
Ireland	-	-	-	-	-	-	-	-	-	-	-	-	-
Italy	0.1	2.8	- 0.1	0.1	0.0	15.6	0.0	1.7	35.2	2.2	5.9	-0.8	2.4
Japan	44.0	19.3	23.4	17.8	125.2	189.6	144.2	124.0	123.0	100.6	114.5	141.6	225.8
The Netherland	*	*	6.8	0.1	13.3	- 6.2	1.9	3.6	1.4	2.3	0.4	- 2.1	16.3

(Contd...)

	1974	1975	1976	1977	1978	1979	1980	1981	1982	1983	1984	1985	1986
New Zealand	0.1	-	0.1	0.2	0.1	0.1	0.0	0.0	-	-	0.0	-	0.0
Norway	-	-	-	0.0	52.4	30.4	68.0	3.2	2.0	- 2.7	39.0	33.1	33.5
Sweden	-	-	-	-	-	-	-	-	-	- 0.3	- 0.2	-	-
Switzerland	0.1	*	-	0.0	0.0	0.2	- 5.0	- 2.5	0.1	- 2.0	- 2.3	- 0.9	1.6
U.K.	1.3	- 1.0	2.5	3.1	14.3	52.3	42.5	27.3	35.7	9.6	- 2.9	- 5.2	- 20.7
United States	- 1.0	- 1.0	- 1.0	9.0	2.0	-	-	1.0	6.0	4.0	7.0	8.0	9.0
2. OPEC COUNTRIES	-	-	-	-	-	-	-	-	-	-	-	-	-
3. TOTAL	60.2	22.2	42.5	58.8	237.7	413.2	324.6	248.0	310.8	211.3	200.0	254.5	306.1

Source : OECD, Geographical Distribution of Financial Flows to Developing Countries, Paris, various annual issues from 1976 to 1988.
Given in Khin Maung Nyunt, *Foreign Loans and Aid in the Economic Development to Burma: 1974/75 to 1985/86*, (Bangkok : Institute of Asian Studies - Chulalongkorn University, 1990), p.28.

Table 4
Multilateral Foreign Loans and Aid : Net Receipts (Million of U.S.dollars)

	1974	1975	1976	1977	1978	1979	1980	1981	1982	1983	1984	1985	1986
A.S.D.B.	-	3.0	6.6	10.6	60.9	20.9	14.1	21.4	35.0	16.6	24.7	32.4	26.6
E.E.C.	-	-	0.9	0.6	1.4	-	-	-	2.3	1.8	1.9	2.1	14.6
IBRD	-2.3	-2.5	-2.0	-0.7	-	-	-	-	-	-	-	-	-
IDA	1.9	15.9	18.3	19.3	25.0	34.8	26.1	38.2	42.0	43.0	79.4	42.9	43.3
IMF TRUST FUND-	-	-	7.5	23.2	23.5	19.9	0.2	-	-	-	-	-	
UN Agencies	5.6	10.0	-	-	-	-	-	-	-	-	-	-	-
UNDP	-	-	4.0	4.8	4.6	7.1	9.2	10.2	11.0	8.8	7.7	12.4	11.0
UNTA	-	-	0.9	1.1	1.2	1.3	0.3	1.7	1.2	2.2	1.0	2.6	0.0
UNICEF	-	-	1.9	1.6	3.9	9.9	7.2	5.3	3.3	7.0	5.3	8.7	8.1
WFP	-	-	-	-	-	4.0	0.1	-	-	0.1	-	-	-
Other Multinational	-	0.2	0.2	0.2	0.2	0.9	0.9	1.5	2.5	1.8	1.6	1.7	2.0
Arab OPEC Agencies	-	-	-	2.3	-	2.4	0.3	1.4	13.8	4.9	4.4	-0.5	-0.1
Total	5.2	26.6	30.6	47.3	120.3	104.8	78.1	80.0	111.2	86.2	125.9	102.3	107.0

Source : OECD, Geographical Distribution of Financial Flows to Developing Countries, Paris; various annual issues from 1976 to 1988.

Given in Khin Maung Nyunt, *Foreign Loans and Aid in the Economic Development to Burma: 1974/75 to 1985/86*, (Bangkok : Institute of Asian Studies – Chulalongkorn University, 1990), p.32.

of 10 years extending from 1977 to 1986, the country received on an average grant (both from bilateral and multilateral) of US dollar 89.19 million[36]. (See Table 5).

Table 5
Degree of Grant Element in ODA: Bilateral and Multilateral

(in per cent)

	1983	1984	1985	1986
1. DAC Countries				
Australia	100.0	100.0	100.0	100.0
Austria			100.0	
Belgium				
Canada	100.0	100.0	100.0	100.0
Denmark				
Finland	100.0	100.0	100.0	100.0
France	100.0	100.0	100.0	100.0
Germany, Fed.Rep.	75.7	51.1	68.0	92.2
Italy	100.0	100.0	100.0	100.0
Japan	85.4	64.7	70.2	67.7
The Netherlands	**100.0**	**100.0**	**100.0**	**100.0**
New Zealand		100.0		100.0
Norway	100.0	100.0	100.0	100.0
Sweden				
Switzerland	100.0	100.0	100.0	100.0
United Kingdom	100.0	100.0	100.0	100.0
United States	100.0	100.0	100.0	100.0
2. OPEC Countries				
3. Bilateral	**85.8**	**66.8**	**72.5**	**74.5**
4. Multilateral	**81.7**	**85.7**	**90.5**	**84.3**
5. EEC Members	**79.4**	**56.7**	**66.7**	**96.2**
6. Total	**83.4**	**70.1**	**75.6**	**76.7**

Source : OECD, Geographical Distribution of Financial Flows to Developing Countries, Paris,1988.
Given in Khin Maung Nyunt, *Foreign Loans and Aid in the Economic Development to Burma: 1974/75 to 1985/86*, (Bangkok : Institute of Asian Studies - Chulalongkorn University, 1990), p.49.

These industrialised countries gave loans and assistance to lighten economic burden if not for economic recovery. However, the tragic part of the story was that most of these benefits were not utilised properly due to red tapism, corruption, bureaucratic inefficiency, ignorance and lack of experience and technical know how on the part of those who were in power under General Ne Win . Besides, there was poor planning in the choice of industries[37]. Except for petroleum based industries, most of the industries were ignored[38]. There was also a tendency to build new plants rather than to expand or modernise existing facilities[39]. Thus, the amount that could be utilized for solving many of the acute economic problems of Myanmarese economy was scattered in a number of sectors. The investment which could have checked the shrinking economy went down the drain, uninterrupted. And this was also one of the main causes of increased black marketeering and high inflation rate in the country; issues which played an important role in the outbreak of the movement of mass discontentment in 1988.

Here, one more important feature of General Ne Win's rule which we need to recall is the heavy military expenditure of his government. This heavy expenditure incurred on the containment of insurgency had greatly affected the poor economy of the country. During the 25 years of Ne Win's rule, his attempt to solve the country's ethnic insurgency by force rather than by political consensus necessitated his government to spend more and more on military hardware. The money which could have been used for building up the much needed economic infrastructure of the country was, instead, diverted to weapons and soldiers. In fact, Ne Win's entire armed forces underwent a sea change. The rapid increase in the number of soldiers and weapons and insurgency containment campaigns entailed at least 50 per cent of annual government expenditure in the 70s and 80s[40], it was believed. This resulted in a near to complete neglect of the basic necessities and social needs of the people causing a decline in the overall standard of living, contrary to what Ne Win had envisioned.

2.2. Policy Consequences

Above discussions focus on various initiatives taken up by the government under the leadership of General Ne Win to improve its economy through nationalisation. Though in the beginning the government did not encourage foreign investment yet latter on it came to realise that without foreign investment the country's economy could not move forward. However, despite these attempts and initiatives it could not develop its economy up to its expectation. Its economic initiatives, in short, were not without fallouts and setbacks. Some of these fallouts were black market, inflation, demonetisations and Least Developed Country (LDC) status.

2.3. Black Market: The Shadow Economy

The presence of black market in the post-independence history of Myanmarese economy cannot be taken lightly. Existence of a black market economy parallel to the already existing national economy was and is one of the most distinct features of the economy under military regimes.

Though black market was not unknown in the U Nu era yet it became evident mainly after Ne Win came to power in 1962. Emergence of this phenomenon under Ne Win's economic policy based on Burmese Way to Socialism was one of the important factors responsible for the mass movement for democracy in 1988. The prevalence of black market in every sector of the economy completely belittled the very positive motive of the Burmese Way to Socialism.

In 1966, in a rush to bring a socialist economy, the government brought under its control most of the essential consumer goods numbering 426 items. In order to avoid the government control of essential consumer items people started withholding the commodities from the government. The result was mass scale hoarding and black marketeering. At the same time, the non-availability and scarcity of many essential items compelled the public in trying to get their necessities by illegal means thus resulting in a lucrative trade of black marketeering. Due to wrong and impractical policies taken up by Gen. Ne Win the Myanmarese economy was gradually pushed backward. There were shortages in every essential commodity. The productive sectors were not producing properly. Besides, as mentioned above, the merchants and traders tried their best to hoard whatever goods that could be put up for sale so that they might sell it at an exorbitant price in the black market. It was artificial no doubt, but the government could do little for it.

Black marketeering under Gen. New Win's military regime was not a phenomenon that was found only in food grain and consumer goods at related sectors of the economy. But it had crept into the remote and deepest units of the economy. Black market even trade in pharmaceuticals, the survival item of the people. In fact, by late 60s, so indispensable the black market had become for the economy that it even came to be known as "Trade Corporation Twenty three"[41], an informal term used in common communication. It was evident in mass scale in and around most of the towns and cities like Rangoon, Mandalay and Moulmein[42]. In the early 1970s an American observer discovered selling of official half-empty bottle of 'Horlicks' powdered health drink at an official equivalent of US $ 12 in Mandalay. Aspirin a common drug was available in open markets of Mandalay and Rangoon[43]. As such, description of the black markets operating openly at the main bazaars in Rangoon and other cities were the subject of "black humour"[44]. Anything could be bought for a price in the markets. The main items ranged from the smallest and most common ones to the largest and most indispensable ones. The turning point came when rice, the very basis of the national economy, became an important item of black market.

Black market in rice was carried out in a very large scale. In 1967 itself, when rice riot broke out due to shortage of rice production, black market price of rice shot up many times more than the official controlled price. Government did try to curb this growing menace of "Trade Corporation 23" but with very little success.

Increasing economic problem and rising scarcity of essential commodities continued in Myanmar and thus prolonged the unwanted trade of black marketeering. Since the Ne Win government did not have the resource to provide either employment or goods, black market activities increased, creating serious problems for the Burma Socialist Programme Party (BSPP)[45]. The starting of economic planning, gradual commercialisation and other new policies for increasing industrial production in the first half of the 70s could do little to curb the growing problem of black market in the economy. Instead, it gave boost to the already spreading phenomenon. And, by 1976, probably 90 per cent[46] of the country's domestic commerce was transacted in this shadow market. The items for this trade came mainly from the neighbouring countries of Thailand, China, India and Bangladesh. The value of this type of trade had been estimated at $ 300 million a year, which constituted more than half the value of Myanmar's above board annual foreign trade of US$400-500 million for each of the past few years[47]. Thus, it will not be wrong to say that whole economy of the country gradually came under the grip of this shadow black market trade.

The 80s marked the complete degradation of Myanmar's economy as a result of the two decades of the wrong socialist based Burmanised economic policies of Gen. Ne Win. Bankruptcy, pervasive state control, very small primary product exports, intense nationalistic seclusion and official autarky were clearly rampant in the economy[48].

Consequently, the economy had to depend more and more on the black market. The increased in the restriction of all legal imports, cutting them by one-third between 1982/83 and 1987/88, at the same time un-officially allowed the expansion of this trade[49]. Though the government knew the presence of black market they were silent because they know that they could not provide what was available in that market. There were instances in 1986/87 when the government quietly opened its borders so that goods from outside could enter the Myanmarese black market without much government and official restrictions. All these show that the Government of Myanmar, in order to substantiate its collapsing economy, supported the nefarious activity of black marketeering, though unofficial in nature. Thus the Ne Win government followed an unofficial economic policy which was contrary to the trade laws of an independent sovereign country.

By 1987, with the rapid economic degradation of the country the situation of black marketeering, tolerated both by military elite and masses for economic survival, went completely out of control. In order to curb this situation government took up certain decontrol measures on trading of rice, maize, beans etc., in September of the same year, but of not much help. For instance, the black market price of rice had reached over 700 per cent above the government distribution price up to March 1988; and by the time Gen. Ne Win resigned from Chairmanship in July it exceeded 800 percent[50]. The same was true of other basic necessities such as cooking oil, fish, *ngapi* (fish paste, a staple of the Myanmar's diet), shrimp, sugar and so on. Thus, composite black market level soared more than 500 per cent above the official price[51]. As a result of this uncontrollable situation people became unhappy with their miserable life under the military regime and ultimately gave their full support to the mass democratic movement. Actually, the event of Rangoon University to which the outbreak of the entire movement was attributed was not the real cause, but was only the necessary spark to start the entire fire of discontentment. There were many long-standing factors of which the problem of black market was one.

Various factors such as neglect of the primary sector, absence of private production units and the inability of government units to supplement the shortage, cheaper goods from across the border etc. were also responsible for the lucrative black market. Lack of necessary economic insight on the part of Gen. Ne Win also further aggravated the situation. Gradually, it led to a widening gap between the haves and have-nots. And ultimately it gave place to the outburst of the pent up emotions in the form of a mass movement in 1988.

2.4. Inflation

Another serious outcome caused by the socialist oriented Burmese way of economy was the increasing degree of inflation in the country. Declining economic condition, highlighted by shortage of rice and other consumer goods, lack of new productive units, presence of a parallel economy in the form of black market, inefficiency and corruption on the part of the military rulers combined together to give wind to the already serious problem of inflation. The neglect of the primary sector by the government in most of its economic policy measures and reforms was also one important cause. Besides, controlling most of the retail items by the government as soon as it came to power led to the growth of black marketeering and hoarding in the economy. The result was an abrupt price rise in the market. There was also lack of production. The decontrol of essential items in September and October 1966 once again brought the share of private trade to about 40 per cent of the total value of internal trade by 1967[52]. Nonetheless, the general situation was such that even the prices of decontrol essential goods continued to be 400 per cent to 500 per cent higher than the pre-control levels.

Up till the early 60s the inflation rate in the Myanmar's economy was more or less steady. However, the picture changed with the coming to power of Gen. Ne Win and the launching of his 'Burmese Way to Socialism'. The administrative and managerial inefficiency on the part of the RC resulted to a higher inflationary trend from the later part of 60s onward. And, in fact, 1967 showed the first serious sign of strains in the economy. There was poor harvest leading to the shortage of rice and other essential commodities. Besides, the rapid action of nationalising and socialising the commercial and industrial sectors of the economy caused shortage in the supply of essential commodities and rapid price rise[53]. A sort of artificial scarcity was created in the economy. An important factor for the rapid price rise during the period could also be attributed to the uncontrolled vast money supply on the part of the government without any clear fiscal and monetary policy. The total supply of money in April 1968 stood at the unprecedented level of Kyat 2.6 million, out of which 72 per cent was currency in circulations[54].

From 1972 onwards there was a shift in the foreign policy of Myanmar. Besides shedding its earlier stand of isolationism it also joined World Bank in 1972 and Asian Development Bank (ADB) in 1973. As a result, assistance in the form of unilateral and multilateral loans started flowing to the country for developmental purposes. However, this increase in money supply as a result of the increasing funds was not utilised properly for productive and progressive purpose. Instead, it was diverted to wrong areas and persons due to mismanagement on the part of the junta. The monetary and financial policies of the regime, in fact, could not grapple with the changing economy of the country. There was vast money supply but less production and fewer commodities. Thus, from early 70s onward inflationary rate shot up. For instance, in 1972, *Bogyoke Market* – the largest in Rangoon – was filled with private traders offering both domestic and foreign goods at prices most people could not afford[55]. During this period, with consumer price index considered as 100 in 1972, what was 91.0 in 1970 jumped up to 156.9 in 1974; in 1976 it peaked up to 252.6, after which it declined slightly but once again rose to 252.6 in 1979[56]. But unofficial black market price often doubled or more official prices[57]. Thus, one reality which the people faced during the period was that when the control of consumer essentials were in the hands of the government it was affordable but not available whereas when the control was in the hands of private individuals who were black marketers and hoarders it was available but not affordable. In short the goods were available but the prices were so high that people could not afford. While wages remained static. Therefore, there was resentment on the part of people against the policies and programmes of Gen. Ne Win.

Knowing the crisis gearing up in the country, at the end of June 1976, President Ne Win advised the Central Committee of the BSPP that rampant inflation was causing undue hardship to all sections of the population[58]. But unfortunately, the BSPP government as a whole could do little to follow the advice as they lacked the expertise necessary for the change. And by the 80s the problem became more acute and unmanageable. While the real GDP growth rate declined from 4.4 in 1983 to 3.7 in 1986, the consumer price inflation rate increased from 5.7 in 1983 to 16.9 in 1986[59]. The above given inflation rate was official – actually, in reality, it was three-four times more than the official rate. Besides, the closing of insurgent smuggling routes in Thailand in 1987 also increased the rate of inflation further. Inflationary pressure still continued as it was beyond the government's capacity to meet the consumer's effective demand for goods and services either by rising domestic production by supplementing it through imports due to shortage of foreign exchange[60]. Deregulation of rice and other basic commodities in September 1987 to solve the brewing economic crises instead led to rapid inflation as the price of those commodities sky rocketed.

Various causative factors had been attributed for the presence of a high rate of inflation in the economy of Ne Win's regime. Supply shortage, stagnation of domestic production, decreased import, increased money supply, over valuation of the Kyat, dual price structure and economic bottlenecks were some such factors. Besides, the policies and programmes of economic development were mainly confined in main cities and towns while the hilly insurgent prone areas were kept out of it. Whatever may be the causes, it was ultimately the common masses who were affected by the problem. It did affect the elites too but that was not a serious problem for them as they could afford anything legally as well as illegally. So differences between the have and have-nots created a schism among the people against the military regime and contributed to the uprising of 1988.

2.5. Demonetisations

As mentioned above one of the serious problems that Ne Win regime faced was how to control the rapidly increasing activity of black marketeering. Black market acted as a parallel economy in the country. General Ne Win and policy planners were of the strong view that demonetisation was a solution to root out black marketeering and hoarding. Therefore, his regime carried out the first demonetisation in 1964. On 27 May the government promulgated his 'Demonetisation Law' and asked the people to surrender all the currency of the denominations 50 and 100 kyats; which would have no longer any legality as currency. This was done mainly to stop the circulation of currency notes of the denominations mentioned above and also to bring down excess money supply so as to curb inflation and black marketeering. While issuing the order the government assured that compensation would be paid in the form of small denominations. But the compensation was limited to kyat 500 per person[61], that also was not to be paid until 3 September 1964. However, demonetisation affected foreigners in general and the Indian community in particular, more than the natives.

There, again, two demonetisations were carried out in 1985 and 1987 in quick succession in the later stage of General Ne Win's rule. However, this time it did not discriminate the Myanmarese and the non- Myanmarese in its impact. It affected the economy and the masses as a whole. No one could escape from the hardship. After a gap of about 20 years, Myanmar had carried out its second demonetisation drive on 4 November 1985. All the currency notes of kyats 100, 50 and 20 denominations were devalued, and replaced them with newly issued 75 kyat notes[62]. Of the currencies devalued, the 100 kyat denomination was in wide circulation. In the initial stage, it proved to be slightly successful in attaining the objective of the government in curbing black market and inflation but, later on, the problem caught up and returned to its original form and went on contrary to the government's expectations. Price of commodities shot up. How much currency was 'caught' and effectively demonetised was not known. The black market value of kyat remained almost four times the official rate[63]. Compensation worked out at 75 per cent of the original value was also very slow in disbursement.

Exchange of old notes for the new currency was done in stages, the intent being to compensate the small and legitimate holders, while the larger holders would be investigated before being allowed to complete the exchange[64]. However, due to the presence of widespread corruption the objective that could have been achieved was defeated. It was discovered that many 'working people' who easily could exchange up to 1000 kyats (3000 in some cases), were actually acting as agents on commission for holders of larger amount[65]. The result was that it did not make much difference.

Myanmar saw yet another demonetisation within a very short period of 2 years. This was Ne Win regime's third demonetisation drive. By an ordinance of the government dated 5 September 1987 all the kyats of 25, 35 and 75 denominations were demonetised. In another sense, any note over $ 1.60 in value became instantly worthless[66]. The objective was the same as the previous one i.e., to curb the increasing black marketeering and large-scale smuggling prevalent in the country resulting in shortages of food and other basic necessities of life. However, one serious defect of this demonetisation of 1987 was that it had no provisions for compensation, contrary to that of 1985 and 1964. As a result, as many as 80 per cent of the currency in circulation became useless. Inclusion of the widely held 25 kyat denomination affected virtually everyone and effectively wiped out the saving of ordinary Myanmarese who could ill afford the loss[67]. Many were left holding with a vast amount of worthless currency notes. The rash action did not even spare the student community. In Rangoon University, for example, the students were caught in the middle of their final examination[68]. In a flash the Students' meagre savings disappeared, their money for everything from lunch to passage home was gone[69]. They were compelled to come out to the streets to protest. In fact, the demonetisation of 1987 devastated the urban middle class and destroyed what little remaining faith people had in the government's economic competency[70]. This policy of Ne Win not only affected the targeted group but also the masses.

The demonetisation of 1987 caused widespread hardship and discontentment that the country had ever experienced. This gradually resulted in the first violent demonstration in the country after that of 1974 funeral of U Thant. This widespread discontentment in the form of demonstrations and riots spread out like wild fire in many cities and towns, besides Rangoon and Mandalay. Though the situation was brought under control for the time being yet it could not remove the anti-government feeling of the people. Above this, the demonetisation, though temporarily succeeded in controlling the circulation of money supply, could not control inflation. Inflation, in fact, became more acute than it was before soon after 2-3 weeks of demonetisation. Price of every essential commodity shot up. People completely lost the faith they had in the government.

Both November 1985 and September 1987 demonetisations, as claimed by the government but never explained properly, were mainly carried out to demonetise some of the vast quantity of bank notes held by black marketeers and drug runners in and outside the country. Besides, it was also targeted to squeeze corruption out of the system and to control inflation by lowering the money supply[71]. However, the result proved otherwise. Everything remained as it was earlier. Further, it resulted in increased social tension, shortages of goods, and demoralisation.[72]. Thus, it was successful only in increasing the economic burden of the people and their hostility against the BSPP government of General Ne Win. Ultimately, it will not be wrong to say from the above observations that the demonetisations were the most extreme economic measures of the regime that had on several previous occasions attempted to flush out hidden wealth [73] - but without success. Lastly, it also brings out clearly that the episodes and issues related with the demonetisation drive of the BSPP government became a catalytic agent, though not directly, for the outbreak of countrywide democracy wave in succeeding year i.e. in March 1988.

2.6. Least Developed Country (LDC) Status

The year 1987 was a turning point in the history of Myanmar. It was on 11 December of that year that Myanmar was declared a Least Developed Country (LDC) by the General Assembly of the United Nations thereby equating it with other least developed countries of the world. Myanmar opted for the status as it expected to receive more aid and grants without interest. By 1987 the country's foreign debt stood at some $ 5.3 billion. This figure was low by comparison with many other developing countries, but Myanmar found it increasingly difficult to service the debt. Moreover, export earning was $230 million in 1986-87 which was far short of the target of $535 million. Annual per capita income shrank from $ 670 in 1960 to $190 in 1987.Official consumer price inflation was around 25 per cent. Forty per cent of the population was well below the poverty line. So serious was the economic decline that at a meeting of the BSPP in August 1987 even General Ne Win, who boasted of a successful Myanmarese economy, now accepted his failure in the economic front [74]. Finding no alternative the government applied for the LDC status so that it could negotiate for more favourable economic terms[75]. However, it hurt the sentiments of the people who were intensely patriotic and proud of its glorious past. Now, its pride was hurt. They started to question their government's competence.

In fact, Myanmar's relegation to the level of an LDC brought home to the people the extent to which economic mismanagement had reduced one of the richest countries in Southeast Asia to penury[76]. The continuing unavailability of necessary consumer essentials, presence of a parallel black market economy, rising inflation, increasing gap between the rich and the poor etc., when coupled with the shameful stigma of LDC could not make the masses remain quiet any longer. It was a wound on the Burmese pride. Thus, this mass discontentment gave the form of the largest mass movement ever occurred in the country against the Ne Win regime, shaking the very foundation of the autocratic rule.

2.7. Factors for the Failure of Ne Win's Socialist Economy

From the above discussion about the Myanmarese economy under the leadership of General Ne Win it can be summed up that there were certain important factors which were largely responsible for the failure of Myanmarese economy run by General Ne Win and his party, the Burma Socialist Programme Party (BSPP). The long span of nearly 25 years of Ne Win's rule, directly or indirectly, revealed an economy which was moving towards regression and stagnation. The result was high inflation, bankruptcy, domestic fall in the foreign exchange, LDC status in 1987, and above all the outbreak of a mass movement in 1988. The factors for all these were structural and lie within the system itself. These were as follows:

First and foremost factor for the declining economy was the lack of experience, and inefficiency on the part of the military rulers. The officers did not have any formal training in the said field. The corporate and managerial experience it had earned during the short caretaker period proved insufficient as well as unsuitable in dealing with the long-term perspective economic development. Ne Win's policy of large-scale induction of the army officers, most of them without any knowledge of administration and economics, created a great deal of in efficiency and incompetence in the government. Junior officers were put as head of many of the economic and business enterprises. Above these, there was also an attitude of ambivalence to foreigners and foreign technology on the part of the Ne Win regime which was a setback in the efficiency of its economy.

Secondly, there was rigid party control and excessive centralisation of the government which obstructed the free development and innovation in the economy. Every decision came from the BSPP (Lanzin Party) in general and Ne Win in particular. In fact, the irony was that the whole economic programme of the largest country of mainland Southeast Asia was carried out according to the whim of a single individual, that of Ne Win, and a party which idolised him. Whether right or wrong, nothing could go against the decisions of the BSPP which were the decisions of Ne Win himself. All power was in the party, and economic enterprises seemed to exist more for their political role than for their productive aspects[77]. Since most of the policies and programmes related with the economy were not the outcome of clear expert views and discussions it was obviously to fail. Besides, lack of economic freedom as was normal under excessive socialist centralisation, reduced the chance for a speedy economic recovery.

Thirdly, another important factor for the decline of Ne Win's quasi-Marxist and quasi-Buddhist economic policies were rigidity and lack of perception of change on the part of leaders and the conséquent intra-party conflict. The military leaders under Ne Win were not ready to change with him. They still confined themselves in their old and outdated orthodox socialist economic ideas. The new generation was not given the chance to acquire creative and innovative ideas. Besides, they were more concerned with their political power which they were careful enough to look after seriously, while the whole economy is left out like a boat without a sail. These military leaders gave more attention to party work rather than to the economy.

Fourthly, the destruction of private enterprises through repressive methods without creating a viable infrastructure was another factor which cannot be ignored. In haste for bringing a socialist economy based on Burmanisation and Buddhism Ne Win had completely forgotten to set up the necessary socialist infrastructure to fill up the vacuum created by the absence of private enterprises. The necessary steps to convert the available resources, both for infrastructure development and for further economic progress, were left out. Thus, the absence of private enterprises was felt in the economy.

Fifthly, the presence of age old socio-political problem of ethnic insurgency was also another factor for decline of Ne Win's economy. Owing to the said problem one third of the national budget was earmarked for defence thereby depriving of the developmental programmes a sizeable amount[78]. Besides, the available rich natural and human resources in the areas occupied by insurgents could not be utilised for national cause.

Sixthly, ironical but which could not be ignored was the orthodox and occultist nature of many of the military leaders including Ne Win himself. In fact, many of the ill timed and ill-conceived policies of Ne Win were carried out as per the direction of astrological and numerological forecast. The economic policies and programmes that should be based on well calculated data and expertise were, on the contrary, left out to the ideas of some pseudo-educated and ill informed astrologer or occultist. The policies which were going to decide the fate of the nation were left to these persons.

Seventhly, clash between ideology and reality was another factor for Ne Win's economy to decline. In the context of Myanmar, in most cases, there was a clash between ideology and reality. Most of the economic policies and programmes were based on Ne Win's ideology of "Burmese Way to Socialism" which could not work when faced with actual reality. Besides, several plans and policies, while clearly enunciated in general term remained fairly vague on specific practicability.

Eighthly, red-tapism and corruption were common phenomena under the military administration. Inefficiency and ignorance on the part of the Ne Win regime was transformed into red-tapism and strict official secrecy. Regarding corruption it was rampant from the highest echelon to the lowest. The amount of salaries of the employees could not meet with the increasing rate of price rise in the country. The government's own financial crises were such that it could not raise the salary. Thus, this very tendency of excessive red tapism and corruption greatly hindered the economic progress of the country.

Apart from the aforesaid factors there might be many more other factors which also largely contributed to the deterioration of the strict economic and political system of Myanmar under Ne Win regime as it was full of complexities. In fact, the vast structure of the Myanmarese economy during the 25 years of Ne Win regime was broken down from within itself by the factors mentioned above. They acted like cancer within the system. In a way, the centralised, regimented and oppressive political rule and the socialist economic rhetoric acted and reacted upon each other to produce a real national crisis, especially from the economic point of view[79]. All these gradually led to the deterioration and stagnation of the Myanmarese economy. This created lots of discontentment and dissatisfaction among the people. Since their illusion of an efficient government disappeared they started preferring the previous democratic set up under premier U Nu. Students' and workers' unrest erupted periodically. People were not really happy with the changing economic status of the country despite the presence of vast human and natural resource. They gradually realised that a change could be brought about in view of the deteriorating economy only by establishing a democratic set up, where everyone would have the freedom to share and express; and that could be possible by ending the authoritarian and autocratic rule of the military regime. Thus the entire discontentment created by the economic failures combined with this realisation led to the first outbreak of a mass movement for democracy in 1988 throughout the country. Finally it will not be wrong to say that the picking up momentum for democracy movement in Myanmar owed much to the static and degrading nature of the country's economy combined with the intolerable military dictatorship at a time when the world as a whole was moving towards democracy.

NOTES

1. The sixteen Officers were : Commodore Than Pe (Navy Chief); Air Brig. Clift (Air Force Chief); Brig. Aung Gyi, Brig. Tin Pe, Brig San Yu, Brig Sein Win, Col Thaung Kyi, Col Kyi Maung, Col Aung Shwe, Col. Than Sein, Col. Kyaw Soe, Col. Saw Myint, Col. Chit Myaing, Col. Khin Nyo, Col. Hla Han and Col. Than Yu Saing.

2. Josef Silverstein, *Burma: Military Rule and Politics of Stagnation* (Ithaca, New York: Cornell University Press, 1977), p.80.
3. Khin Maung Nyunt, *Foreign Loans and Aid in the Economic Development of Burma (1974/75 to 1985/86)*, (Bangkok: Institute of Asian Studies - Chulalongkorn University, 1990), p.136.
4. Ibid.
5. Ibid, p.137.
6. Robert A. Holmes, "Burmese Domestic Policy: The Politics of Burmanization", *Asian Survey* (Berkeley), vol.7, no.3, March 1967, p. 190.
7. Ibid.
8. D.R. Sardesai, *Southeast Asia: Past and Present* (New Delhi: Vikas Publishing House, 1983), p.346.
9. Maung Maung Gyi, "Foreign Policy of Burma since 1962: Negative Neutralism for Group Survival" in F.K. Lehman (ed.), *Military Rule in Burma since 1962* (Singapore: Maruzen Asia, 1981), p.15.
10. S.K. Jayasurya," Technical Change and Revival of the Burmese Rice Industry", *The Development Economies*, vol. 22, no. 2, June 1984, p.144.
11. n. 8, p. 253.
12. *Encyclopaedia Britannica Vol.3* (Chicago: Encyclopaedia Britannica Inc, 1980), 15th Edition, p.509.
13. Robert H. Taylor, *The State in Burma* (London: C. Hurst & Company, 1987), p.299.
14. Ibid, pp.343-344.
15. n. 9, p.15.
16. David I. Steinberg, *Burma's Road Towards Development: Growth and Ideology Under Military Rule* (Boulder: Westview Press, 1981), p.115.
17. n. 13, p.347.
18. F.S.V.Donnison, *Burma* (New York: Praeger, 1970), p.199.
19. n.8, p.346. By 1967, as a result of the decontrolling, private trade again raised to 40% of the total value of internal trade.
20. Kalyani Bandyopadhyaya, *Burma and Indonesia: Comparative Political Economy and Foreign Policy* (New Delhi: South Asian Publishers, 1983), p.86.
21. Lawrence D. Stifel, "Burmese Socialism: Economic Problems

of the First Decade", *Pacific Affairs* (Vancouver), vol.45, Spring 1972, p.63.

22. *Far East and Australasia 1996* (London : Europa Publication, 28th Edition, 1997), p.622.
23. n.20, p.70.
24. Ibid.
25. David I. Steinberg, "Burmese Economies: The Conflict of Ideology and Pragmatism" inF.K.Lehman (ed.), *Military Rule in Burma Since 1962*, (Singapore: Maruzen Asia, 1981), p.44.
26. Nilufar Choudhury, "Burma's Foreign Policy: Continuity and Change", *BIISS Journal* (Dhaka), vol. 7, no.2, April 1986, p.188.
27. Main donor countries were Japan, Germany (West), Australia, USA, France, Denmark, UK, Canada, Italy and the Netherlands.
28. Main donors concerned with multilateral foreign assistance to Myanmar were: IDA, ADB, UNDP, UNICEF, EEC, IMF, OPEC, UNTA etc.
29. n. 3, p. 27.
30. Ibid, p. 28.
31. Ibid, p.31.
32. Ibid., p.32.
33. Ibid., p. 48.
34. Ibid, p.46.
35. Ibid.
36. Calculated on the basis of the datas of OECD given in Ibid. p.44.
37. n.16, p.144.
38. Ibid.
39. Ibid.
40. John Bray, *Burma: The Politics of Constructive Engagement* (London: Royal Institute of International Affairs, 1995), p.27.
41. There were twenty two corporations owned by the government and each one of them controls one particular area or sector of the economy. For e.g., trade corporation one looks after agricultural products.
42. n.20,p.133.

43. Frederica M.Bunge(ed), *Burma: A Country Study* (Washington D.C : American University,1983), p.63.
44. F.N. Trager, "Burma, 1967-A Better Ending then Beginning", *Asian Survey*, vol.8, no.2,February 1968, p.110.
45. n.16, p. 43.
46. Richard Butwell, "The Burmese Way of Change", *Current History* (Philadelphia), December, 1976, p.208.
47. n.20 , p. 133.
48. David I Steinberg, "Neither Silver, Neither Gold: The 40th Anniversary of the Burmese Economy", in Josef Silverstein (ed.), *Independent Burma at Forty Years: An Assessment* (Ithaca: Cornell University, 1989), p.40.
49. Ibid.
50. Mya Maung , "The Burma Road from the Union of Burma to Myanmar", *Asian Survey*, vol. 30, no.6, June 1990 , p.615.
51. Ibid.
52. n.20, p. 86.
53. n.20, p.156.
54. n.2, p. 94.
55. n.2, p.162.
56. n.16, p.801.
57. Ibid.
58. Frank N. Trager and William L. Scully, "The Third Congress of the Burma Socialist Programme Party: The Need to Treat Continuity and Dynamism of Leadership", *Asian Survey*, vol. 17, no. 9, September 1977, p.831.
59. As per the data given in GVC Naidu , "Burma : A Nation in Turmoil", *Strategic Analysis* (New Delhi), October 1988,p.805.
60. n. 20, p.94.
61. n.18,p. 202.
62. Hugh C.MacDougal and Jon A.Wiant, "Burma in 1985", *Asian Survey*, vol.26, no.2, February 1986.
63. Ibid,p.189.
64. Robert O. Tilman, "Burma in 1986", *Asian Survey*, vol. 27, no. 2 , February 1987,p.256.
65. Ibid.

66. Maureen Aung Thwin, "Burmese Days", *Foreign Affairs* (New York), Spring 1989,p.151.
67. John B. Haseman, "Burma in 1987", *Asian Survey*, vol.28, no.2, February 1988.
68. n.66.
69. Ibid.
70. Martin Staurt Fox, "Whither Burma", *World View* (Queensland), vol .30, n. 4, December, 1991,p.36.
71. Robert H. Taylor, " Change in Burma: Political Demands and Military Power", *Asian Affairs* (New York), vol.22, no.2, June 1991,p.136.
72. Ibid.
73. n.48, p.43.
74. G.V.C.Naidu, "Burma at the Crossroads", *Economic and Political Weekly* (New Delhi), 8 October 1988,p.2101.
75. John Bray, *Burma: The Politics of Constructive Engagement* (London: Royal Institute of International Affairs, 1995), p.28.
76. n.70,p.36.
77. David I. Steinberg, "Crisis in Burma", *Current History*, April 1989,p.197.
78. n.25,p.50.
79. n.20,p.225.

3

Government and Politics in Myanmar Before 1988

The Revolutionary Council (RC) started ruling the country with a strong anti-Communist and anti-Western nationalistic ideology. This could be found in two of the documents brought out by the RC viz., "The Burmese Way to Socialism" (BWS), issued on 30 April 1962 and "The System of Correlation Between the Man and His Environment" (SCME), issued on 17 January 1963. The BWS, a mixture of militarism, socialism and Buddhism, was the explicit ideological base of the RC whereas the SCME acted as its philosophic underpinning[1]. The RC sought to establish a democratic socialist state through its 'Burmese Way to Socialism'. However, we should be free from the misconception regarding the term 'democratic' used here. The concept of 'democratic' used by RC was quite different from what is actually meant in Western sense. In fact, the new military government had gradually removed most of the institutions, norms and ideas symbolising Western democratic values. One by one the government suspended the Constitution, dismissed the Parliament, abolished the Supreme Court, the High Courts, and the Secretariat. At the same time, it tried to form a united political party as it strongly felt that the intra-party fight within the then ruling AFPFL was largely responsible for the process of national disintegration during U Nu's regime. When it failed to form such a political party with the support of other parties for executing policies and programmes the RC formed its own political party. The Burma Socialist Programme Party (BSPP) thus, came into being in July 1962. All the potential political leaders opposed to it were arrested; and, on 28 March 1964, the RC took its final step by banning all political parties except its own BSPP or *Lanzin* Party (means New Way)[2]. It was the only legal party allowed to function as such. Thus, an age of one party rule was inaugurated for the first time.

Now, the RC Government spoke for decentralisation of power though in practice it was not so. It took over all the powers given in the constitution. The Chairman as the head was the absolute master of all these legislative, executive and judicial powers. And it was none other than Gen. Ne Win himself who actually held the power of the new military government. Power was centralised in his hands. The whole administration was carried out in the name of the Chairman of the RC. As mentioned, many existing political institutions were dissolved while many new ones came into being on *ad-hoc* basis, which lacked systematic nature. Everything under the government was on the personal whims of Ne Win as the leader. Unrestricted by the challenges that could have been posed by a constitution, a legislature, or an electorate this government governed by decrees and proclamations[3]. All its pronouncements had the force of law and remained in effect until they were withdrawn or replaced[4]. However, all these did not mean that the RC government in particular and the country as a whole, in general, was free from all sorts of political vices. It is a fact, no doubt, that the magnitude was slightly low in this period as compared with those in later stages. For, in the beginning of this period the people as well as the officials were generally not very clear with the motives and nature of the new government. But the most serious problem for the military regime, which would result in political crisis in the later stages, was that the entire responsibility of running the government was given wholly to the army officers. And these officers knew next to nothing about education, welfare programmes, economics, politics and international relations. Here the tragedy was that the RC did not trust civilians to be professional bureaucrats[5]. Experts known in different fields were completely ignored. Loyalty to Gen. Ne Win was the sole criteria for appointment of these military officers. Ultimately, most of the problems during this period cropped up from the inability and inefficiency of the officials holding responsible post in the government set up.

Not surprisingly General Ne Win had tried to justify the coup as well as the formation of the Revolutionary Council on the pretext of keeping the territorial integrity of the country intact; though many leaders from minority groups were not ready to accept it. He had also justified the legalisation of one party rule on the ground of speeding the achievement of the ideological goals given in the 'Burmese Way to Socialism' and to take the country towards rapid development and progress. But the real motive behind all these was to concentrate power. "With the armed forces as its power base, party apparatus such as mass elite communication conveyor belts and control mechanisms and administrative apparatus as the guiding and goading instruments, Ne Win had everything to check in for a power monopoly"[6]. This does not, however, mean that he had total control over the political conditions and affairs of the country. To the contrary, political crisis of all size and magnitude soon cropped up in the post coup period from various quarters. The coup was followed by a sudden disorientation in the economy which further aggravated the political scenario of the country. Besides, most sections of the society were not very eager to co-operate with military regime and its BWS based economic policies. Not only this, but also opposition came from minorities, leftist rebels, remnants of erstwhile political parties and, in some cases even prominent individuals.

Of all those who were opposed to the Ne Win regime, the most vocal and active over ground opposition, in the initial stage, came from University students and Buddhists monks. The students were the first to protest against the destruction of parliamentary democracy by the army in Myanmar. They were not ready to endure quietly the injustice and highhandedness of the junta government. And to make the situation worse, the students were in most cases assisted by the monks. Though not openly, the activities of the students and the monks during this period were more or less intermingled. And this created more difficulty for the government in controlling the already degrading politico-economic situation. To face the challenge arising from these two groups the RC Government imposed restrictive regulations on student movements and activities of Buddhists *Sanghas*. But this could not restrain the spirit of both students and monks. Instead, as a challenge to these restrictions the first protest by the students against the regime was staged in the form of a huge demonstration organised by Rangoon University Students' Union (RUSU) on 7 July 1962. The monks also challenged the military by refusing in 1964 to register in a new government sponsored organisation[7]. But in both cases the government retaliated strongly. Contrary to traditions, the government responded to by firing at the students, and the monks. The RUSU office which was a symbol of freedom and justice was also demolished by dynamiting on 8 July 1962. All these incidents created frustration on the parts of the students and the monks. They considered the actions of the government as a challenge to the spirits and tradition of democratic set up and freedom - a plot to destroy the remnants of the 'parliamentary democracy' era. They also considered it as an attempt of the junta to remove the ideas related with democracy from the minds of the people. Though the RC could subdue the monks up to 1974, in case of students it was not possible. The student movements failed to cease completely though the regime had subdued it up to a certain manageable level. All these formed an important part of the ongoing political crisis.

Political problems faced by the Ne Win regime were not however confined only to the activities of the students and the monks. In fact, this first phase of military rule started with opposition from various quarters. Besides the two groups, the Ne Win government had to encounter lots of tension and problems from ethnic rebels and leftist undergrounds. Insurgency still continued to be a serious political, military and diplomatic headache for Chairman Ne Win[8]. The growth and stability of the nation had been subjected to constant threat due to the activities of insurgent groups[9]. Their continuous attack did not make it easier for the government in their struggle against the ensuing political turmoil in the country. While the regime could not bring about any practicable solution to the problem, opposition from the side of the ethnic and other rebel groups was increasing. Groups related with Karens, Shans, Kachins and Mons were openly fighting against the government. The most active were the Karen National Union (KNU), established in 1947 by Saw Ba U Gyi; the Kachin Independence Organisation (KIO), established in 1961 by three brothers: Zau Seng, Zau Tu and Zau Dan; and the Shan State Independence Army (SSIA), established in 1960 by Shan students on the Thai border. Besides, the communist inspired rebel coalition front, the National Democratic United Front (NDUF)[10], consisting of the Communist Party of Burma (CPB-White Flag), the Chin National Vanguard Party (CNVP), the Karen National United Party (KNUP), the Karenni National Progressive Party (KNPP), and Pao rebels, also became active. All these developments were not something to be taken lightly for the government. In fact, in most part of the territory inhabited by the ethnic minorities the authority of the Union Government was hardly recognised — certainly off the main roads[11]. Not only this, the activity of non-ethnic insurgent groups like CPB, both Red and White Flag, and Communist Party of Arakan (CPA) also increased. But on its part the most important task for the new government and its army was to subdue the insurgents, both ethnic and non-ethnic, in all parts of the country in order to remain in power it had seized forcefully[12]. However, it could not succeed much. Its attempts to negotiate with these warring rebels in 1963 were also not fruitful. No solution came out from the negotiation. By late 60s CPB controlled 20,000sq.km., large areas along the China border down to the Mekong River[13]. Insurgency remained active and political crisis for the government persisted.

During the same period another serious problem for the Revolutionary Council was posed by the armed resistance started by U Nu, the former Prime Minister. In the later part of 1969, with his secret headquarters based in Central Bangkok, U Nu started his Parliamentary Democracy Party (PDP) whose armed wing, the Patriotic Liberation Army (PLA) established a string of bases along the Thai Myanmar border[14]. The PDP even signed an agreement with Karen and Mon rebel groups for fighting unitedly against the military regime of Gen. Ne Win[15]. Various former army officials joined the party. In fact, at one time it was considered to be a political force of enormous significance because of its democratic tag and clandestine international support. This continued up to 1972. Thus under the leadership of Gen. Ne Win there was no improvement in the issues related with insurgency as compared to the former parliamentary democracy of U Nu. Much to the dismay and frustration of the people the chances of peaceful solution to the existing problem was remote because of using excessive force and coercion by the RC. Peace negotiations became impossible and problems multiplied fast. To add to this, economic related crisis and the anti-Chinese riots in the late 60s' also further worsened the situation in the political front of the country.

Above all these, another serious and most complicated political problem faced by the RC government was inconveniences and discontentments which started emerging within the party structure due to regular purging among its ranks and file. In a way, it was something inherent in the rule of the military regime. Gen. Ne Win primarily directed senior military officers to implement his ideas of governance, and they were forced to resign when his programmes failed, taking the heat themselves and always protecting the chief[16]. This was the style he practised. And in fact, this habit of purging those long time comrades under mere pretext, particularly to satisfy Ne Win's whim, created dissatisfaction and insecurity among the members of both the RC and the

BSPP. For, Ne Win never hesitated to imprison even the closest. Ironically, the officers or party members purged were not given any room for clarification and no chance at all for explaining their actions. The first victim of this practice was Brig Aung Gyi, the chief architect of the RC administrative set up and the heir apparent to Ne Win, who was removed on 8 February 1963. He was removed because he had voiced criticism about the officially announced economic policies and suggested a much more pragmatic approach[17]. In what amounted to a coup within a coup, Aung Gyi's faction was removed[18]. This started a subdued frustration among the officers loyal to the ousted brigadier. And the first seed of discontentment within the military set up was sown. All these had a negative impact on the government. As a result there was little progress in the area of development and growth because the officials preferred to follow Gen. Ne Win's whims rather than to bring out their progressive and innovative ideas. The phenomenon which started in the initial stage of military rule still continues today. Anyone who started becoming more popular than Ne Win was removed abruptly - a practice initiated by military successors of Ne Win even now.

In this period many more followed after the purging of Brig Aung Gyi. In August 1972, there was again another purge. Two ministers U Maung Shwe and U Sein Mya were purged from the Ne Win Cabinet. They were prosecuted for higher crimes against the state i.e. corruption, in early 1973. Purges, in most cases were made on the flimsy ground of corruption, something that had got very little validity.

As the first decade of the Burmese Way to Socialism ended, the Ne Win government introduced a series of sweeping institutional changes designed to accelerate the revolutionary transformation of Myanmar and reduce the gap that continued to exist between the military rulers and the Myanmarese polity[19]. In 1971, following the First BSPP Congress, the party was also converted from cadre to mass organisation. It was directed to look to the framing of a new constitution. The working of the Revolutionary Government[20], under the RC came to an end and in its place was formed the Government of the Union of Myanmar, while most of the members remained the same. A new council of Ministers was constituted with Ne Win still as the head. The sign of a change, in fact, was made in the government when twenty senior officers including Gen. Ne Win changed into civilian garbs by retiring themselves from the armed forces. The appearance was of being in civilian hands, as military titles were dropped in favour of traditional civilian prefixes[21]. However, the fact remained that though Ne Win and his followers had shed their military ranks in 1972, yet, it was not until 1974 that the whole military based RC was formally dissolved. And with it came the end of the first phase of military rule. Thus, for the first time since the 1962 coup, a nominal constitutional government came into being though the head remained same. This pseudo - constitutional Republic with all its tendencies, nature and practice of an authoritarian military rule, was to ensure the second phase of military rule from 1974. But the prevailing political problems did not reflect any change. Instead, with all its originality, it passed into the second phase of military rule thus creating the same headache for the civilian turned military leaders as it was in the first phase of their rule.

3.1. Constitutional Dictatorship

A new phase of military rule under Gen. Ne Win started in 1974, twelve years after the military coup, with the newly enacted constitution. After the approval of a national referendum in December 1973 the new constitution commonly known as the 1974 Constitution was adopted on 3 January 1974. The country got a new name - the Socialist Republic of the Union of Burma (now Myanmar), and a new flag. It also got a unicameral legislature, the *Pyithu Hluttaw*, with a single legal political party. Further, the country was divided into fourteen political units comprising seven states and seven divisions. And from 27 January to 10 February, elections were held for the new supreme constitutional body, the *Pyithu Hluttaw* [22]. Consequently on 2 March 1974, the twelve anniversary of the military coup, the Revolutionary Council was formally dissolved, and the new government was officially installed[23]. The legislature elected a Council of State, which was the principal decision making body of the government. A Council of Ministers with Sein Win as Prime Minister was also elected. Not surprisingly, Ne Win was chosen the Chairman of this powerful Council of State with 29 members, and, under the constitution, automatically became the President of the Socialist Republic as well. Under the new constitution, the legislative powers were delegated to the "central and local organs of state power", which in their turn were to be controlled by the Council of State. Ultimately, the reality remained that the power was in fact with the Council, which in turn, was in the hands of the strong man, Ne Win. Thus began the second phase of military rule with Ne Win once again at the helm of power.

The new phase or second phase of the military rule was in fact a period of constitutional dictatorship. There still remained the trace of a strong authoritarian nature behind the facade of constitutionalism and civilian rule. Force and fear were still important means of ruling. This is not surprising because the persons in the new government were also more or less the same as that of the RC period except that they had discarded their military garb and military title and that they were elected through a legally held national election.

However, the overall scenario of the country remained more or less the same as it was in the last 12 years. There was not much change in the way of political clashes and turmoil. The reason being that despite changes in name, flag and political system of the country, the persons in power were the same who had ruled in the first phase, with the same psyche. Besides Ne Win's 1974 Constitution and the new structure of government made no alternations at all in the basic realities of Myanmarese politics[24]. Apart from these, the hardships experienced by the people under the Ne Win regime in the last 12 years also made them aware of the true nature of the junta. People were completely fed up with the power hungry, self-centered and hedonistic nature of the military rulers. They wanted this group of former army officers to leave the seat of power; and in its place a strong and genuine democratic government be installed. As a result of all these, political crisis aggravated more in the Socialist Republic period. Political situation became complex. Problems related with students uprising, discontentment of ethnic minority groups, insurgency, and internal tussle within the party set up and the question of legitimacy of the regime became very complicated to solve. And the inability on the part of Ne Win government to bring about viable solutions for the problem from time to time would finally become a combined factor for the outbreak of the "88 Movement". What needs to be remembered is that the stigmatic nature of the 1974 Constitution in itself was a major cause for those problems prevalent during the period.

The new government were confronted with serious threats from the restive workers, students and monks. This made governance difficult for the new government in a situation where there were problems of ethnic minorities and insurgency. Along with this the deteriorating economy marked by high price rise, shortage of essential commodities and low salary brought out the urban wage employees in the streets. Wages were meagre and working conditions of general workers were miserable. In April 1974, at the annual session of the Workers' Council, protests came from workers and reached an explosive dimension[25]. More violence and riots broke out in the month of June. Starting with the oil workers of Chauk, it soon spread to workers at railway construction, spinning mills, dockyards and so on[26]. Many students' bodies took active part in the anti-establishment protest. Consequently the government retaliated by banning all public assemblage and closing all the universities and high schools. However, this was not the solution. The situation could not be brought under control.

Within a few months of workers' strikes student led riot broke out with monks helping them. Serious altercations and clashes broke out once again in December 1974 between the protesting group of students and the government. The issue, this time, was of not showing proper respect to the death body of U Thant, a prominent world figure and former Secretary General of the United Nations. The students vehemently protested against the government's niggardly burial plan for the deceased U Thant in the remote Race Course Cemetery, on the outskirt of Yangon. Government resorted to force to control the protest movement which resulted in killing and wounding of many protestors. Officially, 9 people were killed, 7 wounded and 1, 800 arrested[27]. Refuting this, students who participated in the demonstration claimed that 300-400 of their colleagues were gunned down[28]. In reality however, the U Thant issue was nothing but an expression of general resentment of the masses against the incompetent and repressive government of Ne Win.

However, 1974 was not the only year with political unrest. Further demonstrations took place in the years that followed it. Students and workers launched riots again in 1975, on the anniversary of the 1974 workers' riot. There were demonstration and protest rallies. Government once more retaliated by closing all universities and arresting 213 students out of which 203 were sentenced[29]. This protest was followed by yet another demonstration in early 1976 by students of Rangoon University demanding for the release of their fellows arrested earlier. They also protested against the declining economic condition of the country under the civilian turned military leaders.

The year 1976, was in fact, an unlucky and ominous year for Ne Win. Apart from the protest outside the government this year was also marked by political crises within the government and the party organisation. Ne Win dismissed the defence minister, Brig. General Tin U (or Tin Oo), who had a strong following in the armed forces, without giving any valid reason. This was followed by a serious crisis in the government set up. A plot to assassinate Ne Win, Secretary of the BSPP and of the State Council General San Yu, and National Intelligence Bureau Head Col. Tin Oo (not to be confused with expelled General Tin U) by a group of junior military officers was unearthed. The group of '14th Junior Officers'[30] led by Capt. Ohn Kyaw Myint were ardent admirers of the ousted Gen Tin U. What is peculiar about the group is the fact that they were all products of the country's premier military institute, the Defence Service Academy. Once the coup was unearthed all the plotters were sentenced. Capt. Ohn Kyaw Myint was sentenced to death and later executed. The remaining officers were given either life imprisonment or long prison terms. On its part, though the coup failed and the plotters were sentenced, yet, it clearly showed the degree of discontentment within the armed forces. It was a show of defiance against Ne Win, his whimsical actions and policies as well as to his leadership. It brought to limelight how deeply the social discontentment had penetrated the new military elite[31]. The coup attempt also 'revealed, for all to see, a soldier class divided internally'[32]. Later on, Gen. Tin U was also sentenced for not revealing about the plot of treason despite having prior knowledge about it. He was given 7 years of rigorous imprisonment. Whatsoever, due to the damage that had already been made, the crack had started appearing in the system. It could not be corrected earlier.

The riots, the attempted coup and the trial were storm warnings to the party leadership that something very basic was wrong with the system[33]. The leaders knew it. However, instead of bringing out a pragmatic policy the party carried out purges at the instigation of Ne Win. In fact the purges became trademark of Ne Win's administration which continued, in a large scale, up to the early 80s. Careers of many stalwarts with bright future came to sudden ends. For instance, Brig. Aung Gyi and General Tin U, who were purged, were on one time rumoured to be likely successors of Ne Win. Not only this, in 1976 alone, aftermath the coup attempt, about 54,193 members and leaders of the party were purged[34]. Intelligence Chief Brig. Tin Oo (considered 'heir apparent' to Ne Win) and Home and Religious Affairs Minister Col. Bo Nyi were purged in May 1983. Even their followers were not spared. Thus, instead of taking the party and government towards a combined effort for achieving progress this practice of purge spread the fire of discontentment among the BSPP cadres. Situation of unrest, however, decreased slightly in the capital after the Third Congress of the BSPP held in February 1977. Ne Win was elected Chairman again. In this session certain remedial steps were taken up on the socio-economic front in order to pacify the people. Special emphasis was stressed on weeding out corruption and economic reforms. Besides, the systematic rounding up of anti government elements on charges of treason had also shifted many active student protestors to the border areas. But in the peripheral areas the ongoing political upheaval and civil war continued as it used to be in the time of independence.

Here, in our study of the period of Socialist Republic what we need not to forget is that the unrest was not confined only in students, monks, workers and armed force personnel. In fact, ethnic and political rebellion and the related insurgency was another important aspect for the deteriorating political atmosphere. Despite use of force and repressive measures the government failed to curb the insurgent groups nor could it bring out any pragmatic solution. Since use of force with brutality symbolised the majority Burman's determination to dominate the minority groups, the fear of annihilation by the majority was always there in the mind of the minority people. This impression created more complexity to the problem. Besides, in many backward peripheral areas of the country, where government's development programmes hardly reach, the armed struggle virtually remained a way of life. And ironically, the new phase of civilianising military rule was followed by a new phase of civil war and insurgency in Myanmar.

In 1976, insurgency spread out in a large scale. Taking advantage of the disunity and discontentment which plagued the army and the BSPP, nine ethnic insurgent groups came together to form an umbrella organisation known as the National Democratic Front (NDF), with Mahn Ba Zan of Karen National Union (KNU) as Chairman[35]. This was the first ethnic front of unique significance. With the formation insurgency related activities increased with more strength. This continued up to the 80s'. In 1980, for a short while, it appeared that the amnesty offered to the rebels and dissident groups by the government would solve the brewing political crisis of insurgency and civil war. The event followed, however, proved otherwise. The talks held by the government with two main groups, the Kachin Independence Organisation (KIO) and the Communist Party of Burma (CPB), were not fruitful. The talks could not be materialised in cease-fire for want of sincerity on the part of the government. The government demanded absolute surrender from the side of the rebel groups, but in return offered no concessions[36]. While the rebels wanted to refer to the 1947 Constitution as they were not ready to accept the new one, the government wanted to stick to the new one. Ultimately, the negotiations and talks with the CPB and the KIO broke down in May and June 1981, respectively. Besides, government's offer of amnesty was found unacceptable to most of the other rebel groups, with the exception of some smaller ones. The Karens and the Shans did not even go to the negotiation table as they were determined to continue their fight for freedom. For them no negotiation was worthwhile except complete independence.

Insurgency and civil war therefore continued in the 80s. While fighting with the Kachins and the CPB insurgents in the North and the North Eastern part of the country remained constant over the period, the government's fight with the Shans and the Karens increased in 1985. To make the matter worse, a military agreement was signed between NDF and CPB in 1986 in the latter's headquarters at Pangshang (in Shan State). The main point was to cooperate with each other in their fight against the government forces. And, with the continuing setbacks in the economic front it was not really easy for the government to face the challenge. It continued its effort to solve the problem with force and suppression though it knew its ineffectiveness in the long run, from past experience. Thus the government continued with its effort to end insurgency with the belief that force was the only means to contain them. On the other hand the ethnic minorities were of the view that successive administrations in Myanmar used the ongoing armed conflict to marginalise them from the actual seat of power. Such misconceptions also took the situation from bad to worse. The congenial atmosphere for negotiation, in fact, was not created at all.

During this phase the actual problem with the issue of civil war and insurgency was that Ne Win did not really show any eagerness to entertain Aung San's policy of "Unity in Diversity" in dealing with the ethnic groups of the country. The formula and spirit of "Panglong Agreement" of 12 February 1947[37] was completely ignored. He did not make any genuine effort to continue whatever a little attempt was started by Aung San and U Nu, and to find out a solution. Instead of promoting federal authority to the ethnic groups more and more centralisation of power was carried out. Besides, a genuine political situation seemed to be wanting on the part of Ne Win and his associates.

3.2. Constitution of 1974

Over and above all problems mentioned the most serious one faced by the Ne Win government during the period of Socialist Republic was from the duly enacted new constitution itself, which, in fact, was Ne Win's own making.

With a view to civilianise the regime and to legitimise the military at the same time Ne Win mooted the idea of a new constitution in 1969. That was followed by a long process of drafting a new constitution which was completed in the last part of 1973. Ultimately the new constitution of the Socialist Republic of the Union of Burma was inaugurated on 4 January 1974, the 26th anniversary of Myanmar's Independence. The main architect was Dr. Maung Maung, a London trained lawyer and Ne Win loyalist. However, the duly enacted constitution deepened the problems already faced by Ne Win, further. It became a source of extreme discontentment and a symbol of repression and manipulation of power. The 1974 Constitution included certain features not conducive for a democratic set up in real practice.

First, effort was made to keep the whole governmental set up under a single party i.e., the military controlled Burma Socialist Programme Party (BSPP) - the only party allowed to exist in the country. From *Pyithu Hluttaw*, the highest organ, to the village council, the lowest in the government hierarchy, it was the BSPP which got the final say on any affair. The three organs of the government the executive, the legislature and the judiciary - came under its control. All the functionaries of any level of the state set-up were decided by the BSPP. Ultimately, sovereignty lay with the BSPP, Thus, the constitution, was in a way, of the BSPP, by the BSPP and for the BSPP. This has been clearly mentioned in the Preamble and Articles 11, 179 and 205.

Secondly, the constitution gave a unicameral legislature under a unitary system (Articles 41 and 44) with maximum importance to control leadership. Though the constitution mentioned a sort of functional autonomy at different level of the state and that the *Pyithu Hluttaw* (People's Assembly), with its elected members, was the highest organ of state power in general. Yet in actual practice power was concentrated in the hands of the 28-member Council of State whose chairman was Ne Win. By virtue of being the Chairman of Council of State he was also the President of the country (Article.66)

Thirdly, the constitution greatly undermined the interest of ethnic people even if it tried to portray itself as a means of bringing equality among different groups. It failed to bring any positive change on the ongoing issue of majority - minority relation and the question of national unity. In a way it made the situation more complicated. This constitution denied the ethnic minorities the special territorial and cultural rights as embodied in the former constitution creating enough ground for the majority domination - the minority so believed.

3.3. The End of Constitutional Dictatorship

The second phase of Ne Win's rule had not made much improvement in most of the issues facing the country. Even after three national election held in 1974, 1978, and 1981 under the new constitution the form of government, the party leadership as well as the organisation remained, in most cases, the same. In reality, the type of civilian government that was introduced in 1974 behind a constitutional facade signified little or no change in the nature of military authoritarianism. Power remained largely in the same hands as before with less ability for bringing development. Though Ne Win had resigned as President from the government in 1981, yet, he still held the Chairmanship of the all powerful BSPP - still retaining the power to pull the strings in the country's political set up. As Chairman of the BSPP the power of decision-making remained with him. In fact, during this phase, Myanmar's politics functioned at two levels: the symbol of power was wielded by the leaders and members of parliament while the levers of power were manipulated by the BSPP leadership[38]. And, it was none other than Ne Win who had controlled both levels, and who had got the actual power. But, despite all these, situations went on degrading. The poor policies, administrative inefficiency and economic mismanagement when mixed up with the arbitrary, abusive and xenophobic nature of the government, did not bring any hope of improvement. Consequently, various unwanted issues and events, quite different from earlier ones, started emerging. By 1987 Ne Win had to accept the failure of his 'Burmese Way to Socialism' and his rule. He emphasised the need for an all round reform of the country. Despite this, in the late 1987 the government surprisingly carried out the demonetisation of three denominations viz, 25, 35 and 75 Kyats. This was followed by the U.N. declaration of Least Developed Country (LDC) status for Myanmar as requested by the government. The people were very much infuriated. All these were the results of the government's own making. Finding out any viable solution for the crisis proved too late. The approaching political firestorm of restlessness and frustration could not be stopped. For, the pent up emotions and discontentment had reached the maximum limit of endurance. Only a spark was necessary to ignite the whole issue. And that was provided by the 'tea stall incident' of 12 March 1988 near the campus of Rangoon Institute of Technology (RIT) - on the occasion of the completion of 40 years of Myanmar's independence. The fire had finally started burning with all its furiousness.

The tea stall incident which started as a normal brawl took a different turn. The killing of an RIT student, Maung Phone Maw, in police firing and the high handed nature of the authority in the ensuing altercation provoked the already depressed masses. The situation which otherwise could have been avoided escalated into a full blown violent mass movement. Students played the leading role. On the other hand, the government, instead of pacifying the students and masses, resorted to the only means known to them - force. The dreaded *Lon Htein* or riot police was called out to tackle the unarmed students. It resulted in the killing and injuring a large number of students. Forty-one arrested, died of suffocation inside a small police van[39]. Educational institutions were closed down until June in order to bring the students under control. But massive demonstration broke out once again when the institutions were opened. There was mounting pressure on the government from the side of the masses. With no alternative in sight Chairman Ne Win called for an extraordinary session of the BSPP on 23 July, actually scheduled for 7 July. There, Ne Win and San Yu resigned from their post of Chairman of the party and President of the Union, respectively. But the induction of Sein Lwin in the scene further aggravated the political situation. After the resignation of Ne Win and San Yu, Sein Lwin - known as the 'Butcher of Burma' and the most hated man in the country - was appointed both as President of the country and BSPP Chairman. On hearing the news of his appointment people became very angry. It provoked more demonstrations and riots. His appointment acted as if putting oil in the burning fire. The situation throughout the country was tense. The *Shwe Dagon* Pagoda in Yangon became the rallying point.

On 3 August, martial law was declared in Yangon. However, most of the protestors defied this ban. Many were arrested. And on 8 August, challenging the actions of the government, anti government demonstrations with thousands of people broke out simultaneously in towns and cities all over the country. The strongest centre was in Yangon. Participation ranged from all walks of life. The government retaliated with all brutalities. Hundreds of demonstrators were killed in the wee hour of 8 August and also in days that followed. The *Tatmadaw* continued its assault. Even the doctors and nurses of Yangon General Hospital were not spared[40]. But all these failed to dampen the spirit of the demonstrators. Mass demonstrations further spread to over 40 places all over Myanmar[41]. And one new and interesting development that took place this time was that, for the first time, the demonstrators demanded for the resignation of the military government (BSPP) and the restoration of genuine democracy and human rights in the country. In fact, the idea of a movement purely for achieving democracy was conceptualised during this 'crisis of 1988'.

On 12 August, Sein Lwin had to resign after eighteen days in power due to the mounting pressure throughout the country. In his place, Dr. Maung Maung, a western trained lawyer and Ne Win loyalist, was appointed as the new Head of State. But his appointment could not bring much change to the already prevailing scenario. Instead, it became uglier and uglier. Various student organisations and opposition groups came out in defiance of the ban of the government. Opposition leaders came on the scene. These groups and leaders, demanding democracy, were to play pivotal role in the democracy movement that was to pick up momentum in the later stage.

Situation in the country remained grim. In the beginning of September, even some fifty towns and cities were under the control of protestors[42]. Anarchy prevailed throughout the country. Army was everywhere spreading the message of brutality. To quell the uprising, in an emergency meeting on 11 September, the *Pyithu Hluthaw* decided to hold general election as proposed by the BSPP the previous day. But the protestors were not ready to call off their protest or to accept anything, unless the BSPP government resigned and an interim government was formed before holding the election. Situation remained tense. And it was in the midst of all these, that on 18 September, a group of army officers under Gen Saw Maung staged a coup within the set up. The pretext was of strengthening the government and its army. This group formed the State Law and Order Restoration Council (SLORC) to govern the country. Soon after the coup all state organs such as People's Assembly, the State Council and the Council of Ministers were abolished. Demonstration of any kind was banned and a nation wide dusk to dawn (8 a.m. - 4 p.m.) curfew was imposed. This time the *Tatmadaw* resorted to utmost brutality against the protestors and demonstrators, without restraint of any kind. Opposition of any form was crushed. Students as well as political dissidents were rounded up. Many were massacred in the streets of cities and towns. In fact, it was believed that Yangon alone, in two months, suffered more casualties than the figure of all the insurgent groups suffered in two years[43]. From the day of the September coup onward the SLORC violently put down the pro-democracy movement[44]. At least one thousand people were killed as the immediate consequence[45]. Myanmar virtually became one of the worst 'killing fields'. Many students and dissidents ran away to the borders, in the rebel areas, to escape the wrath. Thus, the protest was subdued for the time being. However, it was this sign of strong public resentment against dictatorship which sowed the seeds of democracy.

Whatsoever may be the outcome, in the 40 years of post independence political history of Myanmar, the year 1988 was the most significant one. It marked the beginning of a genuine and conscious mass movement for democracy in the country - a challenge to authoritarianism. One can subdue the protestors but not the spirit.

To sum up, the political crisis that had emerged in Myanmar in the first forty years of independence was mainly caused by its political leaders, both civilian and military. It is without doubt that the authoritarian military rulers did the maximum destruction of the country, yet, at the same time, we cannot ignore what the civilian leaders also did. As we know well that the Myanmarese society is a complex one with some 135 discontented ethnic minority groups making various proposals and demands in their own interests. There was never dearth of new problems in Myanmar. Even if one problem was solved another would crop up. And the leaders had taken for granted the love and respect shown to them as the pioneers of Myanmarese Independence, by the people. They never tried to understand what the people wanted. The military hierarchy abused the power delegated to them by the people for their own selfish end, and also in a dictatorial way. This ultimately created a line of enmity between the rulers and the ruled resulting in rapid downfall and regression of the country. The legacy of Aung San was used in a wrong and perverted form. The result was frustration, hatred and discontentment in the minds of the masses against the rulers. In fact, it will not be wrong to assert that the political shortcomings and turmoil of the aforesaid period of the first forty years of independence combined with the economic failures under the Ne Win regime caused the present movement for democracy in Myanmar. In the following pages the movement of democracy is being discussed in the light of these developments already stated.

NOTES

1. Josef Silverstein, *Burma: Military Rule and Politics of Stagnation* (Ithaca, New York: Cornell University Press, 1977) p.80.
2. Ibid, p.99.
3. Ibid, p.90
4. Ibid.
5. Michael Aung Thwin, "1948 and Burma's Myth of Independence, in, Josef Silverstein (ed.), *Independent Burma at Forty Years: An Assessment* (Ithaca: Cornell University Press,1989),p.26.
6. Maung Maung Gyi, *Burmese Political Values: The Socio-Political Roots of Authoritarianism* (New York: Praeger, 1983), p.203.
7. n.1,p.50

8. Kalyani Bandyopadhyaya, *Burma and Indonesia: Comparative Political Economy and Foreign Policy* (New Delhi: South Asian Publishers Pvt. Ltd., 1983), p.139.
9. Ibid.
10. Established in May 1959, the NDUF was the first really successful insurgent nationalities front in Myanmar. It was later dissolved in 1975.
11. F.S.V.Donnison , *Burma* (New York: Praeger , 1970), p15.
12. Ibid.
13. Bertil Lintner, *Outrage: Burma's Struggle for Democracy* (Bangkok: White Lotus, 1990),p. 46.
14. Ibid, p.50.
15. Ibid.
16. John Badgley, "Burmese Ideology: A comment", in Josef Silverstein (ed.), *Independent Burma in Forty Years: An Assessment* (Ithaca: Cornell University Press,1989), p. 71.
17. n.13, p. 40.
18. n.16, p. 70.
19. John A. Wiant, "Burma : Loosening up on the Tiger's Tail". *Asian Survey* (Berkeley), vol.13, no.2, February 1973, p.179..
20. The Revolutionary Government consisted of 8 members - six from RC, one civilian and one army officer.
21. n.1, p. 92.
22. David I. Steinberg, *Burma's Road Towards Development: Growth and Ideology Under Military Rule* (Colorado: Westview Press, 1981), p.65. Also see Josef Silverstein, *Burma : Military Rule and Politics of Stagnation* (Ithaca, New York: Cornell University Press,1977), p.137.
23. Ibid.
24. Richard Butwell, "The Burmese Way of Change", *Current History* (Philadelphia), December 1976, p.206.
25. John F.Cady, *The United States and Burma* (Cambridges, Mass.: Harvard University Press, 1976),p. 277.
26. n.13, p.51.
27. Ibid, p.52
28. Ibid.
29. n.1, p.143.
30. 11 Captains and 3 Majors.

31. *Far East and Australasia 1996* (London : Europa Publication, 28th Edition, 1997), p. 614.
32. n. 24.
33. n. 1, p.144.
34. Ibid.
35. These 9 Groups included KIO, KNPP, KNU, LNUP, PSLP, PNO, ALP, KNLP (it resigned) and SSPP. This further increased to 12. New entries were NMSP (1982), WNO (1983),and CNF (1989).
36. n. 13, p.64.
37. Chao Tzang, "The Burma Military : Holding the Country Together", in Josef Silverstein (ed.), *Independent Burma in Forty Years: An Assessment* (Ithaca: Cornell University Press,1989),p. 82.
38. Josef Silverstein, "Burma in 1981: The Changing of the Guardians Begins", *Asian Survey*, vol.22, February 1982,p.181.
39. Burma Watcher, "Burma in 1988 : There a whirlwind", *Asian Survey*, vol.29, no.2, February, 1989,p.175.
40. Amnesty International, *Myanmar* (London, Amnesty International Publications, November 1990), p.1.
41. no.13, p. 196.
42. n.40, p.3.
43. Moksha Yitri, "Time Crisis in Burma", *Asian Survey*, vol.29,no.6,, June, 1989, p. 553.
44. n. 40, p.3.
45. Ibid.

4

Movement for Democracy in Myanmar: 1988-1990

Now, it is seen that the long period of continuous neglect and inefficient management of the country's socio-economic and political affairs caused the mass uprising of 1988. The faulty policies of the military rulers, based on their perverted version of socialism, brought Myanmar down to the level of begging from being one of the richest countries in Southeast Asia, thereby leading to the United Nations' declaration of the country as the Least Developed Country (LDC). Ultimately, a fluctuating economy characterised by black marketing, inflation and demonetisations; an ethnic based insurgency; social discontents in all the sections of the society; and the question of LDC - all combined together to brought out the simple minded general masses of Myanmar in the main streets of the country in the early summer of 1988. The main purpose was to protest against the military rule and demand for democracy.

The ultimate spark to this chain of reactions was provided by the tea stall incident of 12 March 1988 in the Rangoon Institution of Technology (RIT) campus where a student Maung Phone Maw was killed. He became, in sort, the first student martyr of the present movement. This tiny incident was followed by protest, demonstration, riots and violence of an unimaginable scale. People from all walks of life came out openly against the government. Students, monks, government officials, doctors, nurses, lawyers etc, participated in the demonstration - something quite new in Myanmar. It was a hard time for those in power. The country was completely engulfed in turmoil. Government called out riot police (*Lon Htein*) and regular army units to suppress it.

The students' demonstrations started in March 1988; continued in the months that followed, especially in May, June and July. But the largest pro-democracy demonstration was yet to come out. It occurred in the month of August. On 8 August peaceful anti-government demonstration and procession erupted in all the main cities and towns throughout the country[1]. It was the first of its kind and will always remain in the history of the country's democracy movement as a watermark. On this particular day around 100,000[2] people marched through Yangon alone. Demonstrations and marches were also simultaneously carried out in other cities and towns including Mandalay, Yanangyaung, Pegu, Moulmein, Taunggyi, Sagaing and Prome. In fact, mass demonstrations spread to over 40 places throughout the country[3]. The demands of all the demonstrations were mainly for the resignation of the Burma Socialist Programme Party (BSPP) Government, ending the outdated socialist economy, establishment of multi-party democracy and the formation of an interim government to oversee the election and transition to democracy. These demands were, however, not acceptable to the ruling government. It retaliated with repressive measures. Instead of pacifying the demonstrators with a viable solution order was given to fire upon the unarmed marchers with automatic weapons - something very barbaric. The order was actually executed from around 11.45 p.m. of the fateful day of 8 August. Thousands died within a few days. Western diplomats and independent observers estimated that not less than 1000 people had been killed in Rangoon alone[4]. About 2000 were believed to have been wounded in the five-day carnage[5]. Many were also arrested whose fate no one knew. It was the worst and the first of its kind in the history of Myanmar.

The democratic world was kept awestruck. Immediate suspension of economic aid followed from countries like Japan, West Germany, U.S.A. and European Union members. Educational institutions in the country were closed down while normal life remained more or less paralysed. The worse affected place was Yangon. Resignation of Brigadier General Sein Lwin on 12 August from the presidentship slightly reduced the momentum of the movement or protest for a short while though the tension remained high. However, indecisiveness on the part of Dr. Maung Maung, the new incumbent, once more renewed the momentum of the ongoing movement. Thousands of people took advantage of the lifting of martial law to come openly in the street to protest against the government and its policies and programmes. The government completely failed to contain the resentment of the masses with its few cosmetic reforms and mesmerising acts. The people were no longer under any form of illusion. Thus, besides the students and monks who were known for their political activism in the past, many more people from different walks of life joined the movement.

Even dissatisfied members of the BSPP and the armed forces took to the streets in renewed protest against the government[6]. In between, to bring some sense of organisation to the growing political confusion, at the end of August a General Strike Committee (GSC) was formed to try to bring students, monks, teachers, doctors etc. together under one banner[7]. This uprising of 1988 encouraged many leaders of the past to reappear and involve themselves once more in the political activities. U Nu, the former Prime Minister of the era of parliamentary democracy announced on 9 September the formation of a parallel government with a 25-member cabinet. This information was even circulated to foreign embassies.

The top leaders in the government realised that the situation was gradually going out from their control. Ultimately they planned for a *pseudo*-military coup. As stated earlier the coup was carried out on 18 September by Gen Saw Maung, the Chief of Staff and a hardcore Ne Win loyalist, with 18 other senior military officers. This core group which was largely responsible for the establishment of a military rule came to be known as the State Law and Order Restoration Council (SLORC). Though there were frequent changes in the country's leadership in a short period, the *de facto* leader of the country remained General Ne Win, the *Uno Numero* of Myanmar politics.

Here, what is to be accepted is the fact that the popular uprising of 1988 was a unique experience which the country had never seen in the past. It was unique for the reason that people from every section of society and every walk of life came out openly to challenge the authoritarian system - a system of complete militarised politics without any concession and transparency. Hundreds and thousands of monks, young children, university and high school students, housewives, doctors - even some police and civil servants - took to the streets of major cities of the country in an unprecedented public display of protest[8]. In reality, it was the long subdued and repressed pent up emotions of the general public taking the form of a challenge against the system created by a few military leaders. The events in the summer of 1988 also suggest that the Myanmarese, despite their isolation from world events, desire the same freedom and opportunities enjoyed by the other democratic countries, apart from Eastern Europe, China and the Third World nations in the years that followed[9].

4.1. Aftermath of the September Coup of 1988

The coup of 19 September 1988 symbolised the return of the earlier military administration carried out on the order of Ne Win. It was cosmetic in nature since the members belonged to the same inner circle of the strong man. It was believed that Gen Saw Maung, the coup leader, was summoned to Ne Win's Ady Road residence just a few hours before the coup. Thus, the coming of 19-member SLORC to power once more saw in the country's politics the return of the control of the same military people, but in a more brutal and harsher way than in the past. It completely transformed the political atmosphere of Myanmar from bad to worse. The impact was felt on the movement of democracy also. In fact, the coup ensured a new version of military dictatorship more advanced in nature - which was to start a systematic campaign for removing whatever vestige of democracy found in the country.

Soon after the coup, the whole government set up of Myanmar was completely brought under the control of the newly constituted military body, the SLORC. It quickly assumed all legislative, administrative and judicial powers[10]. All the state legal institutions were abolished. The political party of the ruling junta, the Burma Socialist Programme Party (BSPP), was also dissolved on 24 September though reconstituted as the National Unity Party (NUP) later on. Martial law and military decree was imposed on the people all over the country; and as such; the prevailing constitution of 1974 became meaningless. Press was censored. However, the SLORC made a declaration on 21 September for holding a multi-party general election once law and order was restored in the country. An Election Law known as the *Pyithu Hluttaw* Election or the SLORC Law No. 14/89 was declared on 31 May 1989.

While these changes took place in the existing administrative set up, the immediate aftermath of the September coup was marked by a series of violence all over the country. From the day of the coup itself the ruling junta took a strong stance towards the pro-democracy movement. A propaganda campaign to malign the ongoing movement was also started by the junta under the leadership of General Ne Win's two most trusted ones - his daughter Major Sanda Win and Brigadier General Khin Nyunt, the Military Intelligence Service (MIS) Chief. Through their media campaign, they tried to express that the popular uprising was a conspiracy hatched by CPB and rightist groups from abroad. Not only this, it resorted to a series of repressive measures with utmost brutality against those involved in the movement. Fear and force as weapons were used. The objective was to crush the anti-government elements for which they resorted to both psychological as well as physical methods. Myanmar witnessed turmoil, anarchy and chaos. Arrest and torture became a common feature of day to day affairs. Any form of protest demonstration, peaceful or violent, was retaliated with an iron hand. People were not allowed to say or do anything against the government. Students in the forefront, monks, officials, politically conscious people and self declared political individuals became targets of SLORC's systematic flushing out drive of pro-democracy elements in the country. Even among these, the foremost target of the junta was the student community, particularly the matured and politically conscious university students. They were either killed, arrested, tortured or jailed. At least 1000 people were massacred as the immediate aftermath of the coup: shot dead on the streets or dragged from their houses and summarily executed[11]. Many were arrested, jailed or imprisoned. There was a complete reign of terror in the country which ultimately resulted in the exodus of its population towards the border areas in an unprecedented degree.

Aftermath of the carnage that followed the coup of September thousands of pro-democracy activists including students, monks and others were left with no other alternative than to leave the urban areas for safety. The immediate concern was however to move towards the nearest safe areas and also where one was expected to get help for continuation of the movement. Finally, they landed at those places held by ethnic insurgents or communist rebels in the border areas (Thailand-Myanmar), though the destination or exact site of arrival may be different. Some moved towards places located near Mae Hong Son or Mae Sot awhile some other arrived at places like Pa Jau, Three Pagoda Pass or Manerplaw. The exodus was in three directions - one towards Thailand, another towards India and another one towards Bangladesh. The renegades fanned out toward the border areas without caring much about the direction. And the maximum movement, as observed, was mainly towards the border areas of Myanmar adjoining Thailand. Some from Chin

State, Sagaing Division and Mandalay Division had escaped to Indian border, in the western side of their country. The activists who fled towards India were mainly those who were assured by some of the Indian Embassy officials in Yangon of giving help[12]. In India initially they were settled in Leikhun in Manipur State, and Champai and Saiha in Mizoram State. Beside these students, many activists from Arakan State filtered into South-eastern Bangladesh[13]. Within a very short period of few weeks approximately about 8000 - 10,000[14] people moved out from cities, towns and villages and moved towards the border areas of the country majority of which were given sanctuary in National Democratic Front (alliance of ethnic insurgents formed in 1976) held areas. An estimated 2000 of these largely from Mandalay, Lashio and Upper Myanmar took sanctuary with the Kachin Independence Organization (KIO) and the Shan State Progressive Party (SSPP) in the mountains of far North, while nearly 6000 took refuge with the Karen National Union (KNU) and the New Mon State Party (NMSP)[15] in the Thai border. Majority of the pro-democracy activities remained in the rebel areas - though some returned to an uncertain fate, later on. Thus ensued a mass wave of human exodus toward the border areas which was to increase as time passed. It was to become a common phenomenon of the country's prevailing situation.

The people who fled to the border areas in the hope of food and shelter had to face physical and psychological hardship. Initially, these people mainly the students were encouraged by the rumour that a student army had already been set up in the border areas by some student leader and immense help were coming from abroad. However when they arrived at the place they found it otherwise. This gave them moral setback. Besides, they had to face hardship. The border areas were not conducive for safe and comfortable living. The areas were the worst malaria-zone of the world. Over and above these, there was the paucity of fund for acquiring day to day necessities and also the uncertain attitude of Thai government. However some organised efforts were made and the problem was gradually overcome in course of time, though not fully. The establishment of the All Burma Students Democratic Front (ABSDF) as an umbrella organisation of the students greatly helped in this direction.

4.2. Emergence of New Political Groups and Leaders

Following the political turmoil and massacre the most significant development was the emergence of a number of political parties and their leaders with the sole objective of restoring democracy. It was a unique development which the country had never witnessed in its history. In short the political scenario of Myanmar after the '88' events was marked by the emergence of two opposing forces in the political front - one was represented by the all powerful ruling army officers symbolised by SLORC and another represented by the emerging pro-democracy groups more significantly represented by National League for Democracy (NLD). Consequently, the political affair of the country no longer remained a one sided affair. Though the army was still the dominating force yet the pro-democracy force could no longer be taken lightly.

The emergence of prominent personalities in the political scene gave a strong impetus to the movement for democracy. These personalities were mainly those leaders who had supported the movement for democracy in the early part of 1988. This included, a number of retired army officers once trusted ones of Ne Win. Some of them were Aung Gyi, Tin U and Aung Shwe. Aung Gyi was a former Brigadier General and one time trusted lieutenant to Gen Ne Win. He was also one of the original members of the Revolutionary Council (RC) which was formed after the coup of 1962. He was, however, ousted in 1963 when his pragmatic ideas clashed with those of the strong man. Likewise, Tin U was also a former military commander. He was a former Chief-of-Staff and Minister of Defence, removed for acting contrary to Ne Win. He was, later, imprisoned on suspicion of having link with the abortive coup of 1976. And the same was also with that of Aung Shwe who was a former commander. Other leaders belonged to the category of former political leaders of the parliamentary era.

U Nu was the first Prime Minister of Independent Myanmar and an important member of the legendary 'thirty comrades'. Apart from these personalities the most prominent and charismatic face was that of Daw Aung San Suu Kyi, daughter of Gen Aung San. Educated in India and Oxford she lived in Oxford with her English husband, Michael Aris, who taught there. It was by mere coincidence that she was gradually pulled into the vortex of the movement. Actually she came back to Yangon only to attend her ailing mother. As far as the politics of the country was concerned she wanted to remain far from it. However, incidents of August 1988 completely changed her attitude of remaining apolitical. The incident shook the very core of her conscience. She could no longer keep quite as it would mean betrayal of her father's legacy. She became gradually involved and emerged as a national figure. In fact, her entry into the political scenario filled up the vacuum created by the lack of strong opposition leaders; someone who could act as a rallying point for the whole democracy movement.

The emergence of Aung San Suu Kyi gave a new hope to those who wanted Myanmar to be a democratic country. Her first public speech outside the *Shwe Dagon Pagoda* in Yangon was received with great applause by the masses. Being the daughter of General Aung San, it was also advantageous for her as people had more faith in her than in other leaders. So she kept the legacy of her father and her appearance on the political stage of Myanmar in August was met with excitement and high expectation[16]. In the subsequent months of October and November 1988 she made a nationwide tour. Suu Kyi travelled widely and attracted lots of people despite restriction imposed upon by the SLORC against any pubic gathering. During this short period she travelled to as many as 50 towns, cities and villages throughout the country. Besides Yangon, she visited Bago (Pegu), Magway (Magwe), Mandalay and Sagaing Divisions, and Shan State. She was also able to augment the power of both students and monks and streamlined it in the struggle against the SLORC. Thus, the emergence of Aung San Suu Kyi and many dynamic leaders ushered in a new era in the politics of Myanmar.

Along with the emergence of a new set of political leaders the involvement of students, both underground and overground, became more frequent and intense in the uprising. There was the establishment of the underground student organisation, the All Burma Federation of Student Unions (ABFSU), on 28 August 1988 as an umbrella group for student organisations in Yangon and other towns[17]. It was led by Paw U Tun alias Min Ko Naing[18]. When the first uprising of the present movement was crushed by the regime in 1988 ABFSU's youthful leaders developed a three pronged strategy similar to that pioneered by Aung San during the anti colonial resistance: students over ground, armed underground and party organisation[19]. Min Ko Naing remained in hiding with supporters in Yangon and Mandalay and tried to keep the ABFSU alive until his capture the following year[20]. Another student organisation, the All Burma Students' Democratic Association (ABSDA), led by Min Zeya, an ethnic Mon Law student, also came up. The old All Burma Students' Union (ABSU) was allowed to revive legally. But this time, the ABSU was not like the old one as it acted as a tool for the government with all the leaders being government nominees. Besides, all these were to be followed by the All Burma Student Democratic Front (ABSDF) in the border areas after the September coup.

With the students, in the movement, were the monks. The young monks and the *sangha*, clandestinely as well as openly, contributed to an immense scale to the uprising. Since the protest began in June a number of monasteries, such as the Thayettaw in Yangon and those of the *Yahanpyo* (Young Monks Association) in Mandalay, had been providing safe houses where students could hold meeting, and some 30 to 40 monks had reportedly been shot in the demonstrations preceding Sein Lwin's downfall[21]. An estimated 80 percent of the monks in Myanmar supported the political activities of 1988[22]. It was in the forefront of most of the agitations during the period. Charges by the state that monks actively supporting the NLD were breaking their own code of conduct

(*Vinaya*) had little impact on the Monastic Order[23]. They could not be deterred from their chosen path of full democracy in the country.

Apart from the students and monks another force which emerged was the coming up of political parties. The legalisation for the formation of political parties on 27 September 1988 by the SLORC under the Political Parties Registration Law led to the mushrooming of political parties in the country. The number was so large that there was allegation of parties being formed solely to take advantage of facilities provided, such as telephone, petrol, etc since four telephones and 70 gallons of petrol (16 kyat a gallon) a week were given to each political party. The three main opposition leaders, Aung Gyi, Tin U and Aung San Suu Kyi together established the National League for Democracy (NLD) and registered it on 30 September as a political party. However, due to some internal conflict Aung Gyi left the NLD and formed another party of his own called the Union National Democracy Party. U Nu, the 70 years old first civilian premier of the country, re-emerged as a leading politician with two political parties - the League for Democracy and Peace (LDP) and the Democracy Party. Besides these political parties related with the stalwarts another very prominent group which emerged was the Democratic Party for a New Society (DPNS) led by ABFSU leader Moe Thi Zun. This one-was, in reality, a student group in the guise of a political group. Allied with the NLD, it rapidly built up a mass youth following in Yangon. According to Moe Thi, it was intended to work as a pressure group to revive the ideals and sacrifices made during 1988 in case compromises were made with the SLORC[24]. The period also saw the emergence of political groups led by former leaders with leftist leaning. The old Red Flag Communist, Thakin Soe, came out from political hibernation to announce on 7 October that he had registered the Unity and Developed Party[25]. The People's Democratic Party (PDF) was formed under the leadership of Burma Workers' and Peasants' Party (BWPP) veterans, Thakin Lwin and Aung Than, who is Gen Aung San's brother (elder). Another party, under a BWPP veteran was the Democratic Front for National Reconstruction established by Thakin Chit Maung. Besides, political groups like the National Politics Front (NPF), the People's Progressive Party (PPP), the League for Democratic Alliance (LDA), the National League for Democracy Justice (NLDJ), the Burma United Democratic Party (BUDP), the Patriotic League for peace (PLP), the Old PVO and the Union of Burma Main Anti Fascist People Freedom League (UBMAFPEL) also came up. There were other parties like All Burma Youth League Headquarter (ABYLH), Graduates and Old Students Democratic Association (GOSDA), Peoples Students Democratic Party (PSDP), Students' Revolutionary Party for Democracy (SRPD), Evergreen Young Men's Association (EGYMA) and League for New Generation, which were all student organisations. In between this new spurt of political parties there was the defunct BSPP of the ruling junta taking the new form of National Unity Party (NUP). Thus, within a few months since the SLORC legalisation the number of political parties registered in the country crossed the 200 mark.

Despite the emergence of a large number of parties, only a few remained functioning with significance worth mentioning. Among them NLD remained the strongest and best known, and also the main rallying party with a broad base for participation of any individual or group from any walk of life. The Myanmarese people supported this party en-mass as they considered it something associated with Aung San and had more faith in it. They believed that NLD could lead the movement towards their desired goal. The presence of the charismatic Aung San Suu Kyi was also another factor for this extra popularity and faith. And in the long run it was to be the NLD which would take the main role to lead the whole movement. Every other party would be assimilated in it, which we will find in our study later.

Now we come to another very important aspect of the movement the role of the groups operating in the border areas or outside the country. The ongoing movement of democracy in Myanmar is not the contribution of the parties and groups operating inside the country alone. We need to assess the role of the parties groups operating in the border areas and beyond struggling under harsh conditions, constraints and hardship. The study cannot proceed meaningfully without touching this aspect.

Before the '88 Uprising' it was only the ethnic insurgents, the CPB rebels and some exiled Myanmarese which operated in the border areas of the country and outside. But the picture changed after the uprising. Many new groups came up in these areas as a result of the mass exodus from the cities and towns of Myanmar. The most prominent among these new emergences was the All Burma Students' Democratic Front (ABSDF) - an umbrella organisation formed by those students who had fled to the border areas and based there. It was established on 5 November 1988 at the KNU base of Kawmoorah, in the Thai - Myanmar border. Tun Aung Gyaw, a veteran student activist of the 70s, chaired the 21 members Central Committee of the ABSDF. With its establishment, for the first time since independence, student activists from various generations (1962-1988) united under the banner of the fighting peacock - the symbol of student struggle and also of ABSDF[26]. The 1974-76 generation of student activists acted as its advisors[27]. Initially the main purpose of ABSDF was to bring the scattered students in the border together in the fight for restoration of genuine democracy and federalism in the country. It advocated both armed struggle as well as peaceful means, wherever the necessity arises. Another group which came up was the All Burma Young Monks Union (ABYMU). Led by 37 year old Khemsara, this union has contact with young monks within the country, though based in Manerplaw. Committee for Restoration of Democracy in Burma (CRDB) was another prominent group which came up in the border areas. Originally established by some exiled Myanmarese in USA it was shifted to the Thai Myanmar border after the mass exodus in the post-September coup period. Headed by Tin Maung Win, the son of U Win - a former Burmese Ambassador to the U.S.- the main aim of CRDB was to garner international support for the cause. Apart from these, there were the All Burma Muslim Union (ABMU) and another remnant of U Nu's old PPP of the 70s. But the one to supersede all these border based groups was the Democratic Alliance of Burma (DAB). Most of the existing groups based in the border areas, both ethnic insurgents as well as dissident groups came under the multi-party umbrella organisation. In fact, all the groups related with the democracy movement in Myanmar are to have a direct or indirect relation with it as the movement progressed in the later stage. As such, of all the groups that emerged in connection with the '88 Uprising' DAB need a little more elaboration.

The Democratic Alliance of Burma, as a broad political coalition, was the outcome of combined organised effort of the KNU, the minority ethnic groups belonging to NDF[28], the student dissidents, Buddhist monks and others. It was formed after a long meeting on 18 November 1988 at Klerday, a KNU camp on the Western bank of the Moei River, in the Karen liberated area. General Bo Mya, the head of KNU, became its chairman while Brang Seng of KIO, Nai Shwe Kyin of NMSP and U Thwin of the PPP were elected Vice-Chairmen. Tin Maung Win of the CRDB became its General Secretary which was not welcome by some section. Originally it consisted of 23 dissident and insurgent groups but presently there are 20 groups only. Its main aim was to topple the military regime, install a democratic government, end the civil war and form a federal state[29]. The establishment of DAB was historical in the sense that for the first time so many ethnic and dissident groups with different ideologies combined together under one common organisation and banner to achieve the single goal of restoring democracy and federalism in Myanmar. Besides the various minority groups and student organisations, it consisted of a host of other groups, including one representing Buddhist monks and another two representing Myanmarese Muslims. So, for the first time a common platform for any anti-government group to join and fight against the SLORC came into being. The establishment of DAB gave an opportunity to bring people from different ethnic and regional backgrounds together and to understand one another's problem also. This, in turn, brought them closer and also towards the common objective. And, above all, it proved to be a boon in disguise for those students and dissidents who had fled to the border areas and who wanted to challenge the SLORC by forming an alliance with the various ethnic groups. In fact, DAB was one of the most prominent and successful 'all encompassing alliance' which came up in the liberated area for the democracy movement. As the movement progressed it played an important role.

Despite all these new emergence of leaders and organisations, for the time being, the situation just after the September coup (1988) was that of utter depression. The rebound effect of what happened in the summer of 1988 - the mass killings, executions, arrest etc - struck back very hard on the populace of the Myanmarese society. It seemed that thousands of lives sacrificed senselessly; became, in a way, meaningless as the old military regime still remained in power, stronger than before. Only the announcement of holding a multi-party election in 1990 brought some hope and solace. There were frustration and despair on the part of the masses. But, at the same time, it will be gravely wrong to assume that they had completely given up despite all disappointments[30]. It was only for the time being. The movement continued to pull on though slightly subdued. Contrary to it in the border the preparation was in an upbeat momentum.

The existing melancholic atmosphere changed in the beginning of 1989 with the funeral of Daw Khin Kyi, widow of General Aung San and mother of Aung San Suu Kyi. This funeral of Suu Kyi's mother on 2 January 1989 proved once again to be an important occasion for bringing together those people who aspired for democracy, and also a new hope for them. The procession that marched through Rangoon saw people from different walks of life attending it. About 100,000[31] people were there in the ceremony. And the most disarming nature of the occasion for those in power was that the processions was well disciplined but at the same time the atmosphere was full of anti-government aura. It showed that the main groups leading the movement for democracy, especially NLD, had matured considerably and that a systematic campaign against the military system could be possible. There were lots of student's anti-government slogans during the march which was within a civilised human norm. In fact, it was the biggest as well as the first public march in the country since the coup of September 1988 and the resultant massacre. With it the movement started picking up momentum again.

Altercation, however, increased between the SLORC and the opposition after the funeral march. Junta's repression increased but could not cow down the students. The boosted moral of the students and other opposition groups could not be subdued any longer. They became once more active though in a slightly subdued manner. Preparations were started to commemorate the events of March, August and September of 1988. In fact, in the month of March 1989, despite restrictions, students carried out demonstrations and protests to commemorate the death of Maung Phone Maw and the beginning of the democracy uprising. Processions were carried out in the streets. It was a climax situation created by Min Ko Naing's ABFSU supporters and Young NLD allies. However, once again the movement was effectively crushed. Min Ko Naing, the prominent ABFSU leader, was arrested and sentenced to 20 years imprisonment while Moe Thi Zun of the Democratic Party of a New Society (DPNS) left for the border areas. But Suu Kyi and the NLD supporters continued with their countryside campaign trip. This frightened the regime as they knew of her popularity. The military even threatened to kill her, but could not deter her will. And in June 1989 the name of the country was changed from Burma to Union of Myanmar (*Myanma Naing-ngan*).

By July 1989, the tension between the military government of the SLORC and the pro-democracy groups increased. It deepened further when NLD expressed its intention of commemorating the Martyrs' Day, the death anniversary of Aung San and his comrades, separately from the government. Preparation for a big procession through Yangon was also made. But aware of the situation Aung San Suu Kyi abandoned it in the last moment. She did not want the massacre of 1988 to be repeated, which was very likely to happen if she went ahead with her plan. On the other hand the SLORC, with the motive of crushing the opposition, created military tribunals with summary power. On 17 July 1989, SLORC's Chairman Gen. Saw Maung signed Martial Law Order No. 1/89, which empowered the military to conduct "summary trials" of civilians[32]. Within days of promulgation of this Law 15 tribunals were set up in the three-command regions - Yangon, Central and North West Commands[33]. Soon a mass campaign was carried out against democracy lovers. NLD leaders Aung San Suu Kyi and Tin U were put under house arrest on 20 July for speaking against the SLORC and also by creating discontentment within the ranks and files of it. Besides, scores of NLD workers were also arrested countrywide[34]. Many student leaders were either arrested or went underground. Former Premier, U Nu was also put under house arrest for not agreeing to disband the parallel government he had established in 1988[35]. So, with a brute force the SLORC was once again successful in subduing the movement for time being, but at the same time failed to uproot the movement. And on the other hand, for the pro-democracy opposition, the approaching of 1990 revives a ray of hope as the first multi-party general election was to be held in that year for the first time after 30 years.

4.3. Election of 1990

It was in the midst of the ongoing conflicts between the pro democracy activists and the junta after Daw Khin Kyi's funeral that the SLORC suddenly fixed the date for holding multi-party general election in the country. The announcement was considered to be a shrewd policy to contain the ongoing protest movement. On the other hand it was also a quest for legal and political legitimacy taken by SLORC. With the election it wanted to show the world that it really care for democracy.

In May 1989 the *Pyithu Hluttaw* Election Law No. 14/89,[36] which was promulgated in March, was ratified. The law clearly affirmed once more that the goal of the election was to create a democratically elected parliament through a multiparty election[37]. The law provided for holding the election on 27 May 1990, throughout the country excluding the ethnic rebel held areas. It was the first free democratic poll in 30 years.

Ironically the SLORC had started taking up measures for holding the election in the country soon after it had assumed power. It seemed that the military leaders were eager to hold an election under its announcement No. 1/88. It retained the existing Election Commission in order to hold a multi-party election, though all other organs of power were abolished at the outset of the September coup of 1988. It was follow up of what was previously announced by the BSSP government in August the same year. On 21 September it also enacted a new 'Law of the Election Commission for Holding Democratic Multi Party General Elections'.

Now with the date of election already fixed various political parties came into existence. Ninety-three political parties were allowed to contest the elections. Thirty three political parties were there representing ethnic minority groups and which were formed on a local and regional basis[38]. A total of 2,297 candidates came in the fray for contesting in the announced 492[39] constituencies. The pro SLORC National Unity Party itself fielded 450 candidates. In every constituency there were at least two candidates[40]. The junta promised for a free and fair election so as to enable the candidates as well as the general masses to exercise their democratic rights to the fullest. But it did not seem to be going that way. Despite the above promises, the authority continued to impose martial law condition in the country thus curbing the free movement for any political activity.

Soon after the announcement of the date for election SLORC started a systematic campaign to destabilise the opposition. To many the elections appeared to be just a facade behind which the junta was hatching plots to enable it to return to power legally, with all available forces used to keep the opposition at bay and weakened. Once again, the autocratic and selfish attitude of the rulers emerged. People gradually realised that the election was going to be held by those in power not with the intention of bringing a genuine democracy or for a viable integration of the country's diverse ethnic regime but to strengthen junta's own position. Not surprisingly, there was no room for the ethnic insurgent groups as well as the student dissidents of the democracy movement in the forthcoming election, sealing whatever little chance of their re-entry to the country's mainstream. It resulted in mounting the gulf between the opposition forces and the junta. Even an offer of peace by the NDF, the ethnic alliance, was rejected publicly [41] - stalling a good chance to reduce the ongoing civil war. Not only this, restrictions were imposed, under one pretext or another, solely to throw out likely contenders out of the race. Main opposition leaders like Aung San Suu Kyi, Tin U, U Nu and many other leaders were debarred from contesting the election under one pretext or the other. According to a provision of the *Pyithu Hluttaw* Election Law 1989, those who were imprisoned and sentenced could not contest election. This provision was applied on the dissidents. In fact, right up to the Election Day (27 May 1990), hundreds of different party activists were still being imprisoned[42]. Aung San Suu Kyi was imprisoned on the pretext of having link with underground student groups and also for trying to divide the army-which went against the law of the land. Tin U, the Chairman of NLD, was also imprisoned under the pretext of inciting the public against the military and also for creating disunity within the army. Former Premier U Nu was also placed under house arrest for his refusal to disband the parallel government which he had established during the '88 Uprising'. Besides, other prominent ethnic and student leaders were also arrested. Thus, most of the likely strong contenders were systematically disqualified by arresting or imprisoning them so that only SLORC supported parties could remain and win the election easily.

To make the above campaign effective more restrictions were imposed in the area of campaign, assemblage and movement of individuals. The attitude of the SLORC also became harsher as the time for election went nearer. Free campaigning, assembling and movement were restricted to the maximum. Political parties were effectively barred from organising or campaigning three months before the voting. Many unknown restrictive laws were enforced. Laws such as the 1950 Emergency Measures Act, the 1962 Printer and Publishers Registration Law, the 1975 State Protection Law, Order No. 2/88 prohibiting outdoor assembly of more than four persons, Notification No. 8/88, Martial Law Nos. 1/89 and 2/89 etc. were applied to keep the opposition forces subdued. All party publications were censored and subject to martial law regulations and each of the 93 parties were restricted to one pre-approved ten minutes statement on state television and only 15 minutes on State Radio[43]. In turn, all these measures restricted the right of expression of democracy activists. Censor and martial law became the key words of the day. Nothing went without the notice and scrutiny of the junta's hawk eyes. The opposition was left with no other alternative than to remain quiet or to continue political activities secretly - facing the wrath of the junta. An atmosphere of vagueness and uncertainly still loomed large even when the election date was very near.

As decided in the previous year the election was held on 27 May 1990, in the midst of those repressions and restrictions enforced by the SLORC for the pro-democracy parties. Surprisingly the election process was free and fair contrary to the people's belief that it would be rigged massively in favour of the pro-military NUP. The reason being that the rulers were over confident of their control over the entire population and as such of their victory. They even invited foreign journalists and diplomats to observe the election proceedings. The junta never expected opposition victory, that too in a large scale. Prior to the election the SLORC had adopted a three-pronged strategy - militarily increasing pressure on insurgent groups, reducing socialist control on the country's economy, and efforts to revive relations with neighbouring countries [44]. But ultimately everything went against preconceived expectations. Nothing turned out as visualised by the top leaders of SLORC on the basis of information provided by its intelligence network, the Directorate of Defence Services Intelligence (DDSI). They expected 75 percent of the vote [45] in their favour. Contrary to it the result of the election entirely went in the favour of the opposition pro-democracy groups. The major opponent, the National League for Democracy (NLD), came out with a landslide victory. In a stunning decision of the electorate it alone garnered 80.0 percent[46] of the seats and 59.9[47] per cent of the total valid votes. In terms of actual number of seats it got 392 out of 485, thought it contested in 447 under agreement with allied regional parties which won another 35 seats[48] surprisingly. Thus, with the major chunk of the seats gone in favour of democracy groups the pro-military NUP had to satisfy with only 10 seats[49] and 21.2[50] per cent of the total vote. (See Tables 6 to 8 below).

Table 6

27 May 1990 Myanmar Election Results by State or Division and Party

			Party			
State/Division	*NLD*	*NUP*	*Independent*	*National*	*Regional*	*Total*
Kachin	14	2			3	19
Kayah	4	2			2	8
Kayin	10			1	3	14
Chin	4	1	2		6	13
Sagaing	52	1	2		3	58
Tanintharyi	13					13
Bago	47	1		3		51
Magway	39					39
Mandalay	55		1			56
Mon	16				4	20
Rakhine	9				17	26

(Contd...)

Yangon	59			2		61
Shan	22	1		1	32	56
Ayeyarwady	48	2	1			51
Total	**392**	**10**	**6**	**7**	**70**	**485**

Source: Working People's Daily, 28 May to 3 July 1990.Taken from Robert H.Taylor, "Myanmar 1990: New Era or Old?, *Southeast Asian Affairs*, 1991,pp.203-204.

Table 7
27 May 1990 Myanmar National Election: Numbers of Pyithu Hluttaw Seats and Percentage of Valid Votes Won by Successful Political Parties

Political Parties	*Seats Won*	*Seat Contested*	*Percentage Total Votes*
National Parties			
National League for Democracy	392	447	59.87
National Unity Party [a]	10	482	25.12
Patriotic old Comrades League	1	3	0.02
Party for National Democracy	3	3	0.48
Democracy Party	1	105	0.48
Graduates and Old Students Democratic Association	1	10	0.08
Unions National Democracy Party	1	247	1.48
Regional Parties			
Kachin State National Congress for Democracy	3	9	0.11
Kayah State Nationalities League for Democracy	2	8	0.08
Karen State National Organisation	1	3	0.05
Mon National Democratic Front	5	19	1.05
Democratic Organisation for Kayan National Unity	2	3	0.11
Chin National League for Democracy	3	13	0.38
Mara Peoples Party	1	4	0.04
Zomi National Congress	2	4	0.14

(Contd...)

Naga Hills Regional Progressive Party	2	6	0.08
United Nationalities League for Democracy	1	4	0.07
National Democratic Party for Human Rights	4	8	0.97
Rakhine Democracy League	11	25	1.21
Mro(or) Khami National Solidarity Organisation	1	4	0.17
Kamans National League for Democracy	1	3	0.08
Shan Nationalities League for Democracy	23	58	1.68
Union Paoh National Organisation	3	15	0.27
Union Danu League for Democracy Party	1	4	0.17
Shan State Kokang Democratic Party	1	2	0.05
Ta-ang (Palaung) National League for Democracy	2	9	0.18
Lahu National Development Party	1	7	0.12

[a] Including Peasants Unity Organization , Youth Unity Organisation, and Workers Unity Organisation.

Source: Working People's Daily 1,2,3 July 1990.Taken from Robert H.Taylor, "Myanmar 1990: New Era or Old?, *Southeast Asian Affairs*, 1991,pp.203-204.

Table 8

27 May 1990 Myanmar National Election: Numbers of Pyithu Hluttaw Seats and Percentage of Seats Won by Successful Political Parties

Political Parties	*Seats Won*	*Percentage of Seats Won*
National Parties		
National League for Democracy	392	80.8%
National Unity Party	10	2.1%
Patriotic old Comrades League	1	0.2%
Party for National Democracy	3	0.6%
Democracy Party	1	0.2%

(Contd...)

Graduates and Old Students Democratic Association	1	0.2%
Unions National Democracy Party	1	0.2%
Regional Parties		
Kachin State National Congress for Democracy	3	0.6%
Kayah State Nationalities League for Democracy	2	0.4%
Karen State National Organisation	1	0.2%
Mon National Democratic Front	5	1.0%
Democratic Organisation for Kayan National Unity	2	0.4%
Chin National League for Democracy	3	0.6%
Zomi National Congress	2	0.4%
Naga Hills Regional Progressive Party	2	0.4%
United Nationalities League for Democracy	1	0.2%
National Democratic Party for Human Rights	4	0.8%
Rakhine Democracy League	11	2.3%
Mro(or) Khami National Solidarity Organisation	1	0.2%
Kamans National League for Democracy	1	0.2%
Shan Nationalities League for Democracy	23	4.7%
Union Paoh National Organisation	3	0.6%
Union Danu League for Democracy Party	1	0.2%
Shan State Kokang Democratic Party	1	0.2%
Ta-ang (Palaung) National League for Democracy	2	0.4%
Lahu National Development Party	1	0.2%
Total	**485 seats**	**100.0%**

Source: Mark Weller (ed.), *Democracy and Politics in Burma* (Manerplaw: NCGUB, 1993), pp.187-188.

Now a big question after the announcement of the 1990 Election results - why the assumption of the SLORC went wrong , that also in a massive scale ? This we need to find out in order to enlighten about the ongoing movement for democracy in Myanmar. The exact answer to the above question is not easy but certain contributing factors were there which are very clear even to normal observers. The SLORC was completely under the impression that the people supported the army despite its atrocity against them. And the Myanmarese people tricked the authority by letting them believe that they would do as they (authority) had expected. But, in reality, the general masses were completely fed up with the military rule. Secondly, the atrocities, repression and anti-people measures adopted by the military junta became publicised by the opposition by the time of election. While the military rulers remained overconfident, the people exercised their rights against it. Though many could not come out openly to support the movement and its uprising of 1988, they were morally in favour of it. And the multi-party election provided them an opportunity to translate their desire into action. Most citizens, in fact, regarded the election as a referendum: a straight choice between democracy as represented by the NLD of Aung San Suu Kyi, and a continuation of Ne Win's army dominated rule [51]. Thirdly, SLORC failed to visualise that diverse opposition groups could come together under one slogan i.e. democracy. Besides all these, SLORC had also underestimated the charismatic leadership of Aung San Suu Kyi. Despite her house arrest and exclusion from election fray NLD became synonymous with her name, a comparable legacy that Aung San commanded[52]. All these miscalculations led to the stunning defeat of SLORC in the election.

The election of 1990 was the second most significant event after the uprising of 1988. It was the first major victory of the pro-democracy forces. It helped in bringing to limelight the people's desire for a democratic set up in the country which was manifested by their voting against the junta, represented by NLD. It proved success of the NLD and other democracy groups in striking home the idea of democracy in the Myanmarese society. The election result brought joy and relief coupled with hope for a future democracy government in the country. But, at the same time, there was some doubt on the real motive of the military rulers because people were not new to their hypocritic nature. People knew well that the words of these military rulers could not be relied upon. They ruled without popular support but with force, and force is not based on commitment and promise. In a country like Myanmar even a popular mandate is no guarantee for ensuring a transition to democracy; because in the final analysis it is not the will of people that counts but the military bureaucratic nexus that determines who is going to reign supreme[53]. This people came to realise gradually. And, in fact, the joy and hope of the opposition did not last long. The junta once again came up with its true colour. After a few days of the declaration of result the junta leaders announced their intention to hold on to the reign of power instead of transferring it to the popularly elected group. The simple pretext for their reluctance to transfer power was same as before - safeguarding the unity and integrity of the country.

Due to this reluctance on the part of SLORC to transfer power, the necessity of renewing the efforts and strategy felt once again by those involving in the movement for democracy. At the same time, realising the real strength of the opposition, SLORC also reacted with greater force and harshness. With this the chance for a peaceful transfer of power became very bleak in the country. The junta was not ready to leave the seat of power at any cost. There was also no room for compromise. In fact, the concept of holding the election changed all of a sudden. It was quite different from what it actually meant before the election. Initially the election was held for constituting a new National Assembly or *Pyithu Hluttaw*. But after the election defeat SLORC was not ready to accept it. Accordingly, the so called multi-party election of 1990,it declared, was held solely for forming a Constituent Assembly whose main task simply would be to frame a new constitution for the country as the previous ones of 1948 and

1974 were no longer relevant. SLORC also declared that the constituent assembly would be dissolved after drafting the new constitution and that fresh election would be held once more to form a new *Pyithu Hluttaw* to whom the military could transfer power. However, all these were completely against what actually were mentioned in the Election Law 1989 which was promulgated by SLORC and under that the election was held.

Here another question arises - why this reluctance on the part of SLORC ? This was mainly because of the fact that the rulers never expected their own defeat; that too, in such a large scale. They were stunned. The military regime was completely unprepared for the situation and that there was simply no mechanism available for a smooth transfer of power[54]. Besides, another important factor for the reluctance was the vindictiveness from general public once the power is transferred to them. The junta was very much conscious of the fate of military rulers and dictators like them in countries like Philippines, Bangladesh, South Korea, Haiti, Romania and many more countries in Latin America and Africa. The cases of Ferdinand Marcos (Philippines), Roe Tae Woo and Chun Doo Hwan (South Korea), Mohammad Ershad (Bangladesh), Nicolae Ceausescu (Romania) were still fresh in their minds. These power crazy leaders could not imagine themselves in a situation without power and authority. They were frightened of the revenge and retaliation that might follow because of their past atrocities. Thus, there was a "*Nuremburg Syndrome*" in the psyche of the military leaders (though they denied this concept) which compelled them to cling to power rather than giving it up unless some rigid policy is framed in their favour.

Whatsoever maybe the factor, as the time after the election results became longer, the intensity of creating conflict situation between the two opposing forces - those demanding the transfer of power for constituting a new National Assembly and those who were not willing to transfer the power at any cost - increased. The two came toward a major clash threatening to ruin the country's hope for democracy[55]. Democracy groups, particularly NLD and its allies, were on the warpath. What could have been resolved peacefully was moving towards a conflict situation.

Since the transfer of power in any form was not in sight, the NLD leaders pressurised for dialogue with the SLORC leadership for a speedy move towards a democratic rule. However, the military leaders instead of agreeing to it, became more repressive in nature. It came down heavily on the students, democracy activists and others. Even the Buddhist monastic order, the most respected section of the society, was not spared. They were assaulted because of its pro-democracy stance[56]. NLD became the main target of military wrath as it happened to be the largest and strongest political party opposed to the military junta. To contain it there was large scale persecution of its members. And above all, while dealing with the NLD the junta applied a dual strategy - (i) to delay as far as possible the transfer of power; and (ii) to crush the leaders to the extent that they either give up or are subdued[57]. Further, these military leaders also propagated to discredit the party that since NLD was a combination of various centrifugal elements it could not maintain unity and integrity of the country. While the unity and integrity was under threat, army said that power could not be transferred. This was a pretext though the real intention was to remain in power. It was evident from historical events that centrifugal forces were always there in the Myanmarese society. And there was no much change during the period also. Whether a democratic government or a military government, one will always feel the presence of this element or factor. This is something which has become part and partial of Myanmarese body politics. The factor alone cannot be the cause for non-transfer of power. Political uncertainty and complexity had always been there in the political set-up, this need to be tackled. However, behind this entire pretext the ultimate reality lies in the fact that the junta was not ready to accept any political outcome in which it did not have a lion's share. SLORC insisted, time and again, that Myanmar's national salvation requires a long term military tutelage over any process of political change, including any eventual transfer of power of civilian authority or reformulation of inter ethnic relations.[58]

This view was unacceptable to the NLD. Popular masses were also not very eager to accept. What they wanted was the practice of democracy in Myanmar where the military remain only for defence, and also far from the country's politics. Thus, the stalemate persisted.

It was in between this tussle for power that the SLORC suddenly declared its infamous Order No. 1/90 on 27 July 1990 with the sole objective of subduing the popular demand of the pro-democracy groups led by NLD. The order stated: that the SLORC government was the only one recognised by countries of the world and UN; it was not bound by any constitution since it was ruling by martial law; and that the SLORC would give priority in safeguarding the three cause of (i) prevention of disintegration of the union, (ii) prevention of disintegration of national unity, and (iii) perpetuation of sovereignty[59]. The order further mentioned that it was the responsibility of the elected members to draft a constitution for the future democratic state[60]. It infuriated the NLD and other pro-democracy groups. Various opposition leaders considered the order 1/90 as nothing but a shrewd ploy of the SLORC, an illegal one, for retaining power by ignoring the popular mandate of the Myanmarese people. It was a means to cling to the seat of power even after being decided to establish its legitimacy once more, though not a foolproof one. In essence, the junta was trying to convey the message that nothing of sort could happen without drafting a new constitution accepted by all the main 135 ethnic groups and races. Further it tried to ascertain that any form of effort by the elected groups to draft an interim constitution to obtain state power and form a government would face dire consequences from it. But even before the constitution, a national convention was to be formed first to lay down the guidelines of the constitution. However, all these terms and conditions were not acceptable to NLD. Everything was rejected outright by the party. Countering the declaration NLD, in its meeting, held in Gandhi Hall in Yangon on 28-29

July, drafted a "1990 Provisional Constitution" and called on the SLORC government to convene the National Assembly by September 1990. The terms and resolutions of this meeting known commonly as the 'Gandhi Hall Declaration' also demanded for the release of its leaders and the transfer of power.

By August, following the issue of the aforesaid order, demonstrations and protest marches were organised by the pro-democracy activists. When it started picking up momentum military repression, as a reaction, was a natural course. Confrontation between the two opposite forces became more frequent. Intensification of confrontation resulted in the deterioration of the country's political atmosphere, which affected every section of the Myanmarese society. Once again students and monks in thousands demonstrated in the holy city of Mandalay to commemorate the killing of 8-8-88. Four monks were killed in police firing. This time the monks were also very much angered by the extreme repressive and confrontationist attitude of SLORC and its army. Monks decided to boycott all personal and religious services of armed personnel and their families. This threatened the army set up as majority of army personnel were devout Buddhists. Though effective, unfortunately, this social boycott could not last long. There was heavy clampdown on the *sangha*. The military government even empowered its commanders to pass death sentences on rebellious monks[61]. With no alternative at hand the monks had to withdraw their stand and once more faced the repression. The monks were arrested, tortured and imprisoned. But the monks were not the only exception. There was a systematic arrest of members of pro-democracy groups. And it was during this same period, on 30 August, that National League for Democracy and an allied party, the United Nationalities League for Democracy, announced to convene parliament in September 1990 unless the SLORC tried to do so[62]. This was retaliated by SLORC by a second round of mass arrest and disqualification of NLD leaders in early September. On 6 September 6 NLD members including acting Chairman U Kyi Maung and acting General Secretary,

U Chit Kwaing were arrested. In the following weeks over 40 MPs were imprisoned, two of whom quickly died soon in jail, amidst allegation of torture, allegedly for refusing to sign the 1/90 declaration renouncing any right to form a government[63]. Further 111 elected MPs were disqualified[64]. From all these developments it became clear to the pro-democracy groups that the junta had no intention of meeting any of the demands put forward in the Gandhi Hall Declaration and the NLD's announcement of 29 August 1990. So these groups started looking for a second alternative.

4.4. Formation of NCGUB: A Government in Exile

It was during this political turmoil and chaos - marked by excessive abuse of human rights, repression and mass arrests throughout the country - that the plan for the formation of a parallel or provisional government struck the minds of some politicians. This was the second alternative before the pro-democracy groups. The frustration felt by many NLD leaders, pressurised by student leaders who were unwilling to compromise with the military government on its terms, forced them to think of forming a parallel government within the country or along border areas[65]. The idea was first introduced in a secret meeting of the dissident groups in Mandalay on 29 September 1990. Although the original plan to hold the meeting of 42 NLD MPs, 3 each from the 7 divisions and 7 states, could not materialise. Yet roundabout 100 MPs and NLD organisers attended it from 6 divisions viz. Mandalay, Sagaing, Bago(Pegu), Yangon, Ayeyarwady(Irrawaddy) and Magway (Magwe) and Kachin State[66]. All the MPs present at the meeting were given to understand that the formation of a parallel government was the underlying objective. Originally the principal motive of the group was to set up the parallel government in Mandalay or another suitable place within the country if the support of at least 50 percent of elected representatives was extended[67]. The second alternative base for the parallel government was to establish in the liberated zones controlled by the insurgents. Luckily, signatures of 250 NLD MPs supporting the movement were collected, while influential groups of monks agreed to help in any endeavour related with the establishment of parallel government. With all these ideas in its favour NLD and its allies started making arrangement for the formation of the said government in the month of October 1990. However, due to leakage of secret plan and the resultant raid of hide outs and arrest of prominent NLD MPs and officials, student leaders and monks, the original plan could not be materialised. Instead, there were lots of clampdowns without the exception of monks. The most seriously affected group in a way was the monks as the original plan was to set up the government in a monastery. Over 350 monasteries were raided and many monks were arrested. Even a law known as SLORC Law No. 20/90 was passed exclusively to restrict the activities of the monks for all the time to come. There was also mass arrest of members belonging to political parties and student groups. SLORC subsequently justified its action by order 6/90 and 7/90, which outlawed all sects not legally recognised and empowered the army to take action against sects and individuals using the cover of religion for political activity[68]. Meanwhile NLD was unable to set up the planned 28 members' parallel government in the main centres of the country. Both its attempt to form the said government first at monastery in Mandalay and then at a foreign embassy in Yangon failed. Ultimately the seat of the parallel government had to be changed to the liberated areas along the international border.

Immediately after the above abortive attempt, in early December of 1990, a team of 8 MPs after hiding sometimes headed for the border areas solely to fulfil the planned objective of a parallel government against the junta government. The team headed by Dr.Sein Win, cousin of Aung San Su Kyi and MP of Paukkaung (Bago Division), after covering a hard and perilous journey through mountains, finally arrived at Manerplaw, the headquarters of DAB and KNU[69]. And it was in this Karen area that the so called provisional government known as National Coalition Government of the Union of Burma (NCGUB) was finally established on 18 December 1990, with DAB support. Dr. Sein Win became its Prime Minister. Like Suu Kyi, U.S. educated Sein Win carried the magic of the Aung San name; his father, Ba Win, had been assassinated along with his uncle Aung San in July 1947[70]. This tag proved beneficial in running the coalition provisional government in exile.

Soon after its establishment in the Karen base in Manerplaw the NCGUB formed a cabinet to run the government in exile. It consisted of 8-members[71] with Dr. Sein Win as its Prime Minister. All the other seven ministers were those MPs who had arrived together with Sein Win. The main purpose of this government in exile, as we can assume, was to establish an independent, prosperous and modernised Federal Union in Myanmar. And for this it laid down certain goals such as: to wage war against SLORC-first opted for non violence but later changed to both violence and non-violence; to convene a national conference of all elected leaders, representatives of DAB, democratic forces and other notable individuals; to draft a new federal constitution, and form a true democratic state. Besides, the establishment of NCGUB also brought certain changes in the set up of those who were responsible for restoration of democracy in Myanmar in the border areas. Apart from this it also led to the emergence of another very important political institution, the National Council of Union of Burma (NCUB). This new political institution included in its fold all the existing organisations and alliances, such as National League for Democracy-Liberated Area (NLD-LA), Democratic Alliance of Burma (DAB), National Democratic Front (NDF) and also NCGUB, operating in the liberated zones of the border areas and acted as the de facto parliament to all of them due to the need for political institution[72]. In a way, NCGUB was the government in exile while NCUB was the parliament in exile. Meanwhile, NCGUB also started its attempt to rally international support and undermine the external legitimacy of SLORC. This effort went on with the passage of time.

On the other side, soon after knowing about the

provisional government in exile SLORC intensified its repressive drive and attack against democratic forces both inside the country and in border areas. It quickly denounces the NCGUB. And towards the end of December of 1990 the Election Commission also announced that NLD, led by Tin U and Aung San Suu Kyi, both detained by the government, was no longer a legal organisation[73]. The move, announced on Rangoon Radio, followed the setting up of NCGUB, as it involved NLD MPs.

Despite all the reactions of the junta, the fact remained that with the establishment of the NCGUB the complexity of Myanmarese politics had increased. It appears symptomatic of the severe polarisation of Myanmarese politics by the end of 1990[74]. Now the situation was such that the NCGUB could not be easily underestimated by the military government like what previous junta government did to that of U Nu's government in exile as well as to his parallel government. It had received wide support. Besides, NCGUB had got the necessary publicity and as such could not be hidden from limelight by the SLORC, though it used to criticise it (NGGUB) and its supporters. But whatsoever may be, it will not be wrong to say that the emergence of NCGUB, and its alliance with DAB - the biggest umbrella organisation - gave a new dimension to the movement for democracy and also hope to its supporters.

NOTES

1. The date i.e. 8.8.88 was chosen especially because it was considered to be astrologically as well as numerologically auspicious.
2. *Keesing's Record of World Events*, vol. 34, October 1988, p. 36223
3. Bertil Lintner, *Outrage: Burma's struggle for Democracy* (London and Bangkok: White Lotus, 1990), 2nd Edition, p. 196.
4. Ibid.
5. John Haseman, "The Destruction of Democracy: The Tragic case of Burma". *Asian Affairs* (New York) vol.20, no.1, Spring 1993, p.18.

6. *Washington Post*, 23 August 1988, quoted in Lawyers Committee for Human Rights, *Summary Injustice: Military Tribunals in Burma*, 1991, p. 14.
7. Martin Smith, *Burma: Insurgency and the Politics of Ethnicity* (London: Zed, 1991), p. 8.
8. Maureen Aung Thwin, "Burmese Days", *Foreign Affairs*, Spring 1989, p.143.
9. Clark Neher; "Democratization in Southeast Asia", *Asian Affairs: An American Review*, Fall of 1991, p.148.
10. n.6.
11. Amnesty International, *Myanmar* (London: Amnesty International Publications, Nov. 1990), p.3.
12. Personal interviews with Myanmarese students taking asylum in India.
13. n.3, p. 147.
14. Ibid.
15. n.7, pp.16-17 .
16. n.3, p. 109.
17. n.11, p. 2.
18. Min Ko Naing which means conqueror of kings is an alias used by the ABSFU leadership, collectively in order to avoid arrest.
19. Dr. Thaung Htun. "Student Activism in Burma: A Historical Perspective", *Burma Debate*, April/May 1995, p. 8.
20. n.7, p. 21.
21. Ibid, p. 27.
22. Bruce Mathews, "Buddhism under a Military Regime: The Iron Heel in Burma", *Asian Survey*, vol.33,no.4, April, 1993, p. 419.
23. Ibid, p. 420
24. n.7, p. 21.
25. n.3, p. 164 .for more detail.
26. n.18.
27. n.7, p.407.
28. National Democratic Front is an alliance of 10 ethnic armed groups formed in 1976 solely to fight against the junta government of Ne Win. It was the biggest alliance before the DAB came into being. Presently it consisted of 11 groups with inclusion of CNF in 1989.

29. Jan Donkers and Minka Nijhuis(ed), *Burma Behind the Mask* (Amsterdam: Burma Centrum Nederland, 1996),p. 69
30. n.3, p. 168.
31. n.3, p. 170.
32. Lawyers' Committee for Human Rights, *Summary Injustice: Military Tribunals in Burma* (New York, 1991), p. 30.
33. Ibid, p. 32.
34. n.3, p. 203.
35. *Far East & Australia 1996*, (London : Europa Publications, 1996), p. 616.
36. This law itself is a collection of various dos and don'ts - solely to enable the junta to return to power legally after the election.
37. Mare Weller (ed.), *Democracy and Politics in Burma* (Manerplaw, NCGUB, 1993), p. 10.
38. S. S. Battacharya, "Political Crises in Myanmar", *Strategic Analysis* (New Delhi), January 1991, p.1142.
39. Election was finally held for only 485 seats with 2,233 qualified candidates.
40. n. 35, p.616.
41. n.7, p. 22.
42. Ibid, p.412.
43. Ibid.
44. Martin Fox , "Whither Burma", *World Review*, vol.30,no.4, December 1991,pp.37-38.
45. n.5.p.22.
46. Election results in n.37, p. 187.(see table 8)
47. n.44, p.39.
48. Ibid.
49. n.46.
50. n.47.
51. n.7, p.414.
52. n.44, p.39
53. Farzana Shakoor, "Burma : An Overview", *Pakistan Horizon* (Islamabad), vol.44, no.2,April 1991, pp. 63-64.
54. Bruce Mathews, "Myanmar's Agony: The Struggle for Democracy", *The Round Table* (London), 1993,325,p.39.
55. n.37, p. 198.

56. n.54,p.38.
57. Jalam Alamgir, "Against the Current: The Survival of Authoritarianism in Burma", *PacificAffairs*, vol.70, p.345.
58. Amnesty International, *Union of Myanmar: Arrest and Trials of Political Prisoners* (London: Amnesty International Publications, December 1991), p. 8.
59. SLORC Announcement No. 1/90, 27 July 1990 given in n. 37, pp.194-96.
60. Ibid.
61. *International Herald Tribune*, Paris, 22 October, 1990.
62. n.37, p. 197.
63. n.7, p. 418.
64. n.54.
65. Robert H. Taylor, "Change in Burma: Political Demands and Military Power", *Asian Affairs*, vol.22, no.2,, June 91, p.139.
66. n.37, p.237.
67. Ibid.
68. n.35, p.617.
69. n.7, p. 419.
70. Ibid.
71. The 8 ministers were: Dr. Sein Win (Prime Minister), U. Peter Lin Pin (Minister of Foreign Affairs) U Win Ko (Minister Finance & Revenue), U Than Kywe (Minister of Trade and Cooperative), U Hla Pe (Minister of Education, Health and Information), U Thein Oo (Minister of Justice), U Bo Hla Tint (Minister of Construction, Mining and Energy Resource) and U Tun Oo (Minister of Social Welfare and Labour).
72. *NCGUB, Political Progress Report* (Chiang Mai: NCUB Information Committee, Nov/Dec. 1995), p.3.
73. *International Herald Tribune* (Paris), 21 December, 1990.
74. Amnesty International, *Union of Myanmar : Arrests and Trials of Political Prisoners* (London: Amnesty International Publications , December, 1991), p. 12.

5

Movement for Democracy in Myanmar After 1990

The early 90's saw a change in the trend of world politics. It was marked by an increasing wave of political liberalisation. In the history of democracy and liberalisation it was indeed a unique period. Everyone saw the signs of change towards democracy and liberal reforms. Maximum changes emerged in former USSR, Yugoslavia, Germany and many other countries in Eastern Europe. Even in Asia some sort of change could be seen in many of the formerly repressive regimes. However, in the midst of all these developments and changing trends Myanmar remained an exception. The fact that the majority of the people of the country had strongly favoured and voted for a democratic government in the country had no positive effect towards change on the military rulers. For them it was their rightful claim to rule the country, they thought, as the army was the only institution in the country which had contributed the maximum for the welfare of the country. Thus, "the patters of hobbled economic liberalisation combined with political stasis and formalistically proper international relations coupled with cultural xenophobia, all continued"[1]. The question of transferring power, it seemed, had already been deliberately forgotten. The facilities they had been enjoying as a part of the military, and the chances of repercussion in case of relinquishing the power was also making them reluctant in transferring the power to a civilian group, even after the election debacle of 1990.

However, despite this lack of change on the part of the junta, the early 90's saw a new phase in the movement for democracy in Myanmar. Some positive changes could be observed in the case of democracy movement which was a change in the trend of the movement itself. A clear picture, though not complete, of the movement gradually emerged. It was a change from the previous trend. It was quite different from what it actually was in the pre-91 period. Aung Suu Kyi and National League for Democracy (NLD) became synonymous with the democratic wave in the country, though their functioning inside the country became virtually impossible. Restrictions were strictly maintained on movements and gathering of NLD and democratic activist. However, NLD emerged the only leading group, with the task of representing the democratic will of the Myanmar people and their struggle for democracy throughout the world. This period also saw the emergence of a polarised concrete democratic alliance among those fighting against the regime in the border consisting of the different groups of students, insurgents and political parties - with National Coalition Government of the Union of Burma (NCGUB) as the main functioning body or de facto government. The Democratic Front of Burma (DFB)[2], a policy making body of Burma Democratic forces, which was formed at the time of establishing NCGUB (18 December, 1990) also started operating. The struggle was further concretised with establishment of the National Council of Union of Burma (NCUB) as a sort of *de facto* legislature in August 1992. But ultimately it was NLD symbolised by Aung San Suu Kyi who guided the whole movement, both inside as well as outside the country.

Starting from the year 1991 onwards the movement became more vigorous. It also saw the functioning of a democratic front with more zeal, particularly in the border areas. Despite the normal ups and downs a sort of stability in the movement could also be observed. The establishment of NCGUB with the support of Democratic Alliance of Burma (DAB) and the subsequent setting up of a broad base coalition in the form of Democratic Front of Burma (DFB) also made the movement more systematised and active one. The constituents of DFB decided to struggle together for return to civilian rule, an end to the ongoing civil war and the drafting of a new constitution which would be truly federal and democratic in dimension. The NCGUB, the government in exile, based in the Thai-Myanmar border, pledged to remove the military dictatorship and set-up a federal Union in which all nationalities can flourish equally. In this direction, it got the full supports of all the major resistance fronts, National Democratic Front (NDF) as well as Democratic Alliance of Burma (DAB). Not only this, the NCGUB, though not recognised as a legal government by any country acted as a platform for launching the movement (besides NLD) to a higher plane. And, the supporters of democracy throughout the world acknowledged its existence as an interim government for a further democratic Myanmar. It acted as a sort of official medium for the movement, particularly for those who were active in the border areas or outside Myanmar. Government of many countries established unofficial contacts with it. Help of all types was extended. For example, the Royal Norwegian Government extended financial help of 2 million kroner in 1991. This fund was utilised in setting up an independent radio station, the Voice of Burma (VOB), in the coast of Norway.

Despite these developments abroad, many democratic activists inside the country were still in prison. They include many prominent leaders of the main party, the NLD. Aung San Suu Kyi who was put under house arrest since 1989 was still under detention. Many of the MPs elected in 1990 election were also in prison. The tussle between the military and the NLD for gaining political legitimacy also became a common feature of Myanmar's body politic. Despite these handicaps the struggle for restoration of democracy became more stable with a firm base both inside and outside the country. There was also a change in the attitude of the people. They were ready to face any eventuality coming out of the uncertain nature of SLORC in the course of the struggle.

Undeterred by rising tide of democratic struggle, SLORC, on its part, continued with its hard line approach of repression on the political activists inside the country. Not only this but they had started large-scale military offensive against the various armed groups operating in the border areas which were supporting the movement. Crackdown on the peaceful demonstration of students and clampdown on the *sangha* and the monks from time to time were clear evidences of SLORC's blatant violation of the minimum basic principles of democracy. This was contrary to their assurances to the Myanmarese people and the international community of leading Myanmar on the path of democracy. The reality was that there was no change at all in the attitude of the SLORC towards liberal reforms in the country. Instead, its actions reiterated its steadfast opposition to any change which might lead to a prompt transfer of power. It continued to refer to martial law as a legal basis for its authority and insisted on remaining in power[3]. And according to the regime martial law means a right for them to do anything. Further, Senior General Saw Maung in one of his speeches on 4 February, 1991 told political parties and democracy groups not to hope for transfer of power[4]. Despite all these contradictions to democratic principles, ironically, the junta propagated the idea that whatever repression and restrictions they were carrying out was mainly for bringing democratic changes in the country. Lt. General Than Shwe, Chief of Defence and member of SLORC, on 3 April 1991, reiterated this idea. He further stated that democracy could be achieved in the country only if it follows the scenario put forward in Declaration 1/90[5]. Yet, all these were just the facades to hide the real intention of the junta. Like any other repressive juntas of the world it continued to issue new orders which would help to remain in power longer and easier. Its newly issued Law No. 10/91 and Order 4/91 of 19 July 1991 gave it the power to disqualify any person from being a member of the *Pyithu Hluttaw* (Parliament) or from contesting election again[6]. With this new order and many more such existing laws and restrictions SLORC continued to keep the members of democratic forces subdued. A sort of psychological terrorism also existed besides the ongoing political terrorism of the rulers. The maximum impact of all these was on the NLD as it remained the leading group inside the country.

One of the most severe pressures was to expel Aung San Suu Kyi from the party. There was also the mounting pressure on the party demanding that all the members imprisoned under one pretext or the other should also be expelled from the party. With this, arrest of party members, as usual, persisted. In the beginning of 1991 itself 45 elected NLD MPs were arrested[7]. In fact, all these were an attempt on the party of SLORC to destroy the very foundation of NLD completely. Due to the effort of the junta the NLD was divided into two - legal and illegal, the vague version of the junta. The original executive body of the party consisting of the imprisoned front-runners was declared illegal[8]. Only the new caretaker executive body led by Aung Shwe was accepted as the legal one. The party was also forced to disqualify Tin U and Aung San Suu Kyi due to the increasing pressure and fear of retaliation. Not only was this, in July 1991, election law of the country was amended in order to keep maximum pro-democracy activists away from any future elections, if any (as already mentioned above). All these harsh measures were adopted to minimize the political activity of the NLD inside the country, though the spirit remained high. However, in the border areas the movement continued with more vigour than usual, unaffected by legal restrictions so placed.

One important change could also be observed in the approach of the opposition during this period. Particularly for those operating in the so-called 'liberated zone' in the border areas both violent and non-violent methods were adopted. By early part of 1991, apart from the main section of National League for Democracy operating inside the country, all the opposition groups in the border including even the democratic civilian based NCGUB opted for or supported an armed struggle as the only choice where peaceful ways failed. The main NLD, though opted for peaceful means, did not reject the armed resistance of the groups operating near the border outright. The setting up of a group known as National League for Democracy - Liberated Area (NLD-LA) on 14 February, 1991 at the KNU's H.Q.s, at Manerplaw, by NLD's elected MPs and party members who had fled to the Thai border, also broadened the activity of the party as well as its sphere of influence. The setting up of this group helped in making those operating outside the country and in the border a better understanding of the working style inside the country. It helped in reducing the ideology gap between the two thus making the common objective of achieving democracy more synchronise.

February 1991 also witnessed the emergence of Anti-Military Dictatorship National Solidarity Committee (ADNSC) - formerly DFB, consisting of members from the newly formed NLD-LA and DAB. Composed of 14 members the sole purpose of this committee was to overthrow the Ne Win-Saw Maung dictatorship by strengthening the democracy movement through well-synchronised and coordinated actions in the fields of mass movement and armed resistance. Efforts were also made to bring more unity between the majority Burmans of Central Myanmar with those ethnic minorities in the peripheral minority areas[9]. It also decided to give a prominent role to the NCGUB. Besides, another very important objective of ADNSC was to establish a genuine federal union of states in the country based on freedom, peace and democracy. All these required first of all, a change in the government and restoration of civilian rule. However, for the time being, these new developments gradually helped in picking up the momentum of the movement towards a positive direction. There was a general tendency towards polarisation without exception.

But all was not well. The movement was not completely free from internal problems. At a time when every democratic elements were moving towards a common goal of restoring democracy, problems of splits and defections arose. This could not be ignored lightly. In August 1991, ABSDF, the main group and rallying force for students in the border split into two.

One was led by the veteran student leader Moe Thi Zun of the former ABFSU and the other by Dr. Naing Aung. This situation put the various constituents of the democratic force in the border into dilemma. The decision to take side with any one of the two became quite difficult, as both were equally important for the struggle as a whole. Over and above this, the same year also witnessed mass defection of ethnic insurgents to the side of the SLORC "just when the entire population of the central plains had turned against the regime following the pro-democracy movement that had swept Myanmar"[10]. These issues could not be ignored. In fact, such situations deprived the movement of a forceful and united opposition against the regime. It was what the SLORC was hoping for. But contrary to their expectation the momentum did not come down despite the setbacks.

Above all, in December 1991, still detained without charge or trial, Aung San Suu Kyi was awarded the Nobel Peace Prize for her "non-violent struggle for democracy and human rights". In fact, it was a joyous moment for all those involved in this movement against SLORC's repression. It was a clear recognition that the world acknowledged the importance of the movement. It gave a new thrust to the millions who were facing hardship of different kinds. For some time all the differences and setbacks were forgotten.

Despite internal problems the winning of Noble Prize for Peace by Aung San Suu Kyi gave a strong moral boost to those who were struggling in the border areas. It instilled a renewed zeal among them. As far as possible efforts were also made among these democratic forces to reduce conflicts like the ones already mentioned above. This was mainly to prevent ever-increasing resistance against the regime for restoration of democracy. New steps were taken up in this direction. In order to give a pragmatic approach to all and also fulfil desires and expectations of various democratic groups an agreement was signed in Manerplaw, KNU Base, on 31 July 1992 by different resistance groups. This came to be known as the "Manerplaw Agreement" - considered a milestone among democratic forces.

The agreement, in fact, was very much the outcome of the ongoing effort on the part of these groups to draft a constitution for a Democratic Federal Union of Burma, started since the exodus of 1988. The agreement was jointly accepted by NCGUB, NLD-LA, DAB and NDF with KNU taking the main initiative. The very essence of this agreement was the establishment of a 'Federal Union of Burma' (they were not ready to accept the name Myanmar) by ending the chauvinistic and fascist military dictatorship and where all nationalities could enjoy equality, right to self-determination, democracy and basic human rights to the fullest extent. The event was also significant for its successful integration of different ethnic groups for a common goal; which was absent for a long time. The coming of National Council of Union of Burma into existence in August made the agreement more meaningful. It acted as an accommodating body for all the existing alliances and groups. Democratic forces like NCGUB, NLD-LA, DAB, and NDF became its constituents[11]. In short, it became a common forum or a *de facto* legislature for the constituents where debates and discussions could take place and as such it gave the struggle a formalised as well as legalised image.

Now the question is what was the attitude of the regime to all these developments. The reality was that all the developments could not intimidate the military rulers much to bring any change in the existing political status quo of the country. During this period there was a change in the military hierarchy. On 23 April 1992 Senior General Saw Maung was replaced by General Than Shwe as the Chairman of the ruling State Law and Order Restoration Council on the ground of the former's ill health. But the reality was that Saw Maung was removed because of his mental instability and increasing insanity. It was a change only in the leadership not of the government there was no positive move towards a genuine political reform, moderation and liberalisation. The very few changes, made at all, were also of very less significance. In fact, the new leadership opted for a hard line stand against the increasing tide of democratic force. Replacement in the hierarchy of the regime itself was mainly that of the moderate by hard liners. Power remained strictly in the hands of the small military caucus with Ne Win still powerful through behind the scene. In short, change was cosmetic in nature. Rather than changing to the tune of the democrats the junta had already started a verbal as well as written propaganda attack against the National League for Democracy and the newly formed government in exile, the NCGUB. The Official newspaper, the *'New Light of Myanmar'*, controlled by the Directorate of Defence Services Intelligence (DDSI) under Lt. General Khin Nyunt, became the main medium for this purpose. Active involvement of Ne Win's daughter Major Sanda Win was also alleged. Rumours started spreading that the government in exile being in touch with the country's armed resistance groups had been disowned by most of the elected M.Ps. SLORC also accused the NLD of disintegrating the military set up as well as the country. However no one in particular, both inside and outside the country, was ready to accept this fabricated version and considered it as cheap propaganda policy of the SLORC. Many were of the view that SLORC carried out this propaganda because of the fear of the increasing popularity of the democratic forces and its leadership. Not only this, but, the government in exile, besides the NLD, was also becoming popular in the domestic as well as in the international arena. In fact, the relationship established by NCGUB with the various ethnic insurgent groups of the country made the chances of ending the ethnic enmity in a future civilian government. This development created a well-founded fear in the mind of the military rulers. So the efforts mainly remained on the part of the regime that NLD be cut off from any meaningful productive role. This, according to them, would also curb the integration activities of the democratic forces in the border areas and outside the country. But this was to be proved wrong.

The period, thus, witnessed the existence of side by side the increasing popularity of the struggle for democracy on the one side and the prevailing fear psychosis in the mind of the military rulers on the other. The later could be substantiated from the actions of the junta itself. Soon after the general election of May 1990 the prison became like a parliament because of the mass arrest of elected MPs. Not only this, Rangoon University students who had simply demonstrated peacefully against the government at the time when Aung San Suu Kyi was awarded Nobel Peace Prize were all arrested and given ten to twenty year prison sentences[12]. In fact, repression, both physical, and psychological emanating from this fear psychosis prevailed under the supervision of the dreaded Military Intelligence Services (MIS) headed by Lt. Gen. Khin Nyunt, the Secretary I of SLORC. Not a single form of free expression was allowed. Those who were working inside the country for restoring democracy, particularly NLD, had to face lots of harassment from the junta. The change in the hierarchy and the resultant ending of martial law on 26 September 1992 (in effect since 18 July 1989) has got no real effect in the direction. The release of 534[13] political prisoners after Gen. Than Shwe assumed power also proved just a political gimmick to mesmerise international human right bodies. According to Amnesty International at least 1500[14] political prisoners remained incarcerated, which included most of the top opposition leaders, irrespective of ethnicity and religion. Thus, the members involved in the movement were always vulnerable to any form of action from the government. The NLD was prevented from holding any meeting or gathering in the office or outside. Under these circumstances it was difficult for the party to operate properly. Sometimes all out efforts on the part of the junta to break down those involved in the struggle, both physically and psychologically, make it really difficult for many of them to keep their psyche and sanity intact. And this was the situation where the leadership of Aung San Suu Kyi came to work. It was she who tried to keep their moral high with her relentless inner strength. The very sense of her presence in the movement, though she was physically unable to participate because of house arrest, provided the required moral boost. At times, surprisingly it was said that the name '*Suu*' was forbidden in Myanmar[15].

To the SLORC Aung San Suu Kyi was not a pure Myanmarese with any right to rule the country at all for being married to an Englishman. The real factor however, was that fearful of her popularity the junta wanted to alienate Suu Kyi from the movement, which was not at all possible. For Aung San Suu Kyi the ongoing demand for the restoration of civilian democratic rule was not something ideological or physical but spiritual. It is corollary to the emancipation process started by her father, Gen. Aung San, in the 40s. She is of the view that a true revolution or struggle has to be that of the spirit. There need to be a genuine desire for democracy in the mind of each individual. Thus, under the leadership of Suu Kyi the movement was progressive because most of the original NLD leaders, having faith in her, remained sincere to the cause. The exception being the case of Aung Gyi. Factionalism was absent at the most. And the junta on its part was concerned more in concentrating the controlling power by suppressing the rivals.

Besides these developments, the early 90s saw changes in the political strategy of the junta with the sole purpose of disintegrating the ongoing movement of democracy in the country since 1988. Efforts were made to counter the challenge posed by opposition democratic forces, both inside and outside the country. Various policies and programmes were introduced as a part of the above strategy. This has got certain impact on the movement. In fact, two such policies orchestrated by the SLORC which has to do with the continuing struggle were the convening of a national convention and the starting of negotiation with ethnic insurgent groups. Both these policies formed the main basis of the whole political strategy of the regime in the domestic sphere. The national convention was introduced with a view to constitutionalise the military set-up of the country and its regime while the cease-fire policy was meant to reduce the attack from the opposition side. In the case of the national convention, if it succeeded in the near future; then it would be a repetition of what the military did in 1974 by creating a new constitution and changing to civilian garb, with some minor changes. These two policies have lot to do with the democracy movement and as such a brief elaboration is necessary for a better understanding of the course of the movement. Here, one thing which need to be remembered is the fact that since the policies are still in a continuing process and as such we cannot confine our discussion of the issues within a time frame. As such we will discuss the formative stage within the brief elaboration and continue to discuss other developments in the later stages of our study, wherever it is relevant.

5.1. National Convention:A Constitutional Gimmick

When the military orchestrated National Convention was introduced in Myanmar it was considered a charade by the general people because in this country constitutional culture has no longer got any meaning since the coup of 1962. Secondly, the move was not from the side the popular mandate. In the initial period after the election of 1990 it was always the demand among democracy groups especially the NLD that the SLORC regime should respect the popular mandate and that power be transferred to the duly elected members so that the constitutional process of running the government could be revived. Contrary to the popular demand it was at this crucial juncture that the so-called 'national convention', with the purpose of drafting a new constitution, came into being. It opened with fanfare on 9 January 1993, but it was adjourned up to February soon after the opening. The intention to hold the national convention was already expressed by SLORC in its Announcement No. 11/92 of 24 April 1992. As expected the junta was in favour of drafting a constitution through the medium of the convention which would give maximum power to the armed force. National League for Democracy and its associates were strongly against it. Decision making power under the military apparatus, would become really difficult to bring a change in the political set up leading towards democracy. Regarded as a tactical move to sideline the popularly elected group and to bring in its place a puppet gathering, many saw nothing new in the convention[16]. Besides, the NLD had been underrepresented in the said convention despite the overwhelming popular mandate it received in the election of 1990. Only 90 out of the 702 delegates were from NLD, and not one of them had been selected to head any of the panel discussions within the eight working groups of delegates[17]. Not only this, but the proceeding of the convention itself was also not conducive to democratic values. Above all, the legality of the convention itself was questionable since the military regime was not a legally accepted or sanctioned body.

It is a well known fact that the convention itself was a tactics on the part of the SLORC to manipulate the power of the state; which could be given only by a constitution, in its favour. It had carefully managed the convention's proceedings and ignored even the limited opposition views[18]. Freedom of speech and expression among the delegates was strictly restricted. The main motive was to formulate a constitution which would guarantee a dominant role for the military in the country's future political structure. Out of the total 702 delegates, except for 156 representatives (elected in 1990) and leaders of political parties, SLORC carefully handpicked all participants in the convention from national races, peasants, workers, intelligentsia and technocrats, and service personnel[19]. This was to make it easier for the military rulers to take the proceedings of the convention in the desired direction without much opposition.

Not surprisingly, however, opposition groups knew well that what the SLORC was doing was wrong. These pro-democracy groups, including NLD, expressed the view that the regime had got no authority at all to convene the national convention since it had failed to get the mandate of the people of Myanmar. There was protest from the ethnic minority races also. On 7 April 1993, the convention was once again suspended even before any purposeful work 'amidst opposition from national minority representatives who disagreed with the military's demand for a highly centralised political structure'[20]. The reality was that the ethnic minorities, contrary to the wishes of SLORC, did not want the existence of a status of military supremacy in the political affairs of the country. A fear existed in the mind of the ethnic races that a military domination of the political structure might lead to majority *Burman* domination. This was because there were still some *Burmans* who were not ready to accept the idea of equality with the minority races[21]. All of them believed that the convention would endanger the process of national reconciliation and also make the country's politics more complex. According to these ethnic races, the process of national convention should be stopped immediately and that power is transferred to the duly elected majority party so that the popularly elected parliament (*Pyithu Hluttaw*) could be constituted. Most of the countries of Europe and the U.S.A. supported this viewpoint. From the very beginning these countries were not in favour of the convention and as such none of its diplomats attended the opening ceremony. All these were because of the fact that many of the guidelines and proposals introduced by SLORC in the convention were contrary to democratic values and principles. Some such proposals which could have a negative impact on the speedy restoration of democracy in the country were:

(i) A strong President with a military background for the country.

(ii) Both the President and the members of the assembly must have resided in the country for at least the preceding twenty years.

(iii) Immediate family members of the head of the country, say spouse or children, shall not be foreign citizens.

(iv) Reservation of seats in legislature, both in the centre and the region, for armed forces personnel. It shall be 33 percent in the *Pyithu Hluttaw* and 25 percent in the regional legislatures. And all these personnel were to be appointed by the army chief with no power to the President on the matter.

Pro-Democracy groups both inside the country as well as in the borders were not ready to accept such principles because it would lead to complete exclusion of Aung San Suu Kyi from the future political system. They tried to exert pressure on the SLORC in various ways so that the proceeding of the convention could be directed towards a democratic transition. Some delegates even went to the extent of sabotaging the convention by 'sending threatening letters to other delegates'[22]. The military government countered these genuine demands by either arresting or suspending any delegate who protested against their proposals. Scholars were of the view that the lack of transparency and accountability on the part of the convention had completely put hurdle on the democratisation process as it curtailed the freedom of political life[23]. And despite all these the convention continued to meet intermittently since its inception.

When Aung San Suu Kyi was finally released in July 1995, the belief at that time among various interested circles was that she might play a role in the constitution making process of the convention by directing her party members to participate in it. Instead, she withdrew her party members from participating in it. Suu Kyi alleged that the work procedures of the convention were not democratic in nature and that the basic principles for the proposed constitution contained some elements which were not consonant with a truly democratic state. She further asserted that if the national convention continued in its present form then it could not assist in achieving national reconciliation, genuine multi-party democracy, or a state constitution that enjoyed the support and confidence of the people. The convention was boycotted by NLD.

Because of the boycott of the convention by NLD members it was almost devoid of any elected representative. With this withdrawal, it seemed SLORC's interest in a formal political ideology, particularly in democratic values, and even in the constitution waned. By now, without the presence of the elected MPs, the constitutional gimmick of SLORC had become an open affair. SLORC was forced to adjourn the sporadically continuing national convention *sine die* on 31 March 1996.

5.2. Cease Fire Policy: A Ploy to Destabilise the United Opposition

With a view to disintegrate the democratic struggle in general and to destroy the ongoing armed resistance in particular SLORC started a policy of cease-fire with real seriousness from the early 1990s' though the precedence was already created in the late 80s', when the four factions of mutineers from the former Communist Party of Burma (CPB) entered an informal agreement with the SLORC not to attack each other in 1989. Formally it was only in April 1992 that Senior Gen. Than Shwe, the Chairman of SLORC, announced for a unilateral cease-fire policy. Formally or informally, it remains one of the most serious as well as clever policy on the part of the military regime in recent times. The cease-fire agreements which started with the CPB mutineers after the collapse of the CPB in April 1989 (the fall of its Pangshang headquarter near China border) continued in the years that followed. These alliances of convenience created lots of rifts and mistrusts among the ethnic alliances waging war against the regime – something which the junta desired. This success on the part of the SLORC in tempting various insurgent groups by using ploys like 'border development programmes' and other business concessions (particularly in drug and narcotics) created some set back for the rebels who were struggling for a federal democratic set up in Myanmar. For time being, the forging of an unholy alliance between the SLORC government and various constituents of ethnic insurgent fronts and democratic alliances created a sort of apprehension of neutralising or weakening the ongoing movement for democracy.

The cease-fire agreements which started with the ex-CPB militias particularly the four main groups viz., the United Wa State Army (UWSA), led by Chao Ngi Lai and Pao Yu-Chang; the Myanmar National Democratic Alliance Army (MNDAA), led by Pheung Kyashin and Pheung Kya-fu; the National Democratic Alliance Army, led by Lin Mingxian (Sai Lin) and Zhang Zhiming (Kyi Myint); and the New Democratic

Army, led by Ting Ying; set a precedence for other groups to follow[24]. Of all the mutineers, the most prominent was the UWSA with strength of 8000-10,000 armed personnel. All these four entered the cease-fire agreement in different periods of 1989 itself. And to add to these four groups, a large faction of Shan State Progressive Party / Shan State Army under Sao Hso Htein made peace with the government on 2 September 1989. Thus, within 1989 itself, five insurgent groups, mainly ethnic based, came to terms with the military government. Main initiative in this direction was taken by Major General (later General) Khin Nyunt, the chief of military intelligence. It was he who neutralised these groups even before they merge with any ethnic alliance or front (say NDF), being tempted by future peace and development. With this, the policy of cease-fire was started as an important political ploy of the regime with Khin Nyunt as the main string puller. Another contributing factor to this process was that some of the insurgent groups were tired of their uncertain long years of struggle with no success in sight. The cease-fire policy provided the necessary opportunity to come to terms.

By early 1996, the SLORC, with the effort of Lt. General Khin Nyunt, had negotiated with 16 groups [25] of various sizes, the last being the Mong Tai Army (MTA) of the notorious drug lord of the 'Golden Triangle', Chang Chifu commonly known as '*Khun Sha*'. Most of these deals with the MTA and the subsequent surrender of its leader in January 1996 were carried out by Lt. General Khin Nyunt, the head of DDSI and Secretary One of SLORC on behalf of the government. Of the above-armed groups the Kachin Independence Organisation (KIO) and the MTA were the two most prominent groups with well-armed men of 8,000 and 12,000 respectively. These two were well organised in terms of manpower, strategy and best of firepower. However, the cease-fire entered into with main insurgent groups did not help the struggle for democracy. It created a sense of insecurity and dislocation among those struggling for democracy as most of the above groups were related with DAB, the pro-democracy rebel alliance, which provided the support base of the movement. Above all, one condition for the cease-fire agreement was that the signatories had to completely break off all contact with DAB and the NLD. This, in turn, greatly reduced the strength of those remaining outside the cease-fire. After the cease-fire, only Karen National Union, ABSDF and some smaller groups remained to struggle against the SLORC. As a result the fighting and bargaining power of DAB greatly declined. Many of the decade old bases of the KNU also fell to the government forces one by one. Despite these handicaps, the remaining groups however vowed to continue fighting the Yangon government. They were of the view that those groups meeting with SLORC individually were politically as well as morally wrong as it would slow down the restoration of democracy in the country.

As mentioned above, the disunity and rifts among the armed insurgent groups also proved a great misgiving for democracy movement. It helped in fulfilling the desire of the regime to divide its opposition. There was a sort of understanding or agreement among the ethnic alliances, particularly between NDF and DAB, that no individual group would have separate talk with the junta; but was of no use as the junta refused to negotiate except with individual organisations[26]. "Despite signed agreements and the best intentions, none of these alliances had held up to external pressure and individual concerns"[27]. In most cases personal interest overrides general interest leading the individual groups to enter into secret deals and negotiations. And on the part of the junta, it was successful in luring most of the insurgent groups with assurance of autonomy in managing their own affairs, border development, free business in drugs and narcotics, and right to maintain its army and weapons. This created mistrust among the opposition groups proving harmful to the movement as a whole while the junta harvested the benefit. In fact, signing of cease-fire agreement by Kachin Independence Army (KIA) with Yangon in February 1994 was the greatest setback for the ethnic opposition as it was one of the most well organised and powerful group free from the divide and rule policy of SLORC. Besides, the entering into a ceasefire by KIA and many other such groups deprived many of the pro-democracy activities of a safe shelter. Many of them, having no other alternative, had either to surrender or to move to some other new safer area. For them everything had to be started anew once again.

Now the big question is how the ceasefire policy was helping those armed groups that had agreed to it. This needs to be analysed. One big irony of the cease-fire policy of the SLORC regime was that it was against any form of negotiation with the main alliance, i.e. Democratic Alliance of Burma (DAB), which represents both the democracy movement as well as the armed struggle. The regime was not interested in negotiating with the united front but with its constituents one by one separately. Not only this, but the regime did not allow any group which had entered into cease-fire agreement to suggest or discuss anything related with political issues. The question of autonomy was completely ignored. They were allowed to put up proposals on economic and trade issues only. This, however, infuriated many of them. To them economic rights without political rights was purely inadequate. It made their long struggle futile. However, ultimately what all these bring out was the insincerity on the part of the junta. It also clearly showed that SLORC was interested only in breaking up the united opposition by offering ceasefire to individual groups while it continued strengthening its military power.

Here, once again, the main questions which arise relating to the above facts are – how long is the ceasefire going to last? Will it be able to bring a lasting solution to the decade old problem of ethnic insurgency? How is it going to deal with the present movement for restoration of democracy? If taken seriously these are questions which are not easy to answer. But this is not the case with the regime. In fact, it seems that the rulers are not at all concerned with the solution, rather, it is more interested in playing a delaying tactics with the intention to annihilate the rebel opposition so that movement for democracy loses its support. No concrete and uniform formula was followed in carrying out the ceasefire agreements. Instead, whenever a ceasefire agreement was made the SLORC media portrayed it as an unconditional surrender on the part of the groups which were party to the ceasefire. This created misunderstanding which, in turn, hampered the process of a meaningful ceasefire. In most cases also SLORC violated the ceasefire agreements, and tried to intrude its troops into the limited territories of ceasefire bound ethnic rebels taking undue advantage of it. It lacked fair play, justice and sincerity. As a result, ceasefire had broken down in case of some ethnic groups. The best example of the regime's unreliability on this issue was what it did to the Karenni people. After its ceasefire with the Karenni National Progressive Party (KNPP) on 21 March 1995 SLORC started sending troops to Karenni areas and occupied 90 percent of it[28]. Within few months of the ceasefire it attacked KNPP bases in June. The regime never stopped its preparation for military offensive against the rebels.

The ceasefire policy was not a permanent solution to the ongoing political turmoil of the country. According to veteran NLD leader U Kyi Maung, the ceasefire was "nothing more than a cooling-off period for the insurgents to regroup and train even more of their population"[29]. In fact, the ethnic people have no faith in the regime and as such has retained their weapons and what is called a ceasefire is just a refraining and regrouping period. Both sides used it for organising its forces. "So it is fair to say that these cease-fires can not guarantee lasting peace", further opined Kyi Maung[30]. The reality of the situation lies in the fact that the junta have got no specific permanent policy to bring diverse groups together and also its governing system does not commensurate to a lasting peace in the country. Instead, it resulted in a flourishing narco-politics in the country, which have nothing to contribute towards the unity of the country. Besides, there were always fluctuations on part of SLORC as regards to its policy of ceasefire. For example, it ended its unilateral ceasefire against the Karens in January 1995, when endowed with opportunity to attack Karen bases. So ultimately the task fell on the NLD and other democratic groups supporting its cause. The ceasefire policy remains just a political gimmick to hamper the process towards a democratic spurt.

5.3. Aung San Suu Kyi – SLORC Dialogue

The first half of 90s was full of surprise for Myanmarese politics. Many expected as well as unexpected events that has lot to do with the movement for democracy occurred. One such even was the Aung San Suu Kyi – SLORC dialogue of 1994. It was, in fact, a major event even though it lacked the expected positive change. Despite the shortcomings, it could be considered as a breakthrough to the long ongoing stalemate between the pro-democracy forces and the military regime.

The dialogue, which was believed to be endorsed by Ne Win, was carried out in the form of two meetings. The first meeting between Aung San Suu Kyi and SLORC Generals consisting of Chairman Than Shwe and Intelligence Chief Khin Nyunt took place on 21 September 1994 at a government guest house in Central Yangon. This was followed by the second meeting on 28 October. The said dialogue was arranged by an exiled monk, U Rewata Dhamma, who resided in Birmingham, England. Whatsoever might be the outcome of the talks it was considered important for the movement because this was the first time that SLORC has taken up her offer for a dialogue which she has been demanding since her entry in the politics of Myanmar in 1988[31]. Another fact of the talk was that it was carried out with Suu Kyi still in the custody under her dialogue partners. For many democracy activists it was a victory for their cause because the junta had accepted Aung San Suu Kyi as the undisputed leader of the democratic movement even if they did not want to accept the fact. Their actions already proved it.

What was actually discussed in the talks was not known as nothing was made public. Aung San Suu Kyi, on her part, assured that there would be no secret deal. She was against any negotiation or deal with SLORC in exchange for her freedom. Indeed there was no deal at all. This was disclosed later on by her husband, Michael Aris, who was visiting her at that time. Nothing positive also came out of the dialogue despite pinning lots of hope on it by democracy supporters. However, there were mixed reactions. Many groups like the government in exile, the NCGUB, were not in favour of any talk so long as Suu Kyi's detention continued. They were of the view that nothing could come out of such a talk. They wanted her release first. And ultimately the talks failed to bring any positive change towards restoration of democracy except some hope for future negotiation.

5.4. Release of Aung San Suu Kyi

The release of Aung San Suu Kyi was one of the important event of the year 1995. Her release from house arrest once more inspired the dampened moot of the democratic forces caused due to the fall of Manerplaw, the headquarters of both KNU and DAB. After keeping 6 years under house arrest Aung San Suu Kyi was finally released on 10 July 1995, just a few days before the expiry of her repeatedly extended detention term. Her sudden release was a surprise. The world public as well as her countrymen were all caught unaware as they never expected that the junta would act so soon to release her though some rumour was afloat. Definitely, on the one hand, international pressure did play a role in her release. Discussions and debates were going on in various international forums on the issue. In the United States, Senator Mitch McConnell, a sympathiser of the democracy movement in Myanmar was about to introduce an economic sanction bill against the country on 11 July 1995 in the U.S. Senate. It was Suu Kyi's release which deferred the introduction of the bill. It was clear that the release was due to external pressure. Even though it was so the military junta did not want to give an impression that it acted on international pressure. This is the reason why there was no coverage about her release in any of the national media. The intention of the SLORC, it seemed, was to marginalise the significance of her release on the political sphere of the country while it fulfilled an obligation of the international community. Another factor could be that the regime was confident of its own capability to challenge the popularity of Aung San Suu Kyi. SLORC was of the view that it was capable of tackling with any uprising that might be caused by her reappearance in the political scene[32]. The rulers were also under wrong concept that people had forgotten her during the long years of cut off from the public view.

Aung San Suu Kyi's release has nothing to do with any transfer of power by SLORC for restoration of democracy. No indication on the part of the rulers in the direction could be seen. Though Aung San Suu Kyi's supporters were happy at the release because they hoped to get her support and direction, yet, there was no sign of opening on the part of the regime towards a democratic transformation. Her release was followed not even by a single step towards reconciliation by the regime. The release was only in physical sense and nothing else. So the continuation of the stalemate between the two forces still lingered. It was very much evident that there was nothing for great rejoicement for the movement as a whole. For the time being it was a wait and see situation with only speculations flourishing. All these, did not mean that the positive implication, though however minor it may be, should be easily ignored. Momentum of the pro-democracy struggle, though slightly subdued, started picking up once more besides concentrating its effort on peace and national reconciliation.

But the important question at this juncture was – where would it all lead to? Aung San Suu Kyi, on her part, said at the time of her release that except that of her release nothing else has changed. According to her it would be too soon to arrive at any conclusion. She asserted not to expect too much from the regime. And, in fact, there was not much progress towards political changes since her release. Her repeated request for continuation of dialogue was ignored. Instead, SLORC continued to adopt its early practice of harsh repression.

In the context, whether SLORC would allow Aung San Suu Kyi to take part freely in the political process of the country was something which needed serious pondering. This left many experts to speculate about the exact outcome. For Aung San Suu Kyi, she had already vowed to continue with her struggle for popular political atmosphere in military ruled Myanmar and rejected government claim that she was inciting the people to take to street. Whatsoever may be the outcome political participation was her duty for the goal of a democratic Myanmar. According to her if anyone would suffer in the fight for democracy in the country it would be her and other leaders of her group, not the ordinary people. She further opined democracy is not a 'cure all' of every ill of the society but at least it would ensure the people's security of life and human dignity.

But with time Aung San Suu Kyi and her party also feel frustrated with the lack of response from SLORC for any viable solution to the ongoing political uncertainty. As a result, "she and the NLD moved from their ineffective conciliatory gestures to a strategy of outright confrontation on 28 November 1995, the day that the adjourned convention was set to reopen", by announcing NLD's boycott of the national convention[33]. The regime too, on its part, retaliated by suspending all eighty-six NLD members present in the convention. Besides, one could see the renewed measures on the side of SLORC which indicated a mass repression of the opposition.

The continued indifference on the part of the SLORC regime to the demand for a federal democratic system and the deteriorating political situation of the country after Suu Kyi's release created lot of resentment among democratic forces. This gradually led towards a situation of renewed political confrontation. There was subdued but intense struggle between the two opposing forces for establishing credibility and legitimacy in the country. The high hope among various sections that the release of Aung San Suu Kyi would lead to opening of grounds for further meaningful dialogue between the two proved wrong. One clear sign which was emerging was that the junta was unwilling to sit down and talk with the democratic groups but was determined to overpower and destroy them. The military appeared to be taking an ever-tougher stance towards their political adversaries[34]. Suu Kyi, though released, was not allowed to move or associate freely. Restrictions were placed on her activities. Her weekend speech to the public from her house, which continued up to September 1996, was scrutinised minutely. Besides, the government media under the aegis of military intelligence continued to carry out an anti-Suu Kyi campaign unabated.

In reply to this confrontationist attitude of the SLORC, Aung San Suu Kyi announced the intention of the National League for Democracy to hold a party congress in May 1996, on the eve of the sixth anniversary of the 1990 election victory. SLORC considered it as an open challenge to its power. In order to sabotage the said meeting over 300 NLD activists were arrested in the largest crackdown since the mass detentions of 1990[35]. Out of the above 273 were elected MPs[36]. Not only this but Suu Kyi's husband was denied a visa to visit her in the spring of 1996, and also by using its captive Union Solidarity and Development Association (USDA) the military has mobilised mass rallies against her and her weekly public meeting held at her doorstep. Undeterred by all these Suu Kyi continued with her preparation for the NLD Congress. And it was held inside her compound as proposed despite the presence of only 30 members of NLD[37]. The Congress also got the response of nearly 10,000 supporters who attended it outside Aung San Suu Kyi's house. And immediately after the Congress Aung San Suu Kyi confirmed that her party was to draft a new constitution for future Myanmar, thus challenging the constitution drafting process of the SLORC orchestrated National Convention. Here, in the whole process of Myanmarese democracy movement, another important event which coincided with the said NLD Congress was the adoption of a draft constitution of the proposed Federal Union of Burma as a first draft constitution by the National Council of Union of Burma (NCUB), the *de facto* parliament for democratic forces working in the border. The NCUB further made it clear that the drafted constitution is to be presented to the constituent assembly or a similar body which will be convened when Myanmar achieves democracy[38]. These two simultaneous processes however, infuriated the regime. Once again SLORC angrily responded to these developments by enacting a new Law No.5/96, prohibiting any body from writing or discussing a state constitution or from criticising the National Convention[39]. Thus, a tussle became evident in the political scenario during this period. As a result, the chances of dialogue between the two opposing forces became very bleak.

But, despite all these confrontations and restrictions, one could not ignore the fact that the holding of the NLD congress in Suu Kyi's compound was one forward step for the democracy movement. It was a clear indication of the renewed progress NLD had made in particular and the movement in general. At one stage the arrest of Aung San Suu Kyi and other frontal leaders of the party had greatly subdued the activity of NLD. In their absence the incumbent party president, Aung Shwe, had not taken any major or radical step which might have created complicacy with the junta at that juncture. The Congress of May 1996 was a break from this subdued atmosphere (or so to say a vicious cycle of fear) and also a sort of new beginning.

At that time one question that frequented the mind of the general masses as well as the political circles was - how much understanding do the SLORC have regarding the problem and actual conditions facing the country? Is it genuinely ignorant about the said issues or just fanning ignorance to avoid the real issues? The real answers to these questions lie only with the rulers. However, for the time being, the regime, it seemed, was more concerned about its welfare and safety rather than the problems facing the country. Neither did the rulers showed the intention even to talk with the opposition for the reconciliation of the diverse groups. This tendency was what actually angered those involved in the movement for restoration of democracy. The degree of difference on the part of the regime was really intolerable.

As a result of the existing gap between the two opposite forces chances of a meaningful solution to the continuing statements was bleak. The atmosphere of constant confrontation and political tension was proving non-beneficial for the cause of democracy and federalism in the country. But unavoidable as it was in the existing circumstances, tension of a greater dimension once more broke out in September 1996 when the National League for Democracy again tried to convene yet another party congress on the occasion of the party's eight founding anniversary. It was to be observed under the banner of All Burma Congress of the NLD from 27 to 29 September. Obviously the military regime responded by arresting activists, cutting party's telephone lines, closing party headquarters, banning activities of the party and so on. Arrests were started from 26 September onwards. According to Amnesty International reports, 'in a swift pre-emptive move beginning on 26 September, the authorities arrested 159 NLD delegates and 414 NLD supporters around the country'[40]. The process of suppression continued. Aung San Suu Kyi's telephone line was cut off. Armed riot police (*Lon Htein*) continued to blockade the compound on the weekend of 28 and 29 September, preventing the Myanmarese people and the international media from entering the area[41]. Besides, to prove its harsh repression drive correct the junta accused Suu Kyi of being engaged in subversion activities in collusion with foreign agents. SLORC further charged that she was trying to destroy peace and integrity of the country by instigating and dividing the country's army, the *tatmadaw*. With these accusations a continuous effort was made to marginalise Aung San Kyi's role in the Myanmarese politics.

Uprising continued in the subsequent months of October, November and December 1996. The month of December witnessed the first largest student demonstration since the uprising of 1988. Thousands of students gathered in Yangon carrying out anti-government demonstrations. There was a heavy clampdown from the side of the regime. Arrest and detention once more followed. Policemen carefully checked identity cards to ensure that people, as few as possible, enter the Yangon Institute of Technology (YIT) campus, which has become one of Myanmar's hot bed of dissent. The student movement that started in and around Yangon University and YIT campuses spread to other Universities situated in other parts of the country. As this student protest started picking up momentum government closed all universities on 9 December. Not only this, Suu Kyi was also confined in her compound thus curbing her movement for any activity related with the student movement. Security forces sealed her lakeside compound. Aung San Suu Kyi protested against this confinement, as it was wrong and illegal restriction. She also rejected government charges that her party was involved in spreading student protests and called on the military rulers to seek new solutions to the unrest. The main demands of the students were more freedom - of association, thought and expression.

The renewed student demonstrations, most feared by the regime, clearly showed that the students were coming out once again in the street signalling a threat to the regime. The SLORC, on its part, was unable to solve the problem. Despite the claim of the military regime, far from being marginalised, the student demonstrations for restoration of democracy and democratic rights could draw the world attention and was also becoming well exposed to the world public.

Now, in between our continuing analysis of the process of the movement for democracy in the 90s, we need to study three more aspects i.e. the existing conflicts and contradictions within the movement, the economic changes, and the question of Aung San Suu Kyi as the guiding force.

5.5. Conflicting Ideas and Contradictions within the Movement

Despite the number of alliances among the opposition groups and the mounting consciousness among the people of the need for a democratic set-up the 90s was also not completely devoid of internal conflicts and contradictions within the democratic forces. This, in fact, formed and important aspect of the ongoing movement during the period, which cannot be underestimated.

Internal conflicts and contradictions started brewing within individual democratic groups, particularly those based in the border areas. Whether the groups belong to students, ethnic insurgents or the exile government the main issue of conflict remained the same that is the question of leadership. Leadership, in most cases, was confined mainly in the hands of well to do, educated and well travelled, so to say the elites. As a result, factionalism became rampant in the critical moments of the movement. Fractionalisation was common among the groups. New groups were continually formed; some appeared by splintering other organisations[42]. The first such fractionalisation among the democratic groups was within the All Burma Students Democratic Front (ABSDF), the main student force for democracy. This happened in 1991 when ADSDF was split into two groups mainly on the issue of leadership between Dr. Aung Naing and Moe Thi Zun, though luckily it reunited again in 1996. This was followed by many more such incidents. In December 1994 there was a split within KNU, the main pillar of all democratic alliances, which led to the desertation of more than 500 Buddhists from the Union to form the Democratic Kayin Buddhist Organisation (DKBO). The main pretext for the split was the allegation that Buddhists were discriminated by the Christian. Some were of the opinion that the SLORC had a role in this split since the DKBO joined the SLORC in attacking the Karen Camps later on. Besides this split there was also a continuing conflict within KNU for the change of leadership from old guards to young bloods. In a meeting of the KNU's Executive Committee in mid 1995 it was proposed that the old guards including Gen. Bo Mya should be retired to give way to new ones. However, the meeting was abandoned due to refusal of Bo Mya to retire from the Presidentship of the Union.

Internal conflicts also emerged within the democratic

opposition as a whole mainly because of differences in the means and also due to the ongoing cease-fire. The combination of different and diverse groups for the common goal of federal democratic set up invited problems in identifying a common strategy. This also led to contradictions and misunderstandings. Differences in the means and strategy of the groups, sometimes, had to do something with the presence of a strong narco-politics in the country. Because, most of the ethnic groups, constituting part of the DAB, except for the Kachins and Karens, base their source of income from narco-trade. This resulted in conflict between the groups on the issue. Some of the groups who were against narco-trade were of the view that the use of it as a part of the democracy movement may dilute the very cause. Disagreement became common. Not only was this, but another factor which created conflict within the democratic alliance was the cease-fire policy of the SLORC. Separate peace talks and cease-fire agreements created mistrust and suspicion among the different armed partners. The real intention of the military regime's cease-fire was to disintegrate the movement, which they had achieved to a certain extent.

Mistrust and displeasure also emerged between the NLD and those ethnic groups which had entered into cease-fire agreement with the SLORC when the former boycotted the National Convention in November, 1995. There was lack of support from these groups who were earlier partner to the democratic force. They became less vocal for the cause of the movement even though they morally supported it. In fact, these groups were enticed by various benefits and facilities promised by the regime. Thus, they were not in favour of supporting the NLD in its move against the SLORC. But what needs to be remembered is the fact that this unholy alliance between the two opposing forces is not likely to last long.

This period also witnessed internal conflicts within the NCGUB, the government in exile. This was a serious problem. "The exile government, whose head quarters was situated in the main Karen camp at the Thai Myanmar border (now situated permanently in Washington, U.S.A.), had been extremely emasculated with its, "Prime Minister" and other top cabinet members remaining in the United States since the end of 1993, ostensibly to garner international support"[43]. The absence of important members from the headquarter make it difficult for the government to take up prompt action and planning when need arise. Co-ordination became difficult because of the existing gap. Besides, there was a continuing disagreement and conflicts among the cabinet members also. Some were even against the leadership of Dr. Sein Win, and two ministers viz. U Than Kywe and U Myint Aung even went to the extent of surrendering to the SLORC in February 1991. This particular problem was slightly minimised when the headquarters was shifted to Washington D.C. Another issue which invited dissatisfaction was in regard to the NCGUB's appointments of 'ambassadors' in a number of countries without any consultation with the local organisations (Myanmarese)[44]. The action resulted in the lack of co-ordination in their activities.

Another important issue was regarding the identification of a common strategy acceptable to both the forces operating inside and outside the country. No doubt for both the forces everyone still accepted Aung San Suu Kyi as their undisputed leader. Some student leaders expressed their unhappiness with the unresponsive nature of the internal forces despite well-publicised propaganda for the cause outside. This may be due to the excessive repression of the military regime on the activities of the NLD in the country. According to them means should be found for a dialogue at the earliest by Suu Kyi and NLD, if not then the movement will become uncontrollable. Some scholars were even of the view that the sign of a differentiated political gap between Suu Kyi and her followers in the NLD over the substance and style of her campaign[45].

The aforesaid factors checked the speed of the movement. However, maximum efforts were taken up in the leadership of the movement to erase out their contradictory features. By now they have realised these defects.

Now, after our discussion of the existing conflict and

contradictions within the movement we come to another important aspect i.e., economic conditions or changes during the period. This is because the discussion on any aspect of the said period cannot be complete unless we discuss a brief history of its economic changes and conditions. The study of the economic dimension is imperative to have a more objective view of the movement.

5.6. Economic Dimension of the Turbulent 90s'

In the case of Third World countries democratisation had always followed a successful economy, whatever the form the government may be. This is one point of view among scholars and also historical fact. Another prevalent point of view is that democratisation always precede a successful economy in Asian countries which is the case with Southeast Asian Countries. Either one may happen first. Both the points of view are correct for particular countries under particular circumstance but generalisation is difficult. In the case of Myanmar also it is not easy to accept one of the view points. First of all the state of economy need to be assessed under the prevailing circumstances. As such, it is very important for us to analyse the Myanmarese economy under the regime, both SLORC and SPDC, in the post 1988 period, particularly in the 90s. Because, this, to a great extent, may decide the future course of democratisation in the country. "The state of economy if it is towards stagnation would produce recurring economic, social and political crises, which would be met with continued political repression", according to scholars like Paul Cook and Martin Minogue[46]. They further opined that this might lead to an Eastern European style political collapse, whose outcome would be highly unpredictable[47]. This is to a great extent, is true for Myanmar. Now to know the exact economic scenario of the period is a must for the continuation of our study. This would help, in a way, in bringing out the real picture of the nature and scope of the movement for democracy at the said context. Besides, the study of the economy of this period will help to a great extent to determine what political trends are discernible and what are the future options for the ongoing movement for democracy.

5.7. Economic Reforms in the Post -88 Period

After the failure of a closed door centralised economic planning leading to rapid economic deterioration, the new regime under SLORC took up various economic reforms in the post - 88 period. Despite the economic aid sanctions due to the 1988 uprising the junta started taking the country towards some sort of economic liberalisation bringing changes in the economy. Change was made from a 'control economy' to 'open door' policy or limited kind of market economy. The regime made progressive reforms in the area of privatisation, foreign investment, border trade, exports promotion etc. Some such reforms were: -

(i) The first major step of SLORC regime towards economic reform was the opening of the economy to foreign investment, capital as well as technical knows how. The Foreign Investment Law was enacted in November 1988. This new law permitted foreign investors to form wholly owned enterprises or joint ventures, especially those engaged in exporting activities[48]. The first ventures were short term licenses to Thai and Malaysian firms to fish in designated coastal waters[49]. This was followed by new investment rights to other countries in sectors like logging, oil, coastal fishing an tourism. Despite the sanction of aid private credit continued to flow into the country. Asian countries like Thailand and Singapore were interested in logging, mining and tourism while European and Western companies like Unocal, Total, Shell etc., were more interested in exploiting the country's oil reserves. In fact, it was a boon for foreign investors to exploit the rich natural resources like timber, oil and precious stones of the country.

(ii) Sizeable growth of private sector industry was another important feature of this liberalisation process. Since the coup of 1962 all the means of production in the country was nationalised but they were not working successfully. Thus, many reforms had been taken up. The law allowing private individuals to take part in business ventures was enacted. Steps were even taken up to privatised the government owned State Economic Enterprises (SEEs); but the real motivation was lacking. In 1993, private banks were allowed to establish[50]. Private sector of the economy started picking up momentum once more. Thus in the later half of the 90s' it accounted for around 70 percent of industrial output and 80 percent of industrial employment[51].

(iii) Another important step in this direction was the legalisation of cross border trade with its neighbouring countries particularly with China, Thailand and Bangladesh, and to some extent with India[52]. The process was speeded up mainly because of the collapse of CPB (earlier supported by China), increasing offensive against the KNU and the government-to-government agreements with its neighbours[53]. Earlier border trade was controlled by the ethnic groups and communist rebels viz. Kachin Independence Organisation, Karen National Union, and CPB. Though flow of commodities started as a result of the cross border trade; yet, some 28 goods including rice, teak, gem, oil, natural gas and weapons were under strict government control. The 'regularisation, in fact, enhanced SLORC's fiscal base, while reducing income for the Karen, Shan and other insurgents in the Thai border'[54].

(iv) The opening of economy also saw more orientation towards export promotion. As a part of it rice export was started again.

These government efforts for economic liberalisation were not completely in vain. It brought certain positive changes in the economy. As a result of the foreign investment law certain amount of foreign capital started flowing into the country despite official trade and aid sanctions imposed by countries since 1988. Most of the capital was of private style. Private sector also expanded giving ample scope for large-scale production. It has been reported that by the end of February 1992, 6477 trading and private enterprises had registered[55]. Export had also grown by over 40 percent during the years from 1989 to 1993[56].

However, despite these initial positive signs of economic liberalisation the problem facing the economy, in reality, was acute. Lack of management efficiency and priority of self-interest above national interest still prevailed. Besides, a sort of state controlled capitalism prevailed. Lack of consistency and cohesiveness in the change was also quite evident. As a result, problems such as inability to control inflation, increasing black market economy, lack of job prospect for the rising unemployment and underemployment, scarcity of essential commodities particularly rice still existed. Above all, lack of foreign aid and funds was also hampering smooth process of the economy. The embargo on aid (due to the killing of 1988) has undoubtedly hampered public sector capital expenditure[57]. There was lack of fund when it was very much needed for infrastructural development of the economy. Thus, except for some new changes the economy as a whole during the period was marked, as usual, by manifold setbacks. Whatever little the economy had achieved after its opening in 1988 once more started declining from 1993 onwards. Here the wrong policies of the regime and the resultant setbacks could be simply assessed.

(i) First, the inability to control the ever increasing rate of inflation remained one of the most serious setbacks both in the pre as well as post 88 period. It remained a distinct feature of the Myanmarese economy during the 90s. Inflation was so high that the buying capacity and standard of living of the people were at its lowest level. In the beginning of the 90s itself the rate of inflation was 60 per cent[58] unofficially, and officially it was about 30 per cent. Even Gen. Khin Nyunt, the Secretary I, acknowledged that the prices might be higher than what the government had admitted[59]. One important factor was the repeated printing of currency notes to supplement the lack of fund resulting in an excess money supply. According to Myanmar Scholar Mya Maung, the main causes for this situation are shortage of domestic production, high cost of production, increased money supply, over valuation of Myanmarese currency, and dual price structures[60].

(ii) Secondly, fluctuating rate of exchange was another crisis of the economy. The Kyat was overvalued by over 5000 per cent[61]. The official exchange rate was normally Kyat 6: US Dollar1. However, the average black market exchange rate was about twenty times the official rate which normally came around Kyat 120:1US dollar. In December 1997 it was worth about 380 Kyat per US dollar in the open market[62]. The irony of the Myanmarese economy is that maximum business is carried out in the unofficial exchange rate or the market price of the Kyat. It is believed that 70 to 75 per cent operate at the actual market rate[63]. Thus it acted as deterrent to the economic progress.

(iii) Thirdly, black marketeering remained rampant. This has been a common phenomenon of the military led economy which can be traced since the time of the 1962 coup. This situation came up as a result of the lack of a reliable production mechanism to meet the consumer needs of the people. Besides, whatever little forms of goods produced by the military controlled economy was of inferior quality when compared with outside goods, though the price remained nearly the same. Above this, the increasing population coupled with the desire to garner more income on the part of the military elites also resulted in the existence of the black market system in a wide scale. It is said that one could get any commodity in Myanmar at a price. And this problem has been made more complex with the involvement of narco-politics.

(iv) Fourthly, another setback for the economy was the high rate of military expenditure which was affecting the national budget. It is believed that at least 40 per cent of Myanmar's estimated public sector spending of 60 per cent of the national budget was diverted for military purposes[64]. It might be even higher since reliable data is not available. Since the military coup of 1988 the armed force had increased from 1,86,000 to more than 3 lakhs during a decade. The intention is to increase the strength further. And during this decade more than US$1 billion has been spent on procuring armaments like fighter aircrafts, frigates, tanks, armour carriers, anti-aircrafts weapons and other military hardware[65]. Maximum deal was made with China. Thus, the fact remained that resources has been diverted from the priority sector of economy to meet military needs.

(v) Fifthly, lack of management skill and administrative efficiency on the part of the military rulers was also another impediment for the economy. Due to this the government was unable to properly plan and implement the economic reforms. Lack of faith on experts by the regime also led to not hiring the experts. And as such the lack of trained staff is making it difficult in carrying out a co-ordinated economic planning involving inter-sectoral consideration[66].

(vi) Sixthly, another serious problem facing the economy was the ever-increasing level of corruption. Corruption from the highest echelons to the lowest strata was rampant and it was a means of survival. Salaries of the employees could not keep pace with inflation[67]. At every level of the official channel corruption is involved in tipping 'tea money'. To curb this government had taken up various steps. In October 1991, for example, Lt. Gen. Khin Nyunt admitted that about 10,516 public service personnel had been dismissed for corruption[68]. However, this could not solve the deep-rooted problem.

(vii) Seventhly, infrastructural development remained very slow and backward making other efforts of economic reform ineffective. The necessary amount of foreign aid was also not available because of the sanction that followed the suppression of 1988. Of the $3.2 billion of investment approved since the first reforms of 1989, only $1.2 billion had been invested by 31 March 1996[69]. Besides, whatever little the government had received was not utilised in this sector. As a result the pace of economic progress could not pick up momentum despite the claims of the military regime.

Briefly, the economic situation in Myanmar during the

said period failed to make a stable growth. Various natural as well as artificial causes obstructed the economic progress. Despite initial success as a result of the opening of the economy the main sector like agriculture, industry and mining began to recede once more in the mid 90s'. The decline of agricultural production, which was the main thrust area of the new economy, was a great jolt. Production of paddy declined further in 1997-98 due to over flooding in the Irrawaddy delta[70]. Its share of GDP fell from 54.1 per cent in Financial Year (FY) 1993/1994 to 51.2 per cent in Financial Year (FY) 1997/1998[71]. The growth rate in the industrial sector also declined. This decline in the growth rate of the various sectors made the negative elements like inflation, unemployment, black marketeering and foreign debt uncontrollable. In fact, the second result was worse. As a result the situation remained such that a teacher could no longer afford to give his or her children an education level, like the one he himself had acquired, with his meagre income or earning. The average salary of 1200 Kyat that a second teacher received was not enough even to buy rice for the family. It was only those who were close to the military hierarchy that could enjoy a prosperous life. The condition of the poor in the country was so bad that they could not afford two meals of rice a day[72]. Some even failed to have one meal and as such had to satisfy with rice water rather than the actual rice. This, in fact, in an irony as well as a tragedy for a country which was once known as 'rice bowl of Asia' for its abundance in rice production. This condition was evident not only in the rural areas but also in the so called satellite towns created by the government for settlement of downtrodden people from cities and towns in the name of beautification. Uneven nature of the economy as a result of the inefficient military planners failed to raise the standard of living. But this does not mean that there were no rich people in Myanmar. In fact, the elite group of rich people could spend thousands of *Kyats* a night only in entertainment and frivolities. They constituted a few top members of the regime and their circle. In short, the gap between the rich and the poor was so wide. A vicious circle of poverty exists in the economy.

Another peculiarity of the economy visible during this period was the presence of too much Chinese influence in most economic sectors. The scarcity in the country was filled up by China with its ever-increasing production under a well-planned liberalised economy. China also took the advantage of cross border trade. The commodities demand of Myanmarese people was met by importing from the mainland China. In fact, Myanmar became a lucrative market for Chinese finished goods. However, all these had nothing to contribute in the growth of the declining economy except benefits going to China. In short, a sort of economic colonisation was gradually imposed on the country.

Besides, foreign aid and investment were also not coming smoothly due to various restrictions imposed by the industrialised economic powers when it was most needed. Many foreign investors felt insecure to invest in the country due to the existing fluid political conditions. Here, what needs to be remembered is the fact that Myanmar's political situation has always been closely linked to the fate of its economy. And in this situation even the 'Visit Myanmar Year', an ambitious tourism campaign to attract tourists was a total failure with brand new luxury hotels standing virtually deserted, some registering and occupancy rate of no more than 10 percent[73] . To add to this lack of fund, unemployment was soaring up with a growth from 5.8 per cent in 1993-94 to 6.7 per cent in 1997-98[74] while schools and universities remained closed since 1996.Workers' strikes and employees demands for higher pay and better facilities became common. Even business circle had expressed the desire for a change as business transaction decline to a large extent with the economy once more slipping down. For the regime it became more imperative to depend on narco-money for its survival.

From all these facets of the Myanmarese economy in the 90s it could be deduced that whatever economic reforms made by the SLORC was not for a genuine opening of the economy. Rather, the economic reforms and changes of the junta could be interpreted as a survival strategy in response to the deteriorating economic conditions. The problem with the SLORC regime was that it could not undertake the extensive reforms necessary to turn the economy around for fear of social and political repercussions[75]. No reasonable monetary or fiscal policy as well as any step to rectify the structural imbalances of the economy were taken up. Not only this but the little change that actually took place was also merely from a 'close economy' to a 'command economy' with some changes. It was still run by soldiers whose idea of economic management was to give orders[76]. State control of the economy continued. A clear example was the minimal decline in the number of State Economic Enterprises (SEEs) from 1,768 in 1990-91 to 1,675 in 1994-95[77]. Besides, many of the newly started big private sectors were also controlled by those privileged few related with these SEEs. There was also curtailment in the large-scale free private production. Thus, the Myanmarese economy remained primarily an inefficient command economy with the existence of large-scale black marketeering. The economy instead of reforming towards progress remained purely a hostage under a repressive political system. Besides, whatever little benefit it had earned benefited only the top military rulers, their followers and a few privileged groups close to them, while the general population remained discarded under abject poverty. The returns of the economy was not utilised for further progress of the country. As a result maximum sections of the population were deprived of the fruit.

By the second half of the 90s the economy goes on deteriorating further as repercussion of the inefficient management of the economic reforms. The amount of total external debt was as high as US $ 5,074 million in 1997[78], though it was slightly less from the previous years. And situation became worse with the imposition of US trade sanction against Myanmar in May 1997 because of deteriorating human rights record of the country and the European Union following suit. This resulted in a rapid decline in the continuing foreign investment. Several large investment companies like Pepsi, Madison Avenue, Levi etc. were forced to leave the country because of the consumer boycott of their companies in their home countries started since 1996. Besides, the economic crises that swept Asia also decreased the investing capacity of many Asian giants like Singapore, Japan, Korea etc. As a result, the total amount of Foreign Direct Investment (FDI) declined. For example, FDI approval declined from US $ 2,800 million in 1996/97 to US $ 1,000million in 1997/98[79]. Added to the problems world financial institution like World Bank was not ready to give loan because of the regime's insolvency. Ultimately, the real GDP growth declined to 4.6 per cent in 1997/98[80] and the economy took a down swing trend. The regime once more returned to its real self with the imposition of various restrictions on the economy. The reform measures were curtailed. What ultimately arises is the earlier form of state capitalism based on hidden agenda of command economy. Here it will be worthwhile to mention that the setback of economic reforms discussed above coupled with the lack of transparent and balanced legal and bureaucratic system and inability to maintain political stability brought about clearly the ineffective nature of the liberalising process. It seems that the military rulers had forgotten the fact that a change from a command economy to a market economy requires, besides institutional and structural, a change in outlook and attitude on the part of policy makers[81]. And this was lacking in the case of Myanmar. Thus a change in the leadership or so to say a political change is of utmost necessity.

Now ultimately, it is in the light of this brief economic dimension that efforts will be made to assess the dynamic nature of Myanmarese politics. The study of future political developments and changes should be done keeping in view of this economic scenario. Here what is also to be remembered is the fact that the impact of declining condition of the economy felt among the ordinary masses helped in hastening the movement for democracy forward. It make the people realised that their pitiable economic conditions will improve only under a democratic government and awaken in them the desire for democracy in their country. This provided a strong moral boost to democratic forces. However, it does not entirely mean that the economy will automatically improve immediately once a democratic government is set up, but then there will be enough room for dialogue and discussion on any complex economic issues, unlike that under the present regime. Finally from all these it is very much clear that the require standard of economic and social development for bringing the political system towards a liberal democracy was lacking. As such, in case of Myanmar, it is the political reform in the form of democratisation which will precede economic development and growth. Once democracy is restored then the required structural changes in the economy could be taken up without fear of repercussion. However, one needs always to remember the fact that the economy and politics are inter-related. And the fact remains as said by Aung San Suu Kyi that struggle for democracy in Myanmar is a struggle for every day life[82].

5.8. Aung San Suu Kyi as the Guiding Force

Another equally important area in our discussion is the role of Aung San Suu Kyi. Daw Aung San came to the Myanmarese political scene in one of the most critical juncture of the country's history. She entered Myanmarese politics in 1988 when the mass uprising for democracy was directionless and leaderless. She acted as a sort of rudder and provided direction to the movement for democracy that followed. It was spur of the moment decision and she could not resist the Myanmarese craving for freedom and democracy - two cardinal principles she was wedded to[83]. According to some experts she has reappeared as a sort of avenging nemesis to haunt Ne Win with the memory of Aung San[84]. And indeed, being a new entrant to the country's politics, though she knew the actual picture, proved an advantage for her. The military regime could not exactly predict what she actually was up to. But reality remain that the movement for democracy was gradually concretised and polarised mainly because of her presence. Besides, the world remembers the '1988 Uprising' and continues to exert pressure on the current regime mainly because it had a symbol personified in Suu Kyi[85]. Today, the general masses as well as the whole democratic forces placed great hopes on her. The ethnic insurgents also considered her as the only bridge for them to come to the country's mainstream and lead a peaceful and harmonious life.

Despite, a tainted picture painted about her by the current regime, the general masses, with exception of some pro military ones, still believe that Aung San Suu Kyi is the only focal point of the Myanmarese movement. Though it does not mean that there is lack of leadership in the movement yet the aura she carried with her cannot be compared with by anyone else. Being the daughter of Aung San she could show her extra ordinary charisma distinct from others. Besides, her long exposure to different free societies also equipped her with necessary knowledge to challenge the authoritarian regime, which is phobic to any form of meaningful change towards a more free society. Thus, many considered her presence in the movement unavoidable as well as essential. According to the general Myanmarese she remains the single most important catalyst for political change[86]. It is because of her presence as a symbol of political change that keep the hope of thousands of democracy activists morally alive, despite many ups and downs. In spite of repeated attempts by the military regime to defame and insult her, she retains vast popularity and respect[87].

The lady is considered as vanguard of the country's democracy movement not only because of the fact that she is the daughter of Gen. Aung San, but also that she possesses certain qualities entirely distinct from other political leaders. Qualities like respectability, wisdom, personal appeal, self sacrifice, gentleness, virtue and grace are all intrinsic in herself. However, the most important trait of her personality was her sincerity and absence of fear of any form in her person, something which she inherited from her parents as well as from her upbringing and growing up in a free environment in the formative stage of her life. However, sometimes her faith in Buddhist values creates complicacy for the movement, but, at time, her extreme practicality and rationality ultimately prevailed over it.

Despite a deep conviction to the cause of restoring democracy in the country, unlike other leaders, she is not orthodox in her thinking and approach. Rather, she is dynamic as well as pragmatic in her approach with a deep and unshakable conviction to the cause. As a pragmatist, she responded to changing conditions, both in her role and speech. She was born with revolution in blood. And it was mainly because of this fact that her relevance to the Myanmarese democracy movement is on the rise.

One of the worthwhile contributions Aung San Suu Kyi made to the Myanmarese movement is her effort to remove the elements of fear inherent among the normal masses; a common trait as a result of long period of subjugation under the authoritarian system. This is very important from Myanmarese point of view. Over and above this, while trying to awaken the consciousness of the people towards restoration of democracy, Suu Kyi also tried to awaken their dormant spiritual values and moral inertia. According to her, this is essential to make the people genuinely interested in understanding and participating in the movement, physically and morally. Further, she asserted that in order to achieve the goal of democracy people need to understand that they are not powerless. She believes in people's power which is the bedrock of the democracy.

For Aung San Suu Kyi democracy means harmony in most aspects of the society. She visualised a democratic Myanmar in terms of less suffering for the people[88]. She did not think of it in terms of an abstract institution rather than in terms of what it can do to contribute towards the happiness and well being of the people[89]. Aung San Suu Kyi accepts that the military or *tatmadaw* will play a key role in Myanmar's future democracy, but that must be within a democratic constitution and framework.

Now in the light of the above facts, despite some shortcomings on her part, Aung San Suu Kyi remains the most important guiding force for the ongoing democracy movement. Her inherent personality and her conviction to the cause make her the undisputed choice. It was she who moulded the pro-democracy forces to become the real threat to the military leadership[90]. As such, her permanent residency in the country created fear and demoralising attitude on the part of the junta. This, in turn, raises the spirit of those involved in the movement. And among the Buddhist Myanmarese, her appeal and inner peace found a ready echo and relevance[91]. Because of all these Aung San Suu Kyi, the charismatic daughter of General Aung San, is gradually emerging as the icon of a possible democratic renaissance in Myanmar.

5.9. Changing Facet of the Movement for Democracy: The Year 1997

Side by side with all these happening, the year 1997 came to add a new dimension to the already complex political scenario of Myanmar. This, in turn, also resulted in an increase in the existing complexity of the ongoing democracy movement. It became really difficult at that juncture to predict the exact direction to which it was moving. The arrival of a new year did not bring any change in the existing stalemate between the two opposite forces i.e., the military regime and those who were opposing it. The mass student unrest, which started in the last part of 1996, continued to 1997 with a renewed vigour. They renewed the movement demanding various freedoms and rights. Street processions and slogan shouting were carried out. Some of them even went to the extent of staging a sit-in-protest near the residence of Aung Suu Kyi, which was forcibly removed by the regime. The regime, on its part, retaliated with repressions.

The student demonstrations are followed by yet another demonstration by farmers in the month of January itself. Farmers mainly from the Shwebo region, protested against the government's efforts to buy rice in large quantity below the existing market price at a time when there was a rise in the price of rice due to the scarcity in production created by the flood of the Irrawaddy river[92]. But this was not the end. Protest against the regime took another form in the month of March. This time the protest was staged by the monks. The monks were quiet for some time in the surface due to excessive curbing and subjugation of the whole *sangha*'s movement in the preceding years. The immediate factor could be traced to the Buddhist-Muslim clash, and the looting of an important monastic relic probably the work of SLORC. However, the real reason lies in the fact that a sort of subdued discontentment were brewing within *sangha* family against the excessive curbing of their freedom by the regime.

Ultimately, successive protests by the students, the peasants, and the monks brought a new change to the existing political scenario of the country which, in turn had an impact on the continuing democracy movement[93]. And the chance of coming together of these three groups was what the regime feared most. These groups together could create danger for the regime, not to mention of already existing democratic forces. As a result, repression and atrocities with all its brutality was committed against these groups. Chances of changes in the top brass which had ordered all these actions was bleak. Even though news started floating in April that Gen. Than Shwe was retiring nothing exactly had happened[94]. There was no relinquishing of leadership post or relaxation of control on the part of the existing junta leadership. Crackdown against Aung San Suu Kyi's NLD and her supporters, and also against other democratic forces within the country was negligibly reduced. And this was the new situation that the movement for democracy under the leadership of Aung San Suu Kyi found itself in the beginning of 1997 with the need for change in the approach.

During this period also, as usual, the activities of the movement continued more openly and freely with those groups in the border areas. Due to close scrutiny and tight restrictions the NLD and Aung San Suu Kyi could not do much remarkable activity inside the country except providing moral boost and advice. Thus most of the concrete activities of the democracy movement were carried out by the democratic forces in the border and outside the country. And, in fact, the first important step or activity of the democracy movement in 1997 was holding of a 'Seminar of Ethnic Nationalities' by the groups in the border in the beginning of the year. This seminar of different ethnic nationalities was held from 7 to 14 January 1997 at Mae Raw Hta in the base area of K.N.U. It was very important for the movement as well as for the future unity of the country. The SLORC could not do anything to dissuade ethnic groups from attending the seminar. It was attended by 111 delegates and observers from nearly "15 ethnic nationality organisations"[95], both ceasefire as well as non-ceasefire ones. The presence of these groups clearly brought out the fact that despite the existence of agreements a federal democratic set-up in the country was the utmost priority of these groups.

In the said seminar the delegates resolved: (i) to carry out democratic changes in accordance with the will of the people of Myanmar, (ii) to establish a genuine federal union based on the equality and self determination of nationalities, (iii) to demand for the dissolution of the SLORC's sham national convention and the start of a tripartite dialogue consisting of the SLORC, Suu Kyi and pro-democracy forces, and the ethnic nationalities for solving the political problems by political means. The seminar itself was significant event for the country's continuing democracy movement. It was an important step for the ethnic groups to come together in a country which is cover by civil war for more than 50 years.

At the same time the ceasefire policy was not working as anticipated in the direction envisioned by the military rulers. By 1997 it was very much clear that though the ceasefire had slightly weakened the movement for democracy yet the policy itself was in a shambles due to insincerity on the part of the regime. Many groups like KNPP, KIO and NMSP were fed up with the ceasefire. Even though they did not immediately return to their earlier activities they were no longer ready to follow the dictates of the military rulers and their ceasefire policy.

Not only these developments but within the opposition democratic forces in the border areas, groups like NCUB started mounting pressure on the junta by urging United

States' sanctions against the regime. The National Council of Union of Burma, an umbrella organization as well as assumed *de facto* legislature for Myanmarese dissident in the border and outside the country, said that the continuing crackdowns against the opposition led by Aung San Suu Kyi and the military offensive against the Karen rebels constituted good reasons for imposing sanctions. And, indeed, President Clinton approved a ban on new US economic investment in Myanmar on 22 April because of the regime's stepped up repression on the pro-democracy groups.

However, all was not well for the movement inside the country; though it had already started mounting pressure on the junta even to the extent of confrontations. Restrictions placed on the movement of Aung San Suu Kyi increased. Although diplomats and supporters were occasionally allowed to see her, yet the restrictions on her movements and contacts were virtually synonymous with house arrest. This was mainly because the junta's equation that Aung San Su Kyi would have no longer any popularity after her long period under house arrest had proved wrong. And when the junta realised its error it once more returned to its original nature of carrying our excessive repression.

Crackdown on the oppositions, particularly on NLD and its allies, increased once more as the month of May came nearer. This is in retaliation to NLD's renewed preparation for a party congress on 27 May to commemorate the 7th Anniversary of its election victory in 1990. The said Congress was to be held at the house of Suu Kyi. The junta took it as a challenge to them. As a result arrest of several NLD supporters and MPs had started in various part of the country even before the scheduled date of commemoration. It is believed that at least 316 NLD activists were reportedly detained or picked up[96]. Thus, the said Congress was restricted though some few delegates were allowed to assemble on the fixed date at Suu's residence.

And when the said congress was not allowed to assemble, the opposition, on its part, increased putting pressure on the regime. The NLD pressurised the regime to convene a parliament at the earliest to honour the result of the 1990 election. The statement which was issued by the NLD Executive Committee further stated that the problem of the country could only be solved through dialogue and not through repression of people's voice[97]. One point which need to be remembered here is the fact that though the Congress could not be held yet the NLD was successful in achieving two important objectives: international attention and increasing psychological pressure on the SLORC. In fact, the very intention of NLD for attempting to hold the Congress was not to commemorate in real sense but to draw international attention to the continuing illegal nature of the regime in holding to the power and at the same time to increase psychological pressure on the rulers. NLD had achieved this.

In July, a jolt for the movement was caused when ASEAN decided to admit Myanmar. The SLORC, on its part slightly softened its stand against the oppositions in order to show its Southeast Asian partners that it was in favour of peaceful mending of the country's politics. And as a part of this charade NLD was allowed to hold the first party congress in seven years at the home of Aung San Suu Kyi on 27 September to commemorate the founding of NLD. In allowing the meeting the govt. spokesman Lt. Col. Hla Min even acknowledged, "there is no question that she is a political force"[98]. Till the beginning of October she was allowed to visit party offices and meet supporters. She was even allowed to hold meeting in Thaketa Township on October 22. But this relaxation on the part of the regime did not last long. Clash ensued once again between the two opposing forces in the domestic front in the last part of October. NLD workers confronted with the authority when Suu Kyi was not allowed to meet the workers of her party of the Mayangon office of NLD during her visit to Northern Yangon on 28 October[99]. This dashed the very hope of agreement between the regime and the democratic forces with assumption that the former was becoming more lenient in its attitude. Instead, the junta accused the NLD of being rigid and confrontational. Not only this, but the regime, through its government sponsored political organisation, the

Union Solidarity Development Association (USDA), tried to immobilise and disintegrate the movement for democracy spearheaded by NLD. Through this organisation the regime tried to create a dividing line between the people and the democratic forces; a challenge for the NLD that could not be taken lightly. And it was in the midst of all these political developments of the country that the SLORC changed its name to the State Peace and Development Council (SPDC).

The said State Peace and Development Council was formed on 15 November 1997. However, the change was very insignificant. Though there were some changes in the 19-member council with the inclusion of regional commanders in place of top brasses, yet the "four top generals"[100] still remained as usual, in the helm of power. The change was cosmetic. It was, in fact, a political charade of the regime to mesmerise the international community and at the same time to impress its ASEAN partners. Many opposition groups considered it a cosmetic change with the same old wind in a new bottle. According to them the change is only facial not intrinsic and has got nothing to contribute towards restoration of democracy in the country. The SPDC, like its predecessor, could contribute nothing towards bringing any change and reformation in the political and economic environment of the country, which could create atmosphere for further progress of the country. The positive atmosphere towards change was completely lacking. Instead, factionalism has emerged within the set-up due to the relegating of many prominent generals simply to various non-descript advisory posts. This gave an indirect boost for the democracy movement. It is the main desire on the part of the democratic groups that a sort of strong contradictory force emerges within the military set-up thereby making it weaker. But the factionalism and dissent, it seems, was not strong enough to break up the military set up from within; as desired by the democratic groups of the country. The entry into ASEAN also reduced its pariah status.

And under the changing circumstances and new developments in the country's political atmosphere it became necessary on the part of the democratic force to completely re-evaluate its existing strategy once more, keeping in mind the new demands of time. With more emphasis on the authoritarian based disciplined democracy on the part of the rulers quick political changes in near future seems bleak unless certain new strategies are streamlined in unified spirit.

NOTES

1. David I. Steinberg, "Myanmar in 1991: The Miasma in Burma", *Asian Survey* (Berkeley), vol.32, no.2, February 1992, p. 146.
2. It was a sort of supreme council for the democratic forces consisting of members from both the DAB and the NCGUB. Composed of six Burmans and five minority representatives.
3. Amnesty International, *Union of Myanmar ; Arrests and Trials of political Prisoners, January-July 1991* (London: Amnesty International Publications, December, 1991), p. 12.
4. Ibid, p. 14.
5. Ibid.
6. Ibid, p. 19.
7. Jan Donkers and Minka Nijhuis(eds), *Burma behind the Mask* (Amsterdam : Burma Centrum Nederland, 1996),p.72.
8. Election Commission Invalidated the original 9 person Central Executive Committee on 23 April, 1991, see n. 3, p. 25.
9. Josef Silverstein, "The Civil War, the Minorities and Burma's New Politics", in Peter Carey (ed.), *Burma: The Challenge of Change in a Divided Society* (London: Macmillan Press Ltd., 1997), p. 144.
10. Bertil Lintner, *Burma in Revolt : Opium and Insurgency since 1948* (Bangkok : White Lotus Co. Ltd., 1994) p. 320.
11. Members of Parliamentary Union (MPU), which is a collection of elected MPs in the border areas, joined it later in 1996.
12. *The Irrawaddy* (Chiangmai), vol.6,no.3, 31 May 1998, p.15.
13. David I . Steinberg, " Myanmar in 1992 : Plus Ca Change.......?", *Asian Survey*, vol.33, no.2, February 1993, p. 176.
14. Amnesty International, *Myanmar , No Law at all: Human*

Rights Violations Under Military Rule (London : Amnesty International Publications, October 1992), p.1.

15. Aung San Suu Kyi and Alan Clements, *The Voice of Hope* (Harmondsworth : Penguin, 1997), p.68.
16. Josef Silverstein, " Change in Burma", *Current History* (Philadelphia), December 1995, p.441.
17. Janelle M. Diller, "Constitutional Reform in a Repressive State: The Case of Burma", *Asian Survey*, vol.33, no. 4, April 1993, p.400.
18. U.S. , *State Department Release*, March 1995.
19. n.17.
20. n.10, p. 384.
21. n.9.
22. Marc Weller (ed.), *Democracy and Politics in Burma* (Manerplaw : NCGUB, 1993),p.261.
23. Janelle M. Diller, "The National Convention : An Impediment to the Restoration of Democracy", in Peter Carey (ed.), *Burma : The Challenge of Change in a Divided Society* (London : Macmillan, 1997),p.40.
24. n.10, p
25. The 16 groups were UWSA, MNDAA, National Democratic Alliance Army-Eastern Shan State, NDA, SSA, KDA, PNA, PSLA, Kayan Home Guards, KIA, KNPLF, KNLP, SSNPLO, KNPP, NMSP and MTA.
26. "Ceasefire Talks: Changing the Subject", *Burma Issues* (Bangkok), vol.7,no. 7, July 1997,p.6.
27. Ibid.
28. *Green Wind* (Chiangmai), no.2, September 1995,p.5.
29. n.15, p.192.
30. Ibid.
31. John Bray , *Burma : the Politics of Constructive Engagement* (London : Royal Institute of International Affairs, 1995), p.12.
32. Ibid, p.13.
33. Mary P. Callahan, " Burma in 1995 : Looking Beyond the Release of Aung San Suu Kyi", *Asian Survey*, vol.36,no.2, February 1996, p. 160.
34. n.7, p.81.
35. Amnesty International, *Myanmar: Renewed Repression*

(London: Amnesty International Publications, July 1996), p.1.

36. Ibid.
37. n.7, p.82.
38. Burma Lawyers' *Council, Legal Issues on Burma Journal* (Bangkok, October 1997),p.27.
39. Ibid, p.28.
40. Amnesty International, *Myanmar: Intimidation and Imprisonment, September – December 1996* (London : Amnesty International Publications, February 1997),p.6.
41. Ibid.
42. "A New Paradigm for Activism", *Burma Issues* (Bangkok), vol . 7, NO. 12, December 1997,p.5.
43. Abu Taher Salahaddin Ahmed, "Myanmar: Road to Democracy nor East Asian Model?" *BIISS Journal* (Dhaka), vol.17, no.1, 1996,pp. 124-25.
44. *The Burma Review* (New York), no. 43, January- March 1995, p.10.
45. P.S. Suryanarayana, "A' trade of' for Myanmar", *The Hindu* (New Delhi), 13 December 1998.
46. Paul Cook and Martin Minogue, 'Economic Reform and Political Conditionality in Myanmar', in Peter Carey (ed.), *Burma: The Challenge of Change in a Divided Society* (London : Macmillan , 1997), p. 199.
47. Ibid.
48. n.46, p. 185.
49. James F. Guyot and John Badgley, "Myanmar in 1989: Tatmadaw V", *Asian Survey*, 30(2), February 1990, p.191.
50. n.46, p.203.
51. Ibid, p.202.
52. Border trade agreement between India and Myanmar was signed on 21 January 1994 represented by Commerce Secretary of India, Tijendra Khanna, and Deputy Minister of Foreign Affairs of Myanmar, U Nyunt Swe.
53. n.49, p.192.
54. Ibid.
55. n.13, p.181.
56. n.46, p.203

57. Ibid, 204.
58. n.1, p.149.
59. Ibid. also see David I. Steinberg, " Priorities for Burma's Development : The Role of International Aid", in Peter Carey (ed.), *Burma : The Challenge of Change in a Divided Society* (London : Macmillan , 1997),p.165.
60. Mya Maung, "Burma's Economic Performance under Military Rule: An assessment' *Asian Survey*, 37(6) June 1997, p. 513.
61. The Burma Project, *Burma: Country in Crisis*, (New York: Burma Project, 1998) p. 17.
62. Mya Maung, 'Burma Road to the Past', *Asian Survey*, vol.39, no.2, March/April 1999, p.280.
63. Allen L. Clark, "Myanmar's Present Development and Future Options', *Asian Survey*, vol.39, no.5, September/ October. 1999, p.775.
64. See n.61, p.17. Also see Chi Shad Liang, " Burma's Relations with the People's Republic of China: From Delicate Friendship to Genuine Co-operation", in Peter Carey (ed.), *Burma: The Challenge of Change in a Divided Society* (London: Macmillan, 1997), p.89.
65. Mary P. Callahan, "Junta Dreams or Nightmares? Observation of Burma's Military since 1989", *Bulletin of Concerned Asian Scholars* (Oakland), 33(3), 1999, p.52.
66. David I. Steinberg, " Priorities for Burma's Development: The Role of International Aid " , in Peter Carey (ed.), *Burma: The Challenge of Change in a Divided Society* (London : Macmillan , 1997), p.171.
67. David I. Steinberg, 'Democracy, Power and the Economy in Myanmar: Donor Dilemmas', *Asian Survey*, vol.31, no.8, August 1991,pp.738.
68. n.66, p.169.
69. Bertil Lintner's article written in *Far Eastern Economic Review* (Hong Kong) which was reprinted in *The Irrawaddy*, vol. 5, no.45, August 1997.
70. James Guyot ' Burma in 1997: From Expire to ASEAN' *Asian Survey*, vol.38, no.2, February 1998, p 192.
71. n.63, p.775.
72. In August 1997 the price of rice rose to Kyat 3120 for a bag of 50 kg.

73. *The Irrawaddy*, vol. 6, no.1, February 1998.
74. n.63, p.775.
75. Martin Stuart Fox, 'Whither Burma', *World Review* (Queensland), vol.30, no. 4, December 1991, p.42.
76. n.31,p.29.
77. Country Commercial Guide, 'Burma', *Burma Debate*, July/ August 1996,p.16.
78. *The Far East and Australasia 2000* (London : Europa Publications, 1999), p. 768.
79. Ibid.
80. Ibid, p. 761.
81. Mya Than, "Economic Transformation in Mainland Southeast Asia : The case of Myanmar" in John J. Brandon (ed.), *Burma / Myanmar, Towards the Twenty First Century: Dynamic of Continuity and Change* (Bangkok : Thai Studies Section, Chulalongkorn University, 1997), p. 112.
82. Aung San Suu Kyi and Alan Clements, *Voice of Hope* (Harmondsworth: Penguin, 1997), p. 81.
83. V. Jayanath, 'The struggle for democracy', *The Hindu*, 24 March 1996.
84. Martin Smith, *Burma: Insurgency and Politics of Ethnicity* (London: Zed Books, 1991), p. 144.
85. Amitav Ghosh , *Dancing in Cambodia, At Large in Burma* (Delhi: Ravi Dayal Publisher, 1998), p.83.
86. Bruce Mathews, "The Present Fortune of Tradition bound Authoritarianism in Myanmar", *Pacific Affairs* (Vancouver), 71(1), Spring 1998, p.17.
87. Ibid.
88. n. 82,p.134.
89. Ibid.
90. n.83.
91. Ibid
92. n.86,p.8. Also see *The Irrawaddy*, vol.5, no.8, 15 January, 1997.
93. Ibid.
94. *Asian Age*, 20 April , 1997
95. The organisations were KNPP, PPLO, WNO, UWSP, PSLF, KIO, AASYL, LDF, NMSP, ALP, KNLP, CNF, SDU and KNU.

96. *The Hindu*, 28 May 1997.
97. *Times of India* (Delhi), 29 May 1997
98. Sandra Burton , "Commotion in the Compound" *Time* (New York), 10 November 1997,p.35.
99. *The Telegraph,* 29 October 1997.
100. The four top generals were Sr. Gen. Than Shwe, Gen Tin Oo, Gen Maung Aye and Lt. Gen. Khin Nyunt. Gen. Tin Oo died recently(19 February 2001) in a helicopter crash.

6

Movement for Democracy in Myanmar: International Reaction–I

The uprising of 1988 which took the form of the present movement for democracy was the first of its kind in the history of Myanmar to receive massive attention of the international community as an issue of great importance. It symbolised the struggle for humanity and human values which civilised societies could not ignore lightly. The issue transcends the political boundary of the country.

6.1. Immediate Reactions

Initially when the uprising was started in the early part of 1988 it was simply taken by foreign countries as the internal affairs of the country. However, the indiscriminate killing that followed from August to September compelled to change their earlier stance. The world was dumbstruck by the degree of brutality committed by the military rulers of Myanmar. The massacre which started approximately at around 11.45 P.M. of 8 August 1988 (8.8.88) continued non-stop for four days[1]. This was further followed in succeeding months. The repression became more brutal, harsher and systematic with the military take-over on 18 September. Participants-students, monks, doctors, nurses, lawyers etc., were mowed down in the street. Those protestors who believed that they would not be shot at if they remained before foreign embassies while protesting were also not spared. Many peaceful demonstrators were shot down in front of the United States embassy before the very eyes of the then Ambassador, Burton Levin. Levin said, "I saw soldiers hunting down students on the streets, and people huddled behind trees being picked up by snipers in building across the road" [2]. He further asserted that whatever he had witnessed from the embassy was little short of murder[3]. Media, both domestic as well as international, were banned. There was even an unofficial order that anyone with a camera in the place of carnage should be shot because they did not want the brutalities reached the international community uncensored.

Economic sanctions, boycotts of trade, condemnations came from many countries and international bodies as a reaction. International pressure in the form of boycott was imposed on the country thus making it, for the first time after independence, a pariah in the international arena. At the outset, except for a few, most of the Asian as well as European countries condemned Myanmar for the massacres of the peaceful demonstrators which were so raw and brutal, destroying the last vestige of humanity that no civilised nation could remain quiet.

United States was the first country to officially condemn the carnage and denounce the act which was followed by economic sanctions. The Senate unanimously approved a resolution condemning the slaughter introduced by Senator Daniel Moynihan on 10 August 1988[4]. This was followed by termination of economic assistance and aid programmes soon after the coup of September. It cancelled its annual assistance of about US $12 million which consisted of US $ 7 million in development assistance and US$5 million for anti-narcotics programme in Myanmar [5]. United States thus became the first country to officially condemn the junta both in words and deeds. However, certain rooms for correction and restoration of assistance were given. In a statement before the Sub-Committee on Asian and Pacific Affairs of the House Foreign Affairs Committee on 2 March 1989, David F. Lamberston, Deputy Assistant Secretary for East Asian and Pacific Affairs stated, "We looked forward to resuming assistance when condition in Myanmar permitted us to do so. We are looking for meaningful political and economic reform in Myanmar before resuming assistance"[6]. US Congressman Stephen Solarz , who visited Myanmar in September 1988 also declared his support for those who were fighting against the junta . Thus, with US, the flow of international sanction ensued. Condemnation and sanction from many countries like West Germany, Australia, Japan, India, U.K., Sweden, Norway and most European Union members followed.

Japan, the largest donor and well-wisher of Myanmar since independence but a close ally of the United States, followed suit of the former. Soon after the outbreak of the carnage and imposition of martial law in August 1988, it suspended all its aid to the country though no formal decision was taken in this direction. This was a serious setback for the country. For, during the period preceding the September coup, Tokyo provided official assistance ranging from 40 to 50 billion yen (US $ 300 to 375 million) annually [7]. Nineteen big aid-projects came to a halt. However, Japan on its part was also slightly cautious in its dealing with the country. On 27 September, the Japanese Ambassador to Myanmar, Hiroshi Otaka, met Ohn Gyaw, a top Foreign Ministry official, to express Japanese Government's desire to resume its aid to the country once normalcy was restored and that democratic political settlement reflecting the general consensus of the people was arrived at[8]. This had no impact on the junta. With no other alternative at hand, Japan formally suspended all aid to the country on 13 January 1989[9]. But paradoxically, in February itself, Tokyo resumed disbursements of funds under aid programme which had already been agreed upon before the 'August 88 Uprising' – although it continued to ban new grants. There was no immediate answer to these sudden changes. Scholars believed that Japan did not want to end the economic relationship suddenly in view of the huge debt of Myanmar to be paid to Japan. The country had accumulated a huge foreign debt of $ 5.3 billion by 1983, nearly half of which was owed to Japan. [10]. And, Japanese law forbids official debt to be written off. Thus, except for some $ 23 million provided for debt relief, no aid was forthcoming.

Sanctions also came from the side of West Germany which is one of the major donor countries. It followed suit of United States and other Western countries by suspending all its assistance to Myanmar on 31 August 1988. This was a major blow to the military rulers as West Germany, at that time, was the second largest donor after Japan. To show off its disapproval to the wanton killing and violation of human rights continuing in the country it cut off its Deutch Mark 65 million (US $ 35.14 million) annual assistance[11].

Condemnations and economic sanctions followed from many more countries. Myanmar's traditionally good relations with many countries of the world as a result of its neutralist policy was greatly affected because of the massacre. Protests and condemnations combined with all sort of sanctions followed. Australia, Sweden, Norway and most of the European Union members, officially as well as unofficially, stopped all bilateral assistance including an embargo on arms trade also. However, these governments were reluctant to impose mandated arms embargo against Myanmar in UN because of apprehension of a China veto. Steps were taken up to stop even the multilateral aid agencies like United Nations Development Programme from giving fund to Myanmar till normalisation was restored in the country [12]. Many of these countries also tried to use international forum like the United Nations to express their protest note. Then British Foreign Secretary, Sir Geoffrey Howe, denounced the mass killing in Myanmar in a speech before the UN General Assembly on 28 September 1988[13]. Criticism of the junta government in Myanmar became a routine one in most of the international forums like UN, NAM or European Union.

India, an important neighbour and a big democracy, strongly condemned the carnage and gross violation of democratic norms and human values. The reaction of India was spontaneous. The young and energetic Rajiv Gandhi, the then Prime Minister of India, was in favour of a civil democratic set up in the country. Despite the need for developing relations with Myanmar because of security and economic considerations he was outright in condemning the suppression. Besides, as a member of the Nehru – Gandhi family, he got a soft corner for those leaders involved in the democracy movement, personally[14]. In fact, India, on 10 September 1988, became the first country to express support to the genuine desire of the Myanmarese people for restoration of democracy [15]. Not only this, but it was stated by many Myanmarese dissidents in India that they were offered asylum much before they arrived in the country and were given permission to stay.

Here, what is most ambiguous was the stand of ASEAN in particular and its members in general. Paradoxically most of the ASEAN members were not very outright on the issue. Even the most important immediate neighbour, Thailand was more concerned in improving tie with Myanmar. China, which is an influencing factor and regional power, remained indifferent to the whole issue. Except for some mild expression most of the ASEAN countries were not a party to the international condemnation nor in favour of any economic and trade sanctions against the Myanmar government. Only country which was vocal on the issue was Philippines; may be because of US influence. To most of these countries, what was happening in that country was treated as its internal affairs and not something which affect the humanity as Western countries thought.

Apart from these indifferent attitudes on the part of the ASEAN members in general what was most surprising were the attitudes of two of its major neighbours, China and Thailand. Both countries failed to join the international community in condemning and ostracising the Myanmar Junta for the violation it carried out, though Thailand was affected by the happenings. Besides, it was well known fact that these two countries were supporting insurgents waging war against Yangon. At a time when countries had even recalled diplomats from the country, these two countries followed a trend of exchange visits of high level delegations; something which was uncalled for.

But despite these degrees of indifferences one general attitude remained negative. There were also reactions from the international financial bodies and international organisations. Financial bodies like World Bank, International Monetary Fund (IMF) and Asian Development Bank (ADB) continued to disburse funds for previously existing assistance projects but negotiations on new projects were completely stopped. David Steinberg, a scholar of Myanmarese affairs, rightly said, 'no new multilateral assistance from the World Bank or the ADB has been forthcoming. Some $400-500 million in annual assistance has thus been forgone by the SLORC which also has discouraged the IMF from reviewing its economy'[16]. Almost all bilateral aid donors suspended development assistance and withdrew support for Myanmerese loans in this financial institutions[17]. For the time being, Myanmar was completely isolated by the international community.

In all these developments United States played a very important role. Though the US government have got very little direct leverage over Myanmar yet it has got its influence over the allies and other members of the international funding agencies in substantial way[18]. Ultimately, to a considerable extent it played important role in curtailing activities of UN agencies, the EEC and even bilateral programmes with Japan, Taiwan and Canada[19]. Thus, because of all these spontaneous international reaction against it the SLORC became isolated from the Western democratic countries and also Japan and India in particular.

6.2. International Support: The Initial Stage (1988-1992)

When we mention about international support we need to make an approach towards the subject from different possible angles. Since the Myanmarese democracy movement has completed more than 10 years we could observe a change in the mechanism and working of the international support system from what it was in the beginning to what it is at present. So when we discuss the international support extended to the struggle in various forms we need to study the very initial stage and the later stage leading to the present, separately.

After the 'August 88 Uprising' of the Myanmarese masses, and the subsequent military coup of September, dissidents belonging to different walks of life started moving towards the border areas en mass. With the military takeover it became very difficult for them to stay inside the country without risking their lives; let alone forget about demonstrating or continuing the struggle against the junta government. And the sole hope of these parties lay entirely on international support for their movement , particularly from the Western countries. This line of thinking was very much obvious because of the large scale condemnation of government excesses by the Western countries giving the implication that they were against the junta while supporting the genuine democratic aspiration of the Myanmarese people. Thus, in the very initial stage, immediately after the carnage, the widespread condemnation from the international community itself acted as a strong moral support for the Myanmarese democracy crusaders, giving the hope of forthcoming international support for the cause in the near future. Now the question is whether this passive support in the form of condemnation of the junta was helpful enough for the movement. How much actual international support, besides the above mentioned form, came in the very initial stage? These are the areas we need to delve into.

The neighbouring countries particularly India and Thailand felt the impact of what was happening under the junta in Myanmar first. And, willingly or unwillingly, these two countries were first among those to extend help to the dissidents and student activists. Among Asian countries particularly among its neighbours it was India alone which supported the movement wholeheartedly and openly. Not only expressing its condemnation and concern for the increasing repression of the Myanmarese people by the ruling junta it also extended full support to the fleeing students by opening three camps – two in Champai and Saiha in Mizoram State and one in Leikhun in Manipur State(India) – for their stay. Though the arrangement was not very accommodating yet it was enough for their security and subsistence. On 25 October 1988, the then External Affairs Minister of India, P.V.Narasimha Rao, clearly stated that no genuine Myanmarese refugee seeking shelter in India would be turned back, thus adopting a clear cut refugee policy [20]. Statements made by Indian leaders made clear that India showed sympathy for the aspirants of democracy and anguish at the suffering inflicted on the common people and the death of a large number of innocent people. Government of India expressed, "in keeping with India's tradition of not turning away people who come to India's border to seek shelter, Burmese citizens crossing into India, as a result of the unrest, were allowed to stay in camps in Mizoram and Arunachal Pradesh"[21]. (Sources from various quarters, however, indicate that it is wrong to say Arunachal Pradesh, but it should be the state of Manipur. There was not a single camp in Arunachal Pradesh at the time mentioned).

As a result of the Indian help extended to the dissidents there were allegations from the junta that India, through its Embassy in Yangon, was involved in instigating and harbouring those involved in the uprising of 1988. Though the charge could not be substantiated with hard facts, it cannot either be denied that the Embassy was involved in arranging passage to India and political asylum for many student dissidents[22]. India also started a programme called "Voice of Burmese People" in September 1989, in the All India Radio's Myanmarese Service to express solidarity with democratic forces[23].

On the other hand, Thailand, another important neighbour of Myanmar, was the unwilling helper or passive supporter of the movement. Though it did not want to help the dissidents, being in the proximity of the country it could not escape the reality. During the whole period of Myanmarese democracy movement leading to the present, the stand of Thailand is always ambiguous. At the very outset of the movement in August 1988 it was somewhat charitable to the cause[24]. Myanmarese students and other dissidents were given asylum despite repeated demand for repatriation from the side of Myanmar government. However, this positive attitude on the part of the Thai government changed after the visit of its Chief of the Armed Forces, General Chavalit Yongchaiyudh, to Myanmar in December 1988. Though they allowed relief agencies to send humanitarian assistance to the Myanmarese students and refugees living in the border areas, yet they tried to stop them from staying permanently in the Thai side or to sneak in the interior part of the country[25]. Besides, many of them were also repatriated to Myanmar through a transition camp established at the Tak province.

Besides the above two countries, Japan and Philippines also expressed some sort of support for a new political transformation in the country though not supporting the democracy movement. Japan announced its desire for a transfer of power to the winners of the 1990 election on the part of the junta. Philippines also expressed its desire in the same. Thus, in the initial stage, except for few the rests of the countries in Asia, in general, and Southeast Asia, in particular, had got very little to do with supporting the movement directly or indirectly. They had got a very indifferent attitude about what was happening in Myanmar at the time. Even ASEAN, the apex regional group of Southeast Asia, had very little to say in support of the uprising. In such a situation there was not much to expect from these countries of the region in the form of material as well as moral support.

In that critical juncture even from among the Western countries and USA, except for some relief assistance for Myanmarese refugees, no actual material or diplomatic help purely for the democracy movement was forthcoming. There were condemnations of the carnage inside the country yet actual support of any form was lacking from these quarters. It was mainly after the formation of National Coalition Government of the Union of Burma (NCGUB) in December 1990 that a meaningful support, whether material or diplomatic started reaching as a result of its continuous intensive lobbying of major countries and international organisations. "The US Congress for the first time, voted in 1989 to provide US $ 500,000 as humanitarian aid to Burmese refugees" and another US $ 250,000 to support the movement opposed to the military junta[26].

Here what is to be understood is that the National Coalition Government of the Union of Burma (NCGUB), All Burma Students' Democratic Front(ABSDF) and the Federation Trade Unions of Burma (FTUB) played a very important role in garnering international support. ABSDF mainly deals with the problems of the youth and students under the junta. It represented the section of the younger generation of the movement. FTUB on the other hand tried to represent the cause of the labour and working class of the country. It tried to focus on the exploitation of human labour inside Myanmar. However ultimately it is the NCGUB that encompassed the whole area related with the democracy movement when it comes to the international arena. Though Aung San Suu Kyi and the NLD are the vanguards of the movement, NCGUB became a government in exile representing the whole cause to the world. It acted as platform for the whole Myanmarese democracy movement in lobbying and garnering international support. This is because NCGUB represents NLD and its constituent parties, the major democratic forces which emerged as a result of 1990 election. So, in the very initial stage of the uprising it was with the establishment of NCGUB that there was a change in the attitude of international community, particularly among Western countries.

At that juncture the most important effort by the democracy groups was to carry on lobbying for their cause. This was followed seriously by NCGUB. Since it has got no clear-cut formal recognition, lobbying became the best means by which they could put their issues before the international fora. As a consequence the movement started getting more positive results rather than being just a news piece. With it the movement as a whole started getting material as well as diplomatic and political support in one way or the other. Besides, NCGUB and its official, representing the democracy movement in the international arena, started getting more response from the world community, both countries and international organisations. In the beginning of 1991, Foreign Minister at that time, Mr Peter Limbin, was invited to attend the United Nations Commission on Human Rights's (UNCHR) meeting on Myanmar at Geneva as a guest of a recognised NGO[27]. Not only this, he was also permitted to speak about the real political scenario of the country despite protest from SLORC[28]. Later, he was invited by foreign ministers of various European states[29]. Prime Minister Sein Win, on his part, traveled to U.S. in October to lobby U.S. Congressmen for a UN sanction in Myanmar. All these efforts were further enhanced with the announcement in October of awarding the Nobel Peace Prize for 1991 to Aung San Suu Kyi. While declaring the award the Nobel Committee stated that she represents "one of the most extra ordinary examples of civil courage in Asia in recent decades"[30]. This award to Suu Kyi gave a strong moral boost to the movement, as it was a sort of *de facto* recognition of the world community. Now the initiatives taken up by NCGUB started yielding fruit. Between November and December 1991, the UN General Assembly and the Inter-Parliamentary Union, in separate occasions, demanded for the release of political prisoners under Myanmarese junta regimes[31]. Thus it was the establishment of NCGUB coupled with the awarding of Nobel Prize to Suu Kyi that attracted a wide international attention towards the Myanmarese democracy movement in the initial stage.

Besides the United States, many countries of the European Union and Scandinavian countries showed serious concern for the political situation in Myanmar and a genuine desire to help the movement for democracy. More attention was given in this direction though some difference in degree could be observed among individual countries. Among them, Norway was one of the first countries which gave strong support to the movement through material as well as diplomatic help. It also became the first country to extend some form of recognition to the NCGUB and that was a very strong moral support to the movement and also a precedent for other democratic countries. So NCGUB got the very much essential quasi-recognition from the Government of Norway[32]. Not only this it also provided the much-needed fund by giving 2 million Kroner (1992) to NCGUB and DAB for political, health and education projects through its Norwegian Burma Council[33]. It also allowed Myanmarese dissidents to establish a radio station called the Voice of Burma (VOB) in one of its islands in the coast of Oslo. This positive attitude on the part of the Norwegian government had got its impact on other European countries. Germany, U.K., France, Sweden and U.S. started taking up a more practical approach to the Myanmarese cause. The government of these countries allowed members of the NCGUB to meet their high officials to discuss about their problems. The European Parliament also called on the junta to establish a close political cooperation with the NCGUB. A resolution was passed in this direction in July 1991[34]. Besides, many NGOs belonging to these countries extended material and financial help to the Myanmarese dissidents. Swiss Aid, a private Swiss aid agency, in March 1992 , gave Swiss Franc(SF) 500,000 to the "ethnic minorities and democratic forces" in Myanmar , and earlier gave SF 300,000 for refugees aid on the Thai border and SF 250,000 for education ,health and agriculture[35]. Agencies like Voice of America (VOA) and British Broadcasting Corporation (BBC) also contributed to the movement by broadcasting Myanmarese programs. UN agencies like the UNCHR also took the allegation of Myanmarese dissidents seriously and sent rapporteurs to look into the issues of human rights violation in the country.

The movement for democracy in Myanmar became an issue of international importance. As the movement progress, it saw the emergence of two forces- one is the force of political groups and another is that of student and youths. Aung San Suu Kyi became a symbol. Many students groups became active outside the country. Political forces comprising National Coalition Government of the Union of Burma (NCGUB), National League for Democracy (NLD), Democratic Alliance of Burma (DAB), and the pre uprising organisation, the Committee for Restoration of Democracy in Burma (CRDB) helped in popularising the cause at the international level to receive support. Labour based organisations tried to highlight the plight of the normal people and the labour class, under the military junta, in the country, in international platforms thus making many of the leaders realise the necessity of democracy. Besides, many of the overseas non-resident Myanmarese also set up associations in their respective countries in order to help those struggling for the movement in particular and the movement for restoration of democracy in general. Over and above all these many associations and groups for the Myanmar's cause also came up in many countries, particularly in Europe and America.

The rapid spread of the movement in the early 90s has got a lot to do with the emerging popularity of Aung San Suu Kyi and the symbolism associated with her personality and commitment. She became the guiding symbol for the Myanmarese cause in the international arena. At time the life and activity of Suu Kyi is considered to be synonymous with the struggle itself. This was further enhanced by the recognition extended to her by awarding the Nobel Peace Prize. With it the world community accepted her as the undisputed leader of the movement. She is sometimes taken as par with Mahatma Gandhi and Nelson Mandela, though politely she herself was not ready to accept it. Scholars like Josef Silverstein were of the view that Aung San Suu Kyi symbolised a new politics in Myanmar. Her increasing popularity is such that campaign like 'Free Suu Kyi Free Burma' was established solely for demanding her release. This involved hundreds of world organisations. Suu's image was also bolstered when she rejected the junta's proposal for her freedom if she leaves the country and stop campaign for democracy. She was ready to endure the hardship and the humiliations under the military rulers rather than to discard the struggle. This stance of strength, commitment and courage won the hearts of more and more supporters for the Myanmarese cause. Above all, her strong belief in democracy and the use of peaceful means for achieving the goal was the deciding point for leaders of major powers of the world to accept her. Her ideas could be easily adjusted with the increasing trend of peace and democratisation in the international scenario. Aung San Suu Kyi said:

> *"... why I object to violent means is because I think it would perpetuate a tradition of changing the political situation through force of arms.....*
>
> *For me its very practical. If you want to establish a strong tradition of democracy in this country one of the basic principles of achieving it is that you bring about political change peacefully through consulting the will of the people via the ballot box and not through force of arms. If you want democracy you must demonstrate its principles; you need to be consistent in politics."*[36]

What is significant about her is that she was not in favour of entirely depending on either East or West for the democracy struggle of her country[37]. But at the same time she acknowledges their need as in this day and age the opinion of the international community cannot be ignored[38]. Democracies of the world were very much attracted towards the struggle because of these ideas of her. And as such, the symbolism emanated from the personage of Suu Kyi formed an important facet of the movement. Thus, despite the lack of much momentum of the struggle in the home front as a result of restriction placed on Suu Kyi and the NLD, in the international circle it started getting a more sympathetic and favourable approach from many countries and organisations, strengthening the cause.

The process of internationalising the issue was further enhanced by activities of various political forces working outside Myanmar. In the political front NCGUB and NCUB are the two platforms for the cause of Myanmarese democracy in the international sphere. The former is the *de facto* government while the latter is the *de facto* legislature (parliament) providing a sort of umbrella to the various democracy groups. The aim of NCUB was to provide a parliament to the government in exile, the NCGUB. Likewise, other groups like DAB, National League for Democracy-Liberated Area (NLD-LA), Member of Parliamentary Union (MPU), CRDB and so on are the other components of the broader framework wherein the NCUB also plays a supplementary role. The NCGUB, being the government in exile representing the popularly elected democratic parties, became a type of an apex political body for the whole movement in the international sphere. It was exalted to this position outside Myanmar due to the restrictions imposed by the junta on the NLD activists inside the country. Initially NCGUB was based in Manerplaw, headquarters of the KNU and DAB in the Thai-Burma border, but with the fall of the place to the government forces, and also for more effective campaigning among major world powers, it is now based in Washington. Based in this strategic place NCGUB's Prime Minister Dr. Sein Win and his ministers (though they don't want to call themselves as ministers) are actively engaged in a lobbying campaign for the Myanmarese cause in the corridors of world powers. Efforts continue to pressurise the junta through major world powers for an effective political transformation in the country. Most of the NCGUB ministers are based in different countries in order to make lobbying and campaigning more feasible and easier. For example, the Minister for South Asian Affairs, Dr.Tint Swe, is based in New Delhi. As far as possible it has also established its office in most of the major cities of the world with the help of overseas Myanmarese living there and NGO's supporting the cause. In the same manner the NCUB, which is the de facto legislature, consisting of NLD-LA, MPU, DAB, NDF and also the NCGUB, has got its office in most of the major democratic countries. However, in most cases the offices of NCGUB and

NCUB are situated in a single premise where the representatives of NCUB's are also attached. This is mainly because of lack of material and manpower and also to make it easy in carrying out a co-ordinated approach. Established in August 1992, with the main aim of providing a common platform for different opposition groups, it has got its main office in Mae Sot, in the Tak province of Thailand. NCUB has been carrying out several political activities in the international front. Its Foreign Affairs Committee is actively involved in this matter. What need to be remembered here is the fact that there is a close co-ordination of activities between NCUB and NCGUB. Most of the delegations to the UN are joint delegation of the two led by Dr Sein Win, Prime Minister of NCGUB and Vice Chairman of NCUB. The Foreign Affairs Committee of the NCUB has also formed a campaign committee comprising NCGUB and NCUB officials and is working very closely with diplomats and embassies in Bangkok and also political leaders of the world who are sympathetic to the struggle. Not only this but it is also trying to garner more and more support from various spheres of influence. It is also an important effort on the part of NCUB that foreign investment in the country be stopped as far as possible. Also it has been organising conferences and seminars in many countries with like-minded groups.

Besides the above two, one organisation which existed much before the uprising of 1988 and which has still got some follower among non-resident Myanmarese is the Committee for Restoration of Democracy in Burma (CRDB). It was originally set up in the United States in 1985 but was officially announced on 4 January 1987[39]. Initially as an umbrella organisation of overseas Myanmar dissidents, it has got certain influence over them and has got its units in US, UK, Germany, Australia, Thailand, Bangladesh and India. But later on, when it joined DAB and thus came under the broader sphere of NCUB, it no longer works independently but contributed usefully to the activities of the said groups. Because of its long activity abroad it still has got certain influence among overseas Myanmarese though no longer very active. It is considered oldest among the existing political groups working for democracy of Myanmar in the international sphere.

Federation of Trade Unions - Burma (FTUB) is another important political force, which emerged in the early 90s' to work for the movement in the international sphere. Though a part of the political forces it has got a separate identity of its own. It has got a vast international network and also far reaching influences because of its connection with many of the labour and worker groups from different parts of the world. Though there is co-ordination with other groups wherever situation demands, it has got a clear-cut separate policy and programs of its own with a different strategy and approach. Its emphasis is mainly to use the labour condition and workers' rights in Myanmar as a medium to catch international response in the need of a transformation in the country. Having contact with most of the international groups, it has got a strong lobby at the international level and could expose before the world community the pitiable condition of the workers in particular and the existing situation of the country in general very easily. It could also put proposals before the International Labour Organisation (ILO). It was mainly the effort of FTUB that a resolution was passed in the ILO in June 1999 suspending the membership of Myanmar from it.

Besides, the help in the form of finance, material and asylum extended to it by NGOs, labour groups and governments were more than enough for its own use. So these facilities were further transferred by FTUB to other main Myanmarese groups who are in real dearth of fund like the NCGUB and NCUB. FTUB, in short, is garnering lots of support from international groups which have been judiciously utilised for strengthening the movement. With the help of International Confederation of Free Trade Unions (ICFTU) the FTUB is trying to make a place in the ILO and through it to the United Nations.

Besides the above political forces, we also see the emergence of another force, that of students and youths, as an important part of the movement for democracy in the international level. In the post 1990 it became active concerning the international aspect of the movement. It started making its own contribution in garnering international support for the struggle. But, here, though many ethnic and non ethnic or common student and youth groups came up, only a few could make its impact felt in the world. These are the All Burma Students' Democratic Front (ABSDF), All Burma Students League (ABSL), Students and Youth Committee of Burma (SYCB), Democratic Party for New Society (DPNS) etc etc. Of all these also the most prominent and the one which can have far reaching impact in the international arena, though in the youth and student front, is the ABSDF. It is also the most powerful and influential group within the youth wing of the movement. In short, it represents the youthful and energetic facet of the movement to the world community. It is successful in forming a base line for the movement among the youth population of the world.

It is always the aim of ABSDF to have both material as well as moral help for the movement from other sections. Established by the first batch of students who came out after the uprising of 1988 in the Thai- Myanmar border it has played an active role over the years, despite some ups and downs within the set-up. Originally it had its headquarters at the KNU base of Manerplaw but with the fall of the place it is now located in Mashariang, in the Tak province of Thailand. In Thailand it has three more units located in Mae Sot, Chiangmai and Bangkok. Besides Thailand, it has got its office in India also where it is established in Manipur, Mizoram and Delhi. The ABSDF in India is known as ABSDF-Western Burma and has got certain autonomy in functioning. Units are also there in China-Myanmar border and also in Australia, though these are not very prominent ones. The main aim of establishing these units in different countries by ABSDF is mainly to garner international support. The organisation knows very much the need of external help in strengthening its movement. Since it has been waging a struggle, both armed and political, against the junta and as such there is always dearth of fund. So it is always the effort of ABSDF to have fund as well as political support from various sources of the international community. And to establish a link with the international community, it tried to lobby various pressure groups in many of the countries and also make the world realise their plight. This they do through means like seminars, conferences and demonstrations.

Besides ABSDF, other organisations like DPNS, ABSL and SYCB also made some contribution in the early 90s'. At a time, DPNS was very active in its effort for gaining support from the international community. Though registered as a political party to escape the harassment and ban of the junta, it is purely students' organisation concerned with activities fostering unity and coordination among students and youth forces. There is also a bonding between DPNS and ABSDF. Inter change of leaders and members are going on between the two groups. Moe Thi Zun the original founder of DPNS was at time the leader and Chairman of ABSDF. Now he is once more back to DPNS and with him some of the members of ABSDF have also shifted to DPNS. Thus, it seems that the two are like the different faces of the same coin. SYCB, which was, established in 1996 in New Delhi, also got certain link with Scandinavian countries, which also proved helpful for the movement.

But whether political force or youth force, the activities remained the same when it is concerned with international aspect of the movement. The efforts among the dissidents remain that there should be an active participation of the major countries for the cause. A strong voice as well as action against the junta in the international sphere is what the pro-democracy activists want side by side with the continuous flow of fund for their activities. Thus, the dissidents are following a strong way of lobbying through their apex body the NCGUB. In fact, NCGUB was mainly responsible for the 'MacConnell's Trade Sanction Bill' (September 1995) introduced in the U.S. Congress which was later withdrawn due to excessive pressure from other Senators - as a result of strong counter lobbying by business groups like Texaco and Unocal. It lobbied strongly for the bill in Washington. A chain system of lobbying is followed. It also followed other activities like arranging conferences and seminars, and also to carry on peaceful demonstration before the Myanmar Embassy in various countries on important occasions related with the movement. Every year when 8 August arrived Myanmarese dissidents all over the world commemorate it by staging protest before the Myanmarese Embassy of that country; the main being the Embassy of Myanmar in Bangkok. New campaigns were also started by dissidents living in different countries with the help of organisations of the parent countries. All these have its positive reactions in many countries. As a result of the effort of these dissidents there is an increase in the number of organisations in many countries, which deal with the movement. In fact it is gaining fruit.

6.3. International Support: Means and Ways

One important international aspect of the movement for democracy in Myanmar is the sustenance provided to it by the international community. The continuity maintained by the movement with a positive attitude despite many ups and downs has lot to do with the international support. This may be in the form of financial help, lobbying or punitive measures taken against the junta. Psychological support given by the world leaders and eminent personalities through international media also is of significance. Above all these, international NGOs and committees like Open Society Institute (OSI) and National Endowment for Democracy (under US Congress) of United States, Burma Action Group of United Kingdom, Norwegian Burmese Council, Denmark Burma Council (Funded by Danish Government), Amnesty International, etc., also made important contributions to the movement. Thus, besides giving asylum, which is a normal international norm, the international community extended various forms of help. This help may be both direct as well as indirect ones. It means that nations of the world can give both direct as well as indirect support to the movement.

Directly it can give material as well as moral support to those involved in the movement. And indirectly it can support the movement by boycotting the junta or in a way pressurising it for a change through various means and media. Either way it could play an important role in the context of the Myanmarese democracy movement.

Since the beginning of the movement in 1988 and the resultant mass scale exodus to the border area, funds had been coming from a number of international sources in various forms mainly for humanitarian purpose. Initially the funds were meant for the relief of Myanmarese living in the border areas - specially those in the Thai - Myanmar border. But gradually with the coming up of democratic forces funds and aid started coming from NGOs, trust, voluntary organisations, projects and even from some governments, though indirectly through some agencies, mainly to be utilised for the movement of democracy in the country. As mentioned, funds are coming from US based group like the National Endowment Fund of the US Congress, the International Republican Institute, the Open Society Institute of the George Soros Foundation etc[40]. Different groups receive fund from different sources. For example, ABSDF is mainly funded by OSI (US), NLD- LA and DPNS are funded by National Endowment for Democracy (US), FTUB got its fund from world trade unions through ICFTU, and so on. To mention a few, the US Congress, for the first time voted in 1989 to provide US $ 500,000 in humanitarian aid to Myanmarese refugees, and another US $ 250,000 to support opposition democracy groups in Myanmar[41]. Norway government also gave the NCGUB some US$300,000 as donation in December 1990[42]. In addition, in March 1992, Swiss Aid, a private Swiss agency, gave Swiss Franc 500,000 to democratic forces in Myanmar, and earlier gave SF 300,000 for refugee aid on the Thai border[43]. Ultimately the financial support so extended meant for one and the same goal i.e., the restoration of democracy in Myanmar. International help to the movement is also extended in the form of lobbying and pressurising carried out by organisations and world leaders in the international fora. In fact, lobbying, pressurising and boycott or sanction are all interrelated actions which are used by international bodies, countries and groups supporting the movement. All these have proved helpful for the cause. Lobbying is used as an important instrument both by the dissidents as well as those who supported the dissidents in their struggle. A clear example was the dialogue between Aung San Suu Kyi and the junta in 1994 and her subsequent release in 1995. Many experts believed that the release of Aung San Suu Kyi itself was a clear indication that the movement was receiving reasonable help from the international forces. It was mainly because of repeated international pressure in the form of financial sanctions, and the desire on the part of the junta to improve its image in the international arena that Suu Kyi was released. The recent talk in January 2001 between Aung San Suu Kyi and the military rulers is also because of the initiatives of European Union. Lobbying in the corridors of power like the US Congress, the EU, and international organisations like the United Nations, the World Bank etc has its impact on the movement . The well wishers of the movement have carried out this lobbying. It was mainly because of heavy lobbying by lawmakers and political leaders in USA that many laws were passed in that country against the military regime of Myanmar. Besides, it was the result of lobbying by countries supporting the movement that resolution demanding quick political transformation had been passed in the United Nations General Assembly. Among the lobbyists many US Congressmen and Senators came to the forefront. The former US Secretary of State, Madeleine Albright, herself is a strong supporter of Aung San Suu Kyi and the movement for democracy in Myanmar.

Anti-SPDC (formerly SLORC) forces have emerged in all major countries of the world as well as in the region, like India, Thailand, Philippines, Malaysia and even in Japan. This may be at official, political and organisational, labour or students' level. The tempo has increased with the awarding of Nobel Prize to Aung San Suu Kyi in 1991 and the resultant international media exposure. The initial demand of the world community for her release gradually changed to the demand for political transformation in the country. And for the achievement of the above goal a strong process of lobbying in various power centres started.

Closely related with the above types of help is the means of sanctions and boycotts carried out by those countries, NGOs, and institutions, which sympathise with the Myanmarese democracy movement. It proved a great help. Many companies and business houses dealing with the junta were selectively boycotted in many countries. Most countries of Europe, to pressurise the junta, also imposed arms embargo and economic sanctions. In extreme case the members of the junta in particular and the junta government in general was not given permission for entry in many Western countries and United States.

In United States, groups campaigning for the Myanmarese issue are gaining ground. Popular activism on behalf of the pro democracy movement has already resulted in increasing American sanctions[44]. Many states and cities had passed laws that impose sort of sanction on Myanmar. Massachusetts became the first US State to sign sanction laws aimed at pressurising American companies to stop doing business in Myanmar[45]. This was followed by cities such as San Francisco, Oakland, Berkley, Ann Arbor, and Madison which banned contracting companies to do businesses with the above. As a result many companies were compelled to withdraw large-scale investment from the country. Companies like Pepsi co, Coca-Cola, Levi-Strauss, Amoco, Reebok etc etc, to name a few, pulled out because of boycotts in home ground. Not only US companies but companies of other European countries also follow suit. Besides, Western governments have introduced a range of sanctions to pressurise the Yangon government for democratic reforms. The junta lost access to most foreign aid. The European Union and the United States had also cancelled the 'preferential tariffs' often accorded to developing nations. On 24 March 1997, the European Union unanimously voted to cancel

Myanmar's 'Generalised System of Preferences' (GSP) privileges, as mentioned above, adversely affecting about $ 47 million worth of Myanmarese exports to Europe[46]. And the United States also suspended the 'Most Favoured Nation' (MFN) status of the country[47]. Not only this, but on 25 July 1996, taking a tougher stand, the US Senate passed a new law which imposed ban on new US investment in Myanmar if the then President Clinton determines that the junta has harmed Aung San Suu Kyi or engaged in "large scale suppression" of its democratic opposition[48]. The law came to be known by the name 'Cohen – Feinstein Law' after Californian Senator Dianne Feinstein and Senator William Cohen of Maine, and was finally passed in mid- September 1996 by the Congress. The exception to it is that investment aid for humanitarian, promotion of democracy and anti - narcotics campaign can continue. This law was finally announced in April 1997, banning new investment by American firms in Myanmar. The announcement was made by the then Secretary of State, Madeleine Albright. The executive order putting the ban into effect was issued in May by President Clinton. As a part of the above law the junta official were also restricted from entry to United States. Though some groups expressed that the sanction is no longer effective but the pro- democracy opposition still finds the sanctions helpful to its cause.

Resultantly when there was crackdown on NLD supporters in October 1996 protest and further sanction threats were carried out by various sections of the international community. Besides US, countries like Australia, Japan and many European countries protested. In Tokyo, Foreign Ministry official Seiroku Kajiyama told a news conference that "Japan cannot overlook moves that run counter to democratisation of Myanmar"[49].

6.4. Implication of ASEAN's Policy of Constructive Engagement

ASEAN's attitude towards the Myanmarese movement for democracy is not very heart warming from the very beginning. At the outset of the movement itself except for some mild expression, the ASEAN in general and most of the member countries were not party to the international condemnation of the carnage and brutal suppression carried out by the military junta. It has got its own reason that has something to do with economic interest, ASEAN unity and the marginalisation of increasing influence of China in the region. Besides, other countries of the region have got its own political and human rights problems.

ASEAN is the only group in the region that has got the leverage to pressurise the junta for a meaningful change in the country. However, contrary to the expectation of many it remained soft in its dealing with the junta. Before 1988 this was not the case as ASEAN established limited relations with Myanmar because of the latter's isolationist attitude. However, post- 88 period saw a gradual development in the relation between the two as a result of the efforts made by ASEAN to fulfil its vision of an 'ASEAN-10'. Thus, it did not try to pressurise the junta government of Myanmar to bring about a democratic transformation in the country. With a view to serve its interests, ASEAN remains in favour of following its neutralist policy of 'constructive engagement', which, in fact, is concerned more with economic aspects.

The policy of Constructive Engagement was the brainchild of Thailand to foster its own economic gain in its relation with Myanmar. Later on it was adopted as a policy for ASEAN in general, which avoided interference in the internal affairs of Myanmar. When the United States appealed to ASEAN in the summer of 1991 to use its good offices and influence to encourage voluntary change inside of Myanmar, it met with a refusal; ASEAN spokesman advanced the argument that by "acting individually and employing constructive engagement they would be more effective in tune with the Asian Way"[50]. Thus behind the shadow of constructive engagement it continued to avoid involving in the internal complexities of Myanmarese politics while trying to take economic advantage. Thus, in the initial stage of the movement, except for Philippines, which under the influence of US is against the junta for its unimpressive human rights record, most of the member countries were in favour of fostering trade and economic relations with Myanmar. For them human rights and democratic government have very little meaning as compared to economic gains. Following this line Singapore with US $ 604 million, Thailand with $ 444 million and Malaysia with $ 227 million were among the top six investing countries in Myanmar in the mid 90s'[51]. Despite pressure from Western countries, particularly a number of countries of European Union, and the United States, ASEAN was not ready to change its policy towards 'flexible engagement' in real practice though theoretically they do mention about a change towards it sometimes. At the same time ASEAN do show concern for the deteriorating situation in the country, but ultimately the regional and national interest overrode it.

Another point which needs to be pondered over is the attitude of the ASEAN as an organisation in the whole and also the organisation as a collection of member nations with changes in leadership and party of that member from time to time. And it is a fact that though most of the member do try to follow the general policy of soft approach of the organisation there are instances where a particular member nation failed to toy the same line. There are also cases where a new government shows strong disagreement with the Myanmarese Junta despite a soft approach from the side of the organisation. For instances, Malaysia and Indonesia, two Muslim dominated countries, strongly expressed their resentment against the junta for its ill treatment to Rohingyas (Myanmarese Muslims). They were not happy in inviting the Myanmarese official delegation at the ASEAN's Annual Ministerial Meeting in Manila in July 1992 by Thai Foreign Minister, Arsa Sarasin. They were in favour of adopting a strong measure against Myanmar at that time for the ill treatment of Muslim minority in the country. Contradiction thus emerged. The differences between the ASEAN as an organisation on the one hand, and ASEAN as a collection of different countries on the other emerge from time to time.

Sometimes, it is difficult to find out the exact stand of this regional grouping. It is not helping the movement in any way also. ASEAN has never adopted a common stand on Myanmar, especially on the constructive engagement policy.

In continuation of the above discussion, the question which arises is - do the members always agree to the general policy of ASEAN which at times seems to be dictated by economically influential country like Singapore? This is highly questionable. We find instances where individual members going to the extent of questioning the validity or relevance of ASEAN's generally accepted policy of 'constructive engagement'. Philippines is one such country. This is same with some of the democratic governments of Southeast Asia. They were critical of ASEAN's policy of supporting the Myanmarese junta at the cost of a democratic government in the country. But, this itself is a dynamic one that may change with a new government. Philippines, to some extent, has got a steady and somewhat stable policy in this regard. However, one difference that we can see in these countries is the NGOs, students, intellectual groups which remain free of any bias. These groups in the ASEAN countries, contrary to the policy of their government, were in favour of the democracy movement. They expressed their concern against the continuing human rights violation and the lack of political stability in the country. Also, they were very critical of their government's indifferent attitude. These groups tried to extend whatever possible help to the democracy groups. In February 1996, 17 Malaysian NGOs, representing human rights, youth, environment, religion, student and the development, condemned the junta for its ongoing human rights violation and its refusal to hand over power to the democratically elected Government led by NLD party[52]. Despite all these efforts, ASEAN, in general, continued with its plan to make Myanmar as one of their member.

By mid 90s, ASEAN was more concerned about Myanmar's entry into the regional association so that the members could extract maximum trade and economic benefits, rather than to think about the restoration of democracy. As a first step towards entry into ASEAN, it was allowed to sign ASEAN's '1976 Treaty of Amity and Co-operation' at the Foreign Minister's Meeting in Brunei in July 1995. Some days before that meeting the junta had also released Suu Kyi from house arrest. Despite certain misgivings from its members from time to time it continued with its effort to bring Myanmar into its fold. It was given a formal status by making it an observer at the 29th ASEAN Ministerial Meeting at Jakarta in July 1996. It was also admitted into the ASEAN Regional Forum (ARF)[53]. This was a major victory for the junta but a setback for the movement. For the legitimacy extended to it by regional forum it became more active in carrying out its repressive policies. As Myanmar moves gradually into the mainstream of ASEAN its illegitimacy tag started fading. On the other hand, many experts question the equation behind ASEAN's policy of giving legal or formal status to the junta despite its tainted political and human rights records. No member protested against the steps of the ASEAN though most of the country had spoken against the military rulers in earlier cases. Many Myanmar watchers were of the view that these countries were concerned more about their national interest. South East Asia Information Network (SAIN), one of the foreign NGOs based in Thailand, was of the view that ASEAN has got two reasons behind its action, one is economic because Myanmar has rich natural resources which they want to exploit[54]. And secondly it will divert the attention of the Western countries from their human rights conditions to that of the problem of Myanmar[55]. But in spite of all these positive response from ASEAN, in general, towards Myanmar, the misgivings of many member countries continued. And the peculiarity remained that whenever a common decision was taken, all these misgivings, despite its merit, were vanished.

It is interesting to know that as time became nearer for Myanmar's entry into ASEAN, leaders of member countries started expressing critical comments against the country. "Philippines President Fidel Ramos insisted on commitment to genuine democratic reform, and former Thai Foreign

Minister Amnuay Viravan, cited SLORC's need to draft a new constitution before considering full membership"[56]. Leaders of ASEAN countries had apprehension that admitting a country like Myanmar would seriously affect its international image and credibility. Besides Philippines, Thailand, and even Singapore hinted reservation about the timing of Myanmar's joining the ASEAN family[57]. However, all these reservations were sidelined on the ground of future trade benefits and the pretext of balancing the ever-increasing Chinese influence on the country. Also they wanted to restrict external influence in their regional grouping. ASEAN family was of the view that the military regime must be allowed to act according to its own timetable and in its own Asian Way [58]. Besides there was the vision of 'ASEAN 10' as visualised by the founding fathers of the association. As an outcome, all these different views of the member countries gave way to the general Asian view and as such Myanmar was finally admitted as a full-fledged member of ASEAN in July 1997, on the 30th anniversary of the regional association. Thus Myanmar was provided a regional protection against the continuing global criticism. It gave the regime the required legitimacy and a strong boost of confidence in the amity of nations.

Here, what need to be understood is besides economic factor another issue that prompted ASEAN to take Myanmar into its fold was the ever-increasing influence of China on Myanmar which posed a threat to the security and strategic safety of the region. This threat perception prompted many members to agree to the general idea of ASEAN despite certain disagreement. ASEAN nations feel insecure with the rapid growth of China's relation with Myanmar and the strategic implications[59]. "Whether or not China's strategic influence in Burma has been exaggerated, the possibility alone of China gaining access to military facilities on the Bay of Bengal has been enough to increase regional suspicions about Beijing's intentions"[60]. Taking Myanmar into broader fold of the association, they believed, could reduce this. Whatever may be the outcome the degree of enthusiasm among members varies. Yet the ASEAN as a whole welcomed the country. It was considered a sign of the association's independence irrespective of pressure from major powers. However, on the side of the Myanmarese junta there was no sign of change in their behaviour. The most important advantage of the Myanmarese regime, which is to the chagrin of the supporters of democracy movement, is that "ASEAN has provided ideological support to Myanmarese authoritarianism, in contrast to the European Union's role in encouraging democratisation in Europe"[61].

With Myanmar's entry into ASEAN there came a change in the relationship between the two. If the changes were put to actual practice then it would have been helpful for the democracy movement. For, some degree of difference between ASEAN's attitude towards Myanmar before and after its entry into the association could be observed. Before its entry, ASEAN had a near to indifferent attitude towards the country and its political happenings. No pressure was given to the country for any political transformation considering it as the country's internal affairs. Aftermath some of the member countries were of the view that much more changes could be brought towards political transformation in the country by taking it in the fold of ASEAN. Myanmar had to follow certain international norms of ASEAN. And, in fact, after the entry of Myanmar into ASEAN in July 1997 due to heavy persuasion from Malaysia, the association protected the country's international interest but at the same time adopted tough stance on certain issues like democracy and human rights. This is because it does not want strained relations with its Western business partners like countries of EU and the US who are very much concerned with the deteriorating political situation in Myanmar. Tussles and conflict of ideas between ASEAN and Western groups in international fora on the issue of Myanmar has become a frequent occurrence. This is not conducive to the broader interest of the association for it needs all the support from these countries for having a better trade and political relation and also for its credibility in the global scenario.

In the post entry scenario, besides the general attitude

of ASEAN, some changes could be seen in the attitude of the individual members. These members wanted to bring changes in the general policy of ASEAN based on "constructive engagement". They wanted a change in the association's stance towards particular member countries and issues from just being a passive observer to an active participant. This may apply to Myanmar also. Especially leaders of younger generation started questioning ASEAN's strict adherence to the policy of constructive engagement despite its lack of relevance in the changing situation of the region. Thai Foreign Minister Surin Pitsuwan proposed for the first time the concept of 'constructive intervention' within the broader policy of 'flexible engagement'. Initially in June 1998, Surin stated, "ASEAN's principle of non-interference should be replaced by his concept of constructive intervention in those cases where 'a domestic concern poses a threat to regional security'"[62]. But because of the objection of its members the term was modified and presented in the Ministerial Meeting of July 1998 in Manila, as 'flexible engagement'. If the new policy is followed 'ASEAN could maintain its creditability by being resolute in meeting global challenges but flexible in dealing with intra-regional issues'[63]. Surin was of the view that there should be an open and frank discussion among members through a flexible engagement policy. Either way the member nations, except for Philippines, were not happy with the very underlying ideas of the concept. Malaysia, Indonesia, Vietnam, Laos and Myanmar were in favour of continuing with the principle of non-interference in the internal affairs of other members[64]. Despite all these one significant change in the working of the association could be observed. Though the Thai proposal was rejected, the sprouting of the policy of flexible engagement increased the interaction among the members and effort was taken up in right earnest to smooth out any shortcomings.

However, in spite of all these changes, the question still remains as to why ASEAN have a soft attitude towards Myanmar's military regime. In recent time, ASEAN, like India, is giving priority to improve its economic, diplomatic and strategic relations with Myanmar in order to balance the growing power and influence of China in that country. According to Prof. Mohan Malik, ASEAN's soft attitude towards Myanmar and its admission into the association has to do with the fact that " the ASEAN countries' interest lie in balancing off one regional power against the other in order to maintain the delicate multi-polar balance of power"[65]. He further asserted that politically the regime's hold to power becomes firmer and thus with it the sign of national reconciliation and restoration of democratic process has become very dim[66]. It seems at the juncture that the advantage of joining ASEAN is more in favour of Myanmar. In a way it has cleverly manipulated the association's 'constructive engagement policy' more to its advantage. And at the same time ASEAN is also not really concerned with a long-term political transformation in the country. As David Steinberg has rightly stated, "... theoretically, this sought to transform Myanmar into a more open society through increasing trade, investment, and economic relation, though in practice it seem more devoted to short term profit making by ASEAN states than Myanmar's long term political reform"[67]. Who is the real gainer, it is very difficult to decide. It will take some time for the real picture to emerge. But ultimately it is the people and the democratic forces that are the real sufferer in Myanmar.

6.5. Role of Thailand: Between Neutralism and Alignment

Among the neighbouring countries in particular and ASEAN countries in general the role of Thailand in the context of the movement for democracy in Myanmar is specifically significant because of its physical proximity coupled with inseparable historical and cultural ties it has with the country. There may be many ups and downs in the relationship, no doubt, but at the same time it can never be ignored at all . The existence of a bitter-sweet relation cannot undermine the inseparable nature that exists between the two countries. Any happening inside Myanmar, in most cases, has got its maximum fall-out, directly or indirectly in Thailand. Thai territory, politics, people and its economy are always affected by the happenings in Myanmar. Even when mass exodus started in the later part of 1988, as a result of systematic persecution by the ruling junta, maximum number moved into Thailand. Despite repatriation by the Thai government, many dissidents stayed back in the country, particularly in the bordering states of Chiangmai, Tak, Mai Hong Son, Kanchanburi etc etc.

Thailand's relations with Myanmar is of a paradoxical nature. There is always frequent change in Thai policy. It is difficult to say that uniform policy has been followed. In most cases it depends on the mood and attitude of the Thai political leaders who are mostly from army background. According to Thai scholars, it is dictated by national interest and economic gains. Thailand has got an acute shortage of natural resources mainly due to depletion of its fisheries, forestry, and mineral and gas resources[68]. Thus it does not want to lose the potential commercial benefit that it could gain from Myanmar though it has got problems related with drugs, refugees and immigrants and border skirmishes vis-à-vis with the country.

Relations between Thailand and Myanmar was never cordial before 1988. Myanmar had always the suspicion that Thailand supported the ethnic insurgents in their war against it. Thailand on its part blamed the Myanmarese regime of supporting the drug lords in carrying on transaction of narco products and drug trafficking in its (Thailand) border areas. Besides, there were allegations from both sides of encroaching upon each other's border areas by their respective army. However, since 1988, many strategic and economic considerations related with its national interest compelled Thailand to change its earlier policy of keeping away from Myanmar. Distancing itself from Myanmar was no longer beneficial. It could no longer undermine the importance of the country because of its abundant natural resources. Thailand needs to have a close relation with Myanmar in order to acquire the rich resources of that country including timber, oil, gemstones and with a lucrative market for its consumer finished goods and service industry. On the other hand Thailand wants to check the increasing influence of China on Myanmar. The growing Chinese economic penetration into Myanmar and also its arming of Myanmarese army and its potential military role in its Western maritime littoral was considered to be a threat on the part of Thailand[69]. It was greatly concerned with the apprehension that China may one day use Myanmar as a springboard for increased political and economic influence in Southeast Asia[70]. It was because of these considerations that the attitude of Thailand was changed to improve its historically strained relations with Myanmar, especially since 1988.

From 1988 onwards Thailand's stand toward Myanmar and its military rulers show a positive change despite having certain misgivings due to public opposition to the Myanmarese crackdown on pro-democracy opposition groups in Yangon and other cities. Thailand came under the broader framework of ASEAN in supporting the Myanmarese regime when most of the countries of the world had neglected it as an outcaste. As a part of ASEAN its attitude towards SLORC regime softened. This was a change in Thai foreign policy. But one thing which need to be remembered is the fact that despite the new developments Thailand's attitude towards Myanmar is marked by a general policy, which is neither wholly neutral nor a complete alignment. A sort of middle path is followed which could change with time and leadership. Thailand was the first among ASEAN countries to officially recognise the SLORC regime. This was more concretised with the visit paid by the Thai Acting Supreme Commander, General Chavalit Yongchaiyudh, on 14 December 1988 to the country - the first ever-foreign dignitary's visit under the SLORC regime after the '88 Uprising'[71]. This development brought commercial gains in the form of logging rights, fishing contracts and construction deals for oil pipelines. But for the democracy movement this visit of Chavalit Yongchaiyudh brought some setbacks.

As a part of an agreement between the two countries a centre was set up on 21 December 1988 in Tak province of

Thailand for sending back those Myanmarese student activists who came over to the Thai side for safety in the wake of the '1988 Uprising'. About 300 students were forcibly repatriated despite threat to their lives. Later on the repatriation was stopped because of protest coming from United Nations High Commissioner for Refugees and other Western countries. Whatsoever may be the outcome for the time being the relations between the two countries improved. The visit of Chavalit was followed by frequent exchange visits of official and commercial delegations of the two countries. His visit was reciprocated with the six-day visit of Myanmar's Commander-in-Chief Gen. Than Shwe in May 1989. To show its goodwill towards Myanmar, between 1989 and 1991, Thai government, particularly the military ,unofficially, allowed Myanmarese troops to cross-over into Thai territory and attack the rebel positions from the rear leading to the fall of many Karen and Mon bases[72]. Karen National Union strong holds of Klerday, Maw Pokay and Mae La along the Moei River were overrun during the period between January and April 1989[73]. The cordiality was marked by a significant step introduced by Thai Foreign Minister Arsa Sarasin in 1991. He favoured a policy known as "constructive engagement" rather than following policy of widespread boycotts and condemnations in dealing with Myanmar. This status remained up to the end of 1992. But changes could be seen with the approach of 1993.

Cordial and cooperative relationship between the two countries once more became strained in 1993. Myanmar alleged Thai government and the newly elected leaders of supporting the ethnic insurgents. The presence on Thai soil of more than 70,000 Karen, Mon and Karenni refugees were branded by the SLORC regime as dependants of insurgents while the Thai government adopted a more humanitarian approach allowing private aid organisations to assist them[74]. It also announced its decision of scrapping the fishing and logging concessions given in 1988. Further it expressed unhappiness over Thai government's decision to allow a team of Nobel Laureates to enter the country in February and campaign against the former. The highly publicised team of six Nobel Laureates[75] and representatives of two Nobel Prize winning organisations – Amnesty International and American Friends Service Committee – visited Bangkok and other border areas of Thailand while demanding at the same time for the release of Aung San Suu Kyi and restoration of democracy in Myanmar. What provoked the SLORC leaders most was the fact that Thai leaders accorded them a warm welcome and also met them. This Thai gesture displeased the SLORC leaders.

The year 1994, despite certain misgivings on the part of the SLORC over the Thai poaching in its water and illegal logging of teak, revealed a generally cordial situation in the Thai–Myanmar relations. Speedy trading and exchange of high level visits followed. In December, the two countries made permanent the three existing temporary border check points – Sai-Tachilek, Mae Sot-Myawaddy and Ranong-Kawthaung[76]. Thailand invested $ 3 million on the 'Thailand -Myanmar Bridge', linking Mae Sot with Myawaddy[77]. However, Myanmar was slightly suspicious of the Thai overture and as such did not allow its (Thai) traders to go up to Yangon. They were permitted to proceed only two to five kilometres into Myanmar territory[78]. Despite this in the political front cordial relations continued. Myanmarese Foreign Minister Ohn Gyaw attended the ASEAN Foreign Ministers' Meeting in July at Bangkok on the invitation of Thailand.

In the beginning of 1995 combined forces of the SLORC and Democratic Karen Buddhists Association (DKBA) – breakaway faction of Karen National Union (KNU) – frequently attacked KNU bases deep into the Thai border which became a source of confrontation between the two governments. On the pretext of chasing Karen rebels the forces attacked refugee camps, NGOs and even Thai soldiers thus causing death and destruction. The Thai government under Prime Minister Chuan Leekpai strongly condemned these acts and at the same time promised for the safety of the Myanmarese Karen refugees numbering about 70,000[79].

On its part, the SLORC regime considered this act of Thailand as a sign of insincerity in maintaining good relations between the two. Resultantly Myanmar closed its borders in March 1995 on the ground of backing Karen, Shan and other ethnic rebels and also of illegal trade practice carried on by Thailand. Not only this but also the work on the construction of the 'Friendship Bridge' was halted and the people of Myanmar were urged to boycott Thai products[80]. Even Thai Defence Minister Chavalit Yongchaiyudh's visit couldn't restore the earlier status of cordial relationship.

In March 1996, however, efforts were made to improve ties between the two countries with the visit of Thai Prime Minister Banharn Silpa Arca to Myanmar - first visit by a Thai Prime Minister in 16 years. It gave a moral boost to the SLORC in their search for legitimacy. As a result some improvement in the relations could be seen but whether it improved to the level expected is still questionable. However, the opposition expressed apprehension that the Prime Minister's stand towards Myanmar could be interpreted in a negative light in the prevailing international situation questioning the timing of Myanmar's entry into ASEAN. It wanted the country to improve its political situation first. It also expressed its concern on heavy crackdown by the junta on NLD members in May, the same year.

In the year that followed bilateral relations between the two countries became strained. Despite Thailand's support for Myanmar's entry into ASEAN under the broader framework of the association friction developed between the two in June and July of 1997 on territorial and drug related issues. In June, there was a confrontation between Myanmar and Thai troops on a disputed island in the Moei River[81]. And in July Thai-Myanmar relations reached lowest possible point in years when Thai anti narcotics official accused Myanmar military officials of helping drug trafficking across the border[82]. Resultantly Thai border post in the Thai-Myanmar border was sealed.

Relation further deteriorated in 1998 when Thailand joined Philippines in openly criticising Myanmar for its lack of political reforms despite its entry into ASEAN. In July 1998, in the ASEAN Foreign Ministers' Meeting in Manila, Thai Foreign minister Surin Pitsuwan proposed ' flexible engagement' policy towards Myanmar rather than the age-old ASEAN policy of constructive engagement. This proposal stemmed out from frequent incursion in Thai territory by Myanmarese troops in pursuit of ethnic rebels, exodus of refugees in its territory because of instability in Myanmar's domestic politics and territorial disputes - all of which affect Thailand's national interest. Though most members, except for Philippines, rejected the proposal it clearly brought about one thing that is the Thai government was no longer going to support the regime in all its activities. It also shows that Thailand wants to play a proactive role in order to bring political transformation and reconciliation with Myanmar. This has something to do with more democratisation and diminishing role of army in Thai politics itself[83]. Thailand also took a very soft stand towards Myanmarese student dissidents when they seized their country's Embassy in Bangkok. They were provided a helicopter and sent to safety in exchange for the hostages. This also further strained the already deteriorated relations between the two countries. Myanmar closed all its border points indefinitely.

Despite the above problems and tensions, efforts were made to improve Myanmar- Thai relations considering mutual benefits. However, despite efforts on the part of both the governments some border problems still remain unresolved resulting in frequent flare-up among troops guarding the border of their respective countries. Territorial disputes still remained unresolved. And as such, Thailand's attitude towards Myanmar is marked by a general policy which is neither wholly neutral nor a complete alliance. A sort of middle path is followed which changes with time and leadership.

Finally, the question is whether Myanmar's relations has anything to do with the Myanmarese democracy movement. Here, what is to be remembered is the fact that in dealing with both the Myanmar government and the democracy groups the foremost issue in the mind of the Thai leaders is the national interest of the country. So, from time to time it deals with both harshly as well as softly, as the situation demands though it tries to maintain a cordial and closer relation with the regime in general. But at the same time, despite some strict actions such as repatriation of dissident Myanmarese students in the 90s', the Thai government is not very harsh to the movement also. Though not formally, but many of the Myanmarese democracy groups were allowed to have their office in many parts of Thailand. Maximum numbers of dissidents are accommodated in this country, with or without official knowledge. Besides, in spite of certain restrictions they were allowed to carry out their activities related with restoration of democracy in Myanmar. In this context, Thailand became a passive supporter to the movement. The emphasis in recent years for a flexible engagement by Thailand, in itself, is to bring political transformation in Myanmar through the medium of ASEAN so that the dissidents and refugees could return to their country and also most of the existing problems related with it could be solved for Thailand. The experts in Institute of Asian Studies of Chulalongkorn University and Thammasat University were of the view that even if flexible engagement is not found possible in case of Myanmar more emphasis on genuine constructive engagement should be given so that a change could be brought about in that country which will be in the interest of Thailand in the long run[84].

NOTES

1. The exact time could not be ascertained.
2. Alan Clements and Leslie Kean, *Burma's Revolution of the Spirit: The Struggle For Democratic Freedom and Dignity* (New York: Aperture, 1994), p.46.
3. Burton Levin, "Reminiscences and Reflections on 8.8.88", *Burma Debate* (Washington), vol.5,no.3, Summer 1998, pp.4-12.
4. Bertil Lintner, *Outrage: Burma's Struggle for Democracy* (London and Bangkok: White Lotus,1990), p.110.
5. Ibid, p.144.

6. United States, *Department of State Bulletin* (Washington), May 1989, p.42.
7. *Far Eastern Economic Review* (Hong Kong), 22 September 1988, p.15.
8. n.4,p.145.
9. *Bangkok Post*, 14 January 1989.
10. John Bray, *Burma: The Politics of Constructive Engagement* (London: Royal Institute of International Affairs, 1995), p.52.
11. n.7.
12. Andrew Selth, "Burma's Military Expansion Program: Plan and Perceptions ", *Journal of Contemporary Asia* (Manila), vol.26, no. 4, 1996, p.472.
13. Far Eastern Economic Review, *Asia 1989 Year Book* (Hong Kong). p.95.
14. The Nehru – Gandhi family had got a close and mutual relationship with U Nu, the former Prime Minister of Myanmar, and Aung San Suu Kyi and her mother, Daw Khin Kyi.
15. FEER, *Asia 1990 Yearbook*, p.97.
16. David I.Steinberg, "Myanmar in 1991: The Miasma in Burma", *Asian Survey* (Berkeley), vol.32, no.2, February 1992, pp.151-152.
17. n.12.
18. James F.Guyot and John Badgley," Myanmar in 1989: Tatmadaw V", *Asian Survey*, vol. 30, no.2, February 1990, p.193.
19. Ibid.
20. n.15,p. 97. In an interview with Myanmarese dissidents they disclosed that there were some minor untoward incidents between them and the Indian security personnel arising out of restrictions placed by the Indians.
21. Ministry of External Affairs, Government of India, *Annual Report 1988-89*, p.3.
22. As told to the scholar by Myanmarese students in India.
23. David I. Steinberg, International Rivalries in Burma: The Rise of Economic Competition", *Asian Survey*, vol.30, no.6, June 1990, p.598.
24. Alan Clements, *Burma: The Next Killing Fields* (Berkeley: Odonian Press, 1992), p.55.
25. n.4, p.156.

26. John Badgley, "The Burmese Way to Capitalism", *Southeast Asian Affairs* (Singapore), 1990, p.236.
27. Josef Silverstein, " The Civil War, the Minorities and Burma's New Politics", in Peter Carey (ed.), *Burma: The Challenge of Change in a Divided Society* (London: Macmillan, 1997), p.144.
28. Ibid,
29. Ibid
30. n.24, p.200.
31. Bertil Lintner, *Burma in Revolt: Opium and Insurgency since 1948* (Bangkok: White Lotus, 1994), p.381.
32. n.27, p.145.
33. Josef Siverstein, "Burma in an International Perspective", *Asian Survey*, vol. 32, no.10, October 1992, p.953.
34. *Far East and Australasia 1996* (London: Europa Publications, 1995), p.621.
35. n.33.
36. Aung San Suu Kyi and Alan Clements, *Voice of Hope* (Harmondsworth : Penguin,1997), p.79.
37. Ibid, p.174.
38. Ibid.
39. n.31, p.423.
40. As told to the scholar by different Myanmarese groups staying in India and Thailand.
41. n.26.
42. David I Steinberg, "Myanmar in 1991: Military Intransigence", *Southeast Asian* Affairs, 1991 p.226.
43. *Burma Focus*, June 1992 and *FEER*, 9 July 1992.
44. C Raja Mohan, 'Myanmar- Isolation or Engagement' *The Hindu* (New Delhi), 21 December 1996.
45. *Bangkok Post*, 27 June 1996
46. *The Asian Age* (Calcutta), 20 April 1997.
47. n.44.
48. *The Irrawaddy* (Chiangmai), 31 January 1997. Also check 31 July 1996 issue of the same publications.
49. FEER, *Asia 1997 Yearbook* (Hong Kong), p.97.
50. n.33,p.958.
51. Editorial, *Bangkok Post*, 8 September 1996.

52. *The Nation* (Bangkok,) 13 February 1996,quoted in *The Irrawaddy*, 15 February 1996.
53. ARF was formally inaugurated in July 1994 in Bangkok to look into security side of the region.
54. *The Irrawaddy*, vol.4, no.13, 31 July 1996.
55. Ibid.
56. *The Irrawaddy*, vol.5, no.10, January 1997.
57. James F.Guyot, " Burma in 1996: One Economy, Two Politics", *Asian Survey*, vol.37, no.2, February 1997,p.193.
58. n.33, p.958.
59. Abu Taher , "Myanmar : Road to Democracy or East Asian Model?", *Bangladesh Institute of International and Strategic Studies Journal*(Dhaka),vol. 17, no.1,1996, p.140.
60. Andrew Selth, " Burma and the Strategic Competition Between China and India", in John Brandon (ed.), *Burma / Myanmar: Towards Twenty First Century, Dynamics of Continuity and Change* (Bangkok: Thai Studies Section, Thammasat University, 1997), p. 153.
61. Jalal Alamgir, "Against the Current: The Survival of Authoritarianism in Burma", *Pacific Affairs*, vol.70, 1997, p.348.
62. Carlyle A. Thayer, "Southeast Asia : Challenges to unity and regional legitimacy", *Southeast Asian Affairs* , 1999, p.4.
63. Allen L Clark, "Myanmar's Present Development and Future Options", *Asian Survey*, vol.39,no.5,Sept/Oct 1999, p.784.
64. *The Irrawaddy*,vol. 6, no.4,August 31,1997.
65. J. Mohan Malik, " Myanmar's Role in Regional Security: Power or Pivot? *Contemporary Southeast Asia*, vol.19, no.1, June 1997, p.60.
66. Ibid.
67. David Steinberg, "Myanmar: Regional Relationship and Internal Concerns", *Southeast Asian Affairs* 1998, p.181.
68. Mark I. Brown & Mark Valencia, "Thailand: Resource Diplomacy in Indo-China and Myanmar", *Contemporary Southeast Asia* (Singapore), vol. 14. no. 4, March 1993, p.342.
69. Farzana Shakoor, "Burma: An Overview", *Pakistan Horizon* (Islamabad), vol.44, no.2, April 1991,p.68. Also see n. 59.
70. Chi-Shad Liang, " Burma's Relations with the People's Republic of China: From Delicate Friendship to Genuine Co-operation", in Peter Carey (ed.), *Burma: The Challenge*

of Change in a Divided Society (London: Macmillan, 1997), p.90.

71. Far Eastern Economic Review, *Asia 1990 Yearbook*, p.96.
72. n.10, p.41.
73. n.71.
74. FEER, *Asia 1994 Yearbook*, p.98.
75. The six Nobel Laureates included the exiled Tibetan leader, the Dalai Lama; South African Archbishop, Desmond Tutu; former Costa Rican President, Oscar Arias; Argentine human rights activist, Adolfor Perez Esquival; and Mairead Maguire and Betty Williams of Northern Ireland.
76. Mary Callahan, "Myanmar in 1994: New Dragon or Still Dragging", *Asian Survey*, vol. 35, no.2, February 1995, p.205.
77. Ibid, p.206.
78. Ibid.
79. Mary P. Callahan, "Burma in 1995: Looking Beyond the Release of Aung San Suu Kyi", *Asian Survey*, vol. 36, no. 2, February 1996, p.163.
80. FEER, *Asia 1996 Yearbook*, p.98.
81. *Far East and Australasia 2000* (London : Europa Publications,1999), p.759.
82. FEER, *Asia 2000 Yearbook*, p. 92.
83. Donald M. Seekins, "Burma in 1998: Little to Celebrate", *Asian Survey*, vol. 39, no. 1, January/February 1999, p.17.
84. The scholar talked with experts in Thailand in the months of January and February 2001.

7

Movement for Democracy in Myanmar: International Reaction - II

The above discussion clearly highlights how reactions came from the industrialised democracies and the ASEAN in regard to the movement for democracy and the military junta. Their views were quite diametrically opposed. While such were their reactions China and India acted differently. The following pages will clearly show how China so strongly stood by the military junta while India adopted an opportunistic policy sometimes with ambiguity while dealing with Myanmar.

7.1. Myanmar – China Relations after 1988

Myanmar's relation with China was never friendly before 1988 because of China's involvement in anti-Yangon activities of the communists and the ethnic insurgents. At that time China's role was that of an instigator creating political instability inside a sovereign country thus having a negative tag. However in the years since 1988 uprising there has been a tremendous change in the relationship between the two countries.

After the military take over in Myanmar its relations with China is marked by (i)frequent exchange of official visits from both sides;(ii)significant increase in bilateral volume of trade ; (iii) Myanmar's heavy dependence on China for arms supply ; (iv) increasing of China's participation in the developmental process of Myanmar; and (v) the expansion of

China's economic activities in India's Northeast through Myanmar. In October 1989 Lt.Gen.Khin Nyunt, SLORC's Secretary -1, paid an official visit to China at a time when Myanmar's military government was at its height of unpopularity. Again in August 1991 another important official visit was paid by General Saw Maung, Chairman of the SLORC. These important visits were reciprocated by the official visit of China's Premier Li Peng in December 1994. During the period of about 10 years there have been a series of high-level political, military and commercial delegations signifying closer ties between the two countries.

As already seen before, in the wake of the popular 'Uprising of 1988' the industrialised countries of West and Japan imposed economic sanctions on Myanmar for anti democratic activities and violation of human rights. These actions created a vacuum which was filled by China. First, China was desperately on the look out for markets for its cheap finished consumer goods; and secondly it became more interested in the contracts for extracting the country's rich natural resources like forest products, oil , gem and precious stones etc.

For a country like Myanmar where the application of modern technology is rare Chinese help for the installation of power generating plants was significant and on the other hand Myanmar could export raw materials like fish, timber and gemstones to the former[1]. The gradual opening of the Myanmarese economy and the country's increasing closeness towards China proved a boon for the latter. As a result, volume of trade between the two countries increased markedly including border trade. In fact, it was China who first formalised border trade with Myanmar. On 5 August 1989 an agreement was signed between Myanmar's Export Import Corp (MEIC) with its counterpart in Yunnan of Southern China[2]. At present the whole of upper Myanmar consisting of northern and central has become purely a Chinese economic zone or trade zone. It has further expanded, reaching South of Mandalay[3]. Mandalay is gradually taking the shape of a 'China town'. Not only this but in order to maximise its influence on the commercial sphere of Myanmar, China extended soft loans, technical know how and expertise and also help in infrastructure development projects. In August 1991, it gave a Rmb 50 million (US$ 9.3 million) interest free loan for unspecified economic projects[4]. Not only this but the two countries signed agreements in July 1993 on areas ranging from timber sales to the construction of hydroelectric power station in Northern Myanmar[5]. With the passage of time the volume of trade increased. Now trade transactions per year is worth about $ 1 billion [6]. But in the late 90s there were fluctuations in the volume of trade - in the fiscal year that ended in March 1999, it was valued at $418 million and accounted for 10.46 per cent of Myanmar's total foreign trade[7]. Percentage of border trade, however, increased.

Myanmar considers China as the main partner which provides it with its strategic needs. On the other hand China considers Myanmar as the medium through which it could fulfil its strategic aspirations in the region. Particularly it could keep an eye on India from a near angle through the Myanmarese army, the *tatmadaw*. With the unofficial arm embargo by Western countries, China became the only major country supplying defence materials as well as training to the junta regime. As a token of appreciation for the support extended to it at the time of its isolation by the world Myanmar started purchasing much of its military requirements from China. For example, "following the October 1989 visit of Lt.Gen. Khin Nyunt and Sr.Gen. Than Shwe to Beijing SLORC procured as much as US $ 1.2 billion worth of weapons from China - the largest arms deal in Myanmar history"[8]. It consisted of heavy military hard wares such as F-7 and F-6 fighter jets, medium tanks, multibarrelled anti-aircraft guns, 120 mm and 150mm howitzers, shoulder missiles, patrol boats, armoured personnel carriers and trucks[9]. The above agreement on military purchase done in August 1990 also included a training programme for some 400-600 Myanmarese personnel at army base and military colleges in nearby Yunnan [10]. Not only this but Chinese experts also helped Myanmar in upgrading its naval bases in

Sittwe, Yangon, and Mergui in 1992. Besides, within a few years another arms purchase agreement followed. China became the largest supplier in Myanmar's drive for modernising its army. In November 1994, SLORC concluded the second arms sale agreement with Beijing, amounting approximately to US $ 400 million[11]. Besides, Chinese experts were involved in the development of naval bases at Hianggyi Island and Coco Island.

In substance, China is trying to spread its sphere of influence in the region through Myanmar. It is also the effort of China to challenge the regional dominance of India in the Indian Ocean and to establish its supremacy as a dominant power in the region. Not only this but having an alliance with Myanmar also give the country a chance to have maintenance base for its large-scale maritime trade and subsidiary surveillance.

Now it is very clear that in order to maintain all its commercial and strategic gain China provided Myanmar with a sort of protection from international pressures caused by increasing lobbying of democratic forces. But the degree of gain is much more in favour of China. So, finally what emerges from the relationship, as Wayne Bert, an American Political Scientist, remarked, "is essentially realist, opportunistic approach that has as a priority the protection of China's security and economic interests by ensuring the presence of friendly neighbours on its immediate periphery"[12].

The improvement of relations between Myanmar and China has its repercussions on India and ASEAN in terms of threat perception. Many ASEAN countries and India are trying to balance the Chinese influence by giving certain concessions. Ultimately, it is an all win situation for the Myanmarese military regime in its fight against those supporting democratic transformation in the country.

7.2. India's Policy Towards Myanmar Since 1988

As already mentioned, India was among the first countries to extend help and support to the movement for democracy as a policy of the government. It was India's view that a democratic regime in Myanmar would be more sympathetic to India's national security interest. Myanmarese student dissidents who crossed over to India were given political asylum. Because of the assistance provided by India it was alleged by the junta that the Indian Embassy in Yangon was harbouring and instigating those involved in the uprising. This was true to a great extent[13]. India's sympathetic attitude towards the opposition was also reflected in the broadcast of the Myanmarese service of All India Radio (AIR), which had overtaken even the BBC's Myanmar Service in popularity. Dissidents were allowed to organise public demonstration and protest movement for the cause in India much to the chagrin of the military regime. Besides, many of the prominent political leaders and national level organisations and associations also provided patronage to these supporters of the Myanmar democracy movement. The former Defence Minister of India, Mr. George Fernandez himself is a strong supporter. The late Mr. Rajiv Gandhi, during his tenure as Prime Minister, also supported the movement. In substance, in the initial stage of the democracy movement in Myanmar India gave full support and encouragement to it from the government as well as the public. At that time the government followed a clear-cut policy on the issue as compared with other nations and much to the displeasure of the junta. India was in the forefront in demanding for the release of Aung San Suu Kyi and many other political prisoners languishing in the jails of the country.

However, in the mid 90s, a gradual shift occurred in the attitude of the Government of India towards the military junta. The change in the stance of India became imperative with the changing strategic, economic, and security concerns. Of all the imperatives, the China factor[14] became the most important one. No doubt the question of internal security, particularly the insurgency in the Northeast India, the problem of narcotics and trade and commercial gains were other considerations which compelled to change India's policy towards Myanmar which was at the cost of the movement for democracy.

Containment of Chinese influence in the region remains always an objective of India's foreign policy that cannot be played down lightly. Increasing Chinese influence over Myanmar is no doubt a disadvantage to India.

After the widespread protest of 1988, relations between China and Myanmar became cordial and co-operative, as we have noted while discussing the relations between the two countries. The fast improvement of relations between the two, Chinese sale of military hardware, extension of aid for both military and of development including Chinese help in building monitoring and surveillance facilities quite close to Andaman and Nicobar islands, Myanmar's repeated encouragement to the insurgent groups in India 's Northeast were largely responsible for the Government of India to reverse its earlier stand.

Another important imperative to reverse India's policy is the increasing narco-trade which flourishes in the states bordering Myanmar. This supply of drug which originated from Eastern and Northern Myanmar, particularly Shan areas, entered the border states of Manipur, Nagaland and Mizoram and then spread throughout the country[15]. Besides the traditional drugs like opium and its derivative heroin, some new synthetic drugs also surfaced in the narco markets in the 90's. These synthetic drugs viz 'methamphetamines'[16] and 'ecstasy', started entering into India in large quantity, as it is much cheaper and easier to produce. During this period the flow of drug in India from Myanmar increased because of large-scale production and multiplication of refineries quite close to the border areas[17]. Efforts for curbing and curtailing their trade have become a big headache for India. This menace, according to experts, could only be curbed with the help of the Myanmarese government.

Then there is also the ever-increasing insurgency problem in the Northeast India. States like Assam, Manipur, Nagaland and Tripura are under the strong grip of insurgency. Most of their insurgency groups whether it may be the United Liberation Front of Assam, National Socialist Council of Nagalim(Issac-Muivah) and National Socialist Council of

Nagalim (Khaplang), Tripura National Volunteers (now nearly defunct), National Liberation Front of Tripura, or Revolutionary Peoples' Front (formerly Peoples' Liberation Army) and United National Liberation Front of Manipur, had their camps for the last many years inside Myanmar- with or without the consent of the government of that country. Many of these groups which were mostly in that country had links with Karen National Union (KNU), Shan State Army (SSA) and Kachin Independence Army (KIA) up to the mid 90's. Therefore, containment of insurgency in Northeast India highly calls for mutual ccoperation between the two countries. This does not mean that India does not want to take advantage for commercial gains. Particularly in the areas of logging, mineral extraction, and capturing market for India's finished goods, mainly industrial goods, also pushed it towards developing the relationship. India was eager to tap the energy resources of the country- petroleum and hydroelectric power.

To fulfil the above objectives, it became necessary to improve bilateral relations between the two countries at the cost of the movement of democracy. Therefore, from the mid 90's India's stand towards Myanmar started softening contrary to the expectation of the democracy groups living in India. Exchange of delegations and exchange visits of high level officials, signing agreements and memoranda, and steps for improving border trade become frequent government business.

The first step to develop relationship between India and Myanmar after the 1988 uprising was taken up when a delegation of the Myanmar Foreign Office was received in August 1992. The delegation which was led by the Director General of Myanmar Foreign Office held discussion with the Indian officials and also " identified concrete areas for bilateral cooperation including border trade, preventing of narco-trafficking and contacts between the civilian and military authorities in the border regions of the two countries to prevent illegal activities"[18]. Initiatives also were taken up on the part of India to develop a better working relationship with the Myanmar government. The reciprocal as well as official visit to the country was made by a delegation led by the then Foreign Secretary of India, Mr. J.N.Dixit, in March 1993[19]. Discussion was made on issues already taken up in the earlier meeting. However, one significant development this time was the initiatives taken up for a border trade agreement. In the same visit, on 30 March, an agreement for reducing and preventing illicit trafficking in narcotic drugs and psychotropic substances and related matters was signed between the two countries[20]. The year 1994 also brought more positive changes in the relationship between Myanmar and India. Some major re-evaluation in the Indian foreign policy could be observed. An MOU was signed in January at the secretary level to concretise border trade between the two. Initiatives were underway to open a border crossing at Moreh (Manipur State) from Indian side and Tamu (Sagaing Division) from Myanmar side. In May the same year, the Indian Army Chief, Gen. Bipin Chandra Joshi, visited Yangon – the first of its kind – to discuss matters related with insurgency and other security related issues with his counterparts. Resultantly, a joint counter-insurgency operation consisting of Indian and Myanmarese army known as 'Operation Golden Bird' was launched in 1995 in the Indo-Myanmar borders thus busting many Indian insurgent bases. Most of these Northeast insurgents later shifted camps to Bhutan and Bangladesh. During the year 1994 several Indian officials and trade delegations visited Myanmar. In all their visits the main area of discussion focussed on 'better border management' which in turn covered issues like insurgency , terrorism, narcotic trade and boundary issue. And on 12 April 1995 the Moreh-Tamu trade post was inaugurated jointly by Trade Minister of Myanmar , Lt.Gen. Tun Kyi and Commerce Minister of India, Mr. P. Chidambaram. This was a landmark in Indo-Myanmar trade relationship bringing a free flow of goods in each other's country. And to further trade relationship between the two in particular and in the regional level in general both India and Myanmar took part as members in formation of an economic alliance called 'Bangladesh, India, Myanmar,

Sri Lanka and Thailand Economic Co-operation' (BIMST-EC) in 1996.

The area of relationship between the two countries was broadened with the visit of India's Foreign Secretary K. Raghunath to Yangon in March 1999. The Hindu (new Delhi) of 3 March 1999, observed,

"The Foreign Secretary, Mr. K. Raghunath, who was in Yangon recently addressed the entire canvas of Indo-Myanmar relationship, with co-operation in the sectors of power, hydrocarbon, railways, highway construction, border trade and counter-insurgency emerging as priority issues."

This developing relationship was further enhanced with the signing of the multi-faceted agreement at the Indo-Myanmar sectoral level meeting in the Indian State of Nagaland in November the same year. "According to the agreement, construction of the Tamu-Kalewa-Kalemyo road in Myanmar with Indian assistance, navigational survey on the Kaleidan river link between Mizoram and Myanmar, maintenance of boundary pillars and building up of necessary infrastructure at the Champai-Reh Trade Centre (Mizoram sector) will be completed. The meeting agreed to open four trade centres in Nagaland to facilitate barter"[21].

With the approach of the new millennium Indo-Myanmar relationship move towards a much more pragmatic and co-operative front. The year 2001 is a very significant year for Myanmar in terms of its relation with India. In February, India's Foreign Minister, Jaswant Singh, visited Myanmar – the first by an Indian minister since the uprising of 1988. He inaugurated the 165 Km long Tamu-Kalewa-Kalemyo Road linking to India's national highway No. 39 on 13 February. This road costing 90 crores constructed by the Border Road Organisation (BRO) of India was a gift to Myanmar as a token of the improving relationship[22]. The road which will link Northeast India[23] to Myanmar and Southeast Asia also reflects the goodwill India would get in Myanmar. Besides, it is sure to speed up the flow of trade between the two countries and to some extent tourism industry also. Thus with this visit of Jaswant Singh the formalisation process has more or less been complete. And, here, it will not be wrong to say that in recent times India has opted for promoting constructive engagement policy towards Myanmar but with greater options.

These changes in the policy of government of India do not mean that India has completely abandoned those who were fighting for restoration of democracy in Myanmar. Still, when all these co-operation and exchange were going on between the two countries, India also went ahead with its initiatives for supporting the democracy movement. It allowed the dissidents to remain in the country without fear despite repeated demand for extradition of many of them from the side of Myanmar authorities. In 1995, Aung San Suu Kyi was conferred the Jawaharlal Nehru Award for International Understanding, considered to be one of the highest international awards conferred by the Government of India. This was given at a time when measures were taken up for improving relationship between New Delhi and Yangon. India government also supported all the United Nations resolutions demanding restoration of democracy in Myanmar and criticising human rights violation of the junta regime.

No doubt democracy supporters considered the effort on the part of the government of India to make an amicable and balanced approach to the issue of improving relation with the regime while supporting the democracy movement ambiguous and contradictory. They felt that the two couldn't go together. Signing trade agreement with the regime while giving the Jawaharlal Nehru Award to Aung San Suu Kyi is meaningless. However according to experts like Mohan Malik, a working relationship with the Myanmar government is no longer seen as undermining India's support for the 'democratic aspirations of the Myanmar people'[24]. In fact, all these changes in the foreign policy is carried out because of the national interest of the country based on its security and commercial needs. This has nothing to do with sidelining the democracy issue of Myanmar as India, being one of the largest democracy, is very much conscious and support the genuine democratic aspiration of the Myanmarese people.

But ultimately India's foreign policy towards Myanmar since 1988 could be divided into three sections – first, strongly critical of the junta regime; secondly, gradual move towards neutrality; and finally, increasing inclination towards the regime.

7.3. Asean, EU and the United States Triangle

An important outcome of the movement for democracy in Myanmar is a conflict between ASEAN on one side and European Union and United States of America on the other. EU and US was well aware that it has got no pragmatic leverage or mechanism against the SLORC regime in bringing a democratic transformation in Myanmar. Both, therefore, tried to persuade ASEAN in the early 90s - particularly 1991 and 1992 - to intervene for a democratic change in that country. However, ASEAN remained insisting on its general policy of constructive engagement which gave preference to a more quiet, conciliatory diplomatic approach[25]. The members were not ready to press upon for the western democratic values as insisted by the United States and the European Union in Myanmar as it could not be adjusted with their authoritarian governments of the East which is based on maximum non-interference. Countries like Singapore, Malaysia and Indonesia even suggested that Western demands for democratic transformation might risk Myanmar plunging into an abyss of violence and destabilisation[26]. Myanmar's SLORC regime took advantage of these soft policies and attitude. It was able to take advantage of ASEAN's style of working on the basis of consensus reached. It knew that ASEAN was much more concerned with conflict avoidance among its members as well as in the region rather than conflict resolution. In fact, controversial subjects were always set aside by ASEAN[27]; and Myanmar's case was not an exception.

The Myanmar issue created complications for both

parties in dealing with each other. With the failure to bring any democratic change in Myanmar EU and US started putting more pressure on ASEAN, the only forum which the two considered, could pressurise the military junta. The Association on its part did not want to provoke US and the European Union while supporting Myanmar at the same time. This put it to a dilemma. However, understanding the importance of each other both sections made certain relaxation from time to time to make normal dealing possible though they remain stuck to their principle stands. A departure from its earlier policy, ASEAN made the unified approach to encourage the US to maintain a military presence in the region[28]. At the same time in the ASEAN Foreign Ministers' Meeting in Manila in July 1992 - attended by US, EU and Japan as dialogue partners - E.U. addressed ASEAN as an economically vibrant bloc and as such should have respect for human rights[29]. This includes Myanmar's case also. United States subscribed to this view. As a result complicacy emerged because of the presence of Myanmarese delegations at the meeting. This became a conflicting point for the otherwise smoothly going meeting. The same issue dogged in most meetings between ASEAN, E.U. and U.S. in the following years. Myanmar became a point of discord among these groups which affected economic and political relations. The issue once again flared up in the same ministerial level meeting in Bangkok in 1994. This time, however, U.S. and Western countries tried to bring some changes in Myanmar by softening its stand towards the same under its broader policy of 'critical dialogue'. U.S. and U.K. sent their emissaries Thomas C. Hubbard, Deputy Assistant Secretary of State for East Asian and Pacific, and David Dain, Assistant Under Secretary of State, respectively to Yangon. Nothing came out of it. And what was more irritating for the West was the firm decision of ASEAN not to interfere in the internal affairs of its member-states while following 'constructive engagement policy'. Thus in most of the successive meetings, prior to Myanmar's entry to ASEAN, arguments and counter arguments followed. In 1995, when

Aung San Suu Kyi was released US and EU expected some positive change in the country which was not to be. And as such the existing tension continued. But the peculiarity remained that despite its protest against Myanmar's existing political turmoil and subjugation of democratic forces United States and E.U. always goes back to its reconciliatory stand in its relations with ASEAN. For example, in the ASEAN Foreign Minister's Meeting in Jakarta in July 1996 when EU and US expressed their unhappiness with the effort of ASEAN to take Myanmar into its fold. There was strong reaction from the ASEAN. Indonesian Foreign Minister, Ali Alatas, who was also Chairman of the ASEAN Standing Committee, even went to extent of saying, "This is our organisation, not theirs"[30]. Here the Western group took a reconciliatory stand. A European official said that the E.U. did not think any issue should be allowed to get in the way of its developing relationship with Southeast Asia[31]. Developing relationship with Southeast Asia particularly with the regional powers remain a priority for economic and security reasons. However, changes could be seen in the ASEAN, EU and USA triangular relationship in the later half of the 90's.

As the time of Myanmar's entry to ASEAN approached the tussle of US and EU with ASEAN became more intense and complicated. Because of intense lobbying from democratic groups US and EU increased its degree of pressure on ASEAN not to accept Myanmar's membership. But ASEAN wanted to go ahead with its objective of unifying all the states in the region despite knowing fully the shortcoming. This resulted in mud throwing and threat between the two interest groups. Despite knowing the negative impact it may create in their relation with ASEAN in general E.U. and U.S. started exerting more pressure on Myanmar by adding other forms of sanctions to the already existing ones. The European Union was prompt in this direction. Besides the already existing arms embargo, announced in July 1991, and suspension of foreign aid in 1993, European Union in October 1996 imposed a broad ban on Myanmar's military and high level officials and their relatives from entering into member states[32]. Not only this but in March 1997 it also revoked the 'preferential trade benefits' for Myanmar's industrial and agricultural exports to the E.U. under the Union's 'Generalised System of Preferences'[33]. The confrontationist attitude and indifference to international democratic norms shown by the country infuriated the United States more. Besides, the indication by SLORC leaders that they were ready to face any eventuality as they got support from its neighbours, particularly the ASEAN members and also the indifference of ASEAN to the issue could not be tolerated by it. The sanctions and punitive actions taken up by the United States against the regime of Myanmar were more severe than any other group or country. EU's ban of Myanmar's officials was a follow up step of the U.S. action. On 3 October 1996 the United States imposed ban on all Myanmar's government officials, both military and civil and also on all persons who implement or benefit from policies that impede Myanmar's transition to democracy and also their immediate family members from entering in its territory[34]. As already mentioned, this was preceded by the law known as 'Cohen-Feinstein Law' passed by the US Congress which give the President the power to impose a ban on new US investment in Myanmar if the political situation in that country deteriorates. And in fact this was announced in April 1997 by the then US President Bill Clinton and was formalised by an executive order on 20 May 1997. All these sanctions were imposed immediately after the harsh crackdown on NLD by the SLORC regime in September 1996. It was a setback for Myanmar in particular and the ASEAN in general. In doing so the main objective was to prevent Myanmar's entry to ASEAN till some improvement in its political situation. However, there was an urgency for the country on its part to enter ASEAN so that it could have legitimacy charade in the international arena. This, EU and US knew and as such, wanted to use the same association as leverage against Myanmar. But both of them failed to persuade ASEAN to follow their line as it was more concerned with its objective of having a combined regional economic block in the form of

ASEAN-10. And to the chagrin of the democracy supporters, Myanmar was accepted as a full-fledged member of ASEAN, with Laos, on 23 July 1997, at a grand ceremony in Subang Jaya, Malaysia.

The entry of Myanmar to ASEAN worsened the association's relation with EU and US in a much greater scale. Already existing ban and sanctions also became harsher. It had far reaching impact. In a way, deteriorating relations of ASEAN with EU and the United States in the post July 1997 period i.e. after Myanmar's entry to ASEAN, was no longer confined in verbal duel but it extended to threats put to real practice. Myanmar became a headache for the association. In November 1997, the EU objected to Myanmar's participation in the EU-ASEAN Joint Cooperation Committee Meeting in Bangkok as a member of ASEAN. The request of the ASEAN Secretariat in favour of Myanmar was rejected by EU. But, at the same time the association "refused to relent to the EU demand to downgrade Myanmar's participation to that of attending informally in a passive capacity"[35]. Its emphasis on Myanmar's participation is based on its principle of consistency and non-discrimination among its members. Consequently the meeting was indefinitely postponed. Not only was this but a schedule EU - ASEAN Meeting in Berlin in March 1999 also was delayed over the same issue of Myanmar attendance[36]. Myanmar was not allowed to participate in any joint meeting of ASEAN, EU and US held in EU countries. Myanmar could not attend for existence of broad ban on its entry.

The worsening of relations between ASEAN, on the one side, and the US and EU countries, on the other, compelled some of the member countries of the former to express the need for a reassessment of ASEAN's policy towards Myanmar based on "constructive engagement". The existing stalemate did not prove helpful for the region. Coupled with it was the prevalent economic crisis which led to more political turbulence in the region for a while. As such in the ASEAN Foreign Ministers Meeting of July 1998 in Manila the then Thai Foreign Minister Surin pleaded for "flexible engagement". The proposal emphasised the need to involve directly in reforming the political situation of each country or to use its influence directly wherever necessary. Though it was not acceptable to majority of the members it, at least, forced the member of this association to rethink. In fact a new concept known as 'enhance interaction', something between the non-interference policy of constructive engagement and direct involvement policy of flexible engagement, became the basis of working for the regional grouping in place of its earlier existing traditional concept. ASEAN, as a whole does not want the existing stalemate to continue as it was proving harmful for the greater interest of the region. For example, Malaysian Prime Minister who was a strong supporter of Myanmar's membership visited Yangon in March, the same year and stunned his Myanmarese host by emphasising the friendship with the EU as a significant factor for ASEAN[37]. Initiative to end the dead lock was taken up by ASEAN.

The deadlock between ASEAN and EU which started since the entry of Myanmar to ASEAN was partially broken on 27 July 1999 when foreign ministers from ASEAN, including Myanmar, and the EU sat at the same negotiating table to discuss future joint meetings of the two groups to be held in Europe. However, in the view of the political scenario in Myanmar whether it will be agreeable for EU to lift the existing sanction over the country so that the meetings could be held in Europe is really doubtful. And that the return of the previous positive relations between the two groups very soon, even if the meetings are possible, is something highly questionable.

The problem for ASEAN is not confined only to the above ones with EU .The tension with the United States over Myanmar still dogged. It is really difficult for the regional grouping to face two giant sections of the world forming important parts of the international politics. In spite of having a need for improving relations with ASEAN, the United States continued with its sanctions over Myanmar as well indirect criticism of ASEAN for its soft stand towards the military grouping and for its indifferent attitude towards the showdown between Aung San Suu Kyi and the Myanmar's regime on the bridge incident of July 1998 and similar one in August-September 2000. In the ASEAN Ministerial Meeting in Manila in July 1998 the U.S. Secretary of State Madeline Albright brought up the issue of human rights violation and lack of political transformation in the country. US also expressed its outrage when heavy crackdown was carried out over NLD executives and Suu Kyi in September 2000. In July the same year, the U.S. Senate passed a resolution reaffirming the support for Suu Kyi, the NLD and the newly formed the Committee Representing the People's Parliament[38]. The resolution was introduced by Senators Moynihan and McConnell.

In spite of all these attempts the impasse between US-EU and the ASEAN still continues though complete separation is also not possible. Despite all the sanctions imposed upon by the West against Myanmar it is undeniable that ASEAN is the only group which can influence Myanmar. No doubt the admission of Myanmar into ASEAN has acquired a 'legitimacy shield' for the military junta to rule. The admission has invited international criticism against it. ASEAN, US and EU on their part also need to give a positive support to ASEAN in its effort to follow enhanced interaction policy towards Myanmar. A clear understanding among the three parties is a must for a successful democratic transformation in Myanmar. The dialogue initiated between Suu Kyi and the SPDC due to the effort of EC in Jan-Feb, 2001 might be recognised as a positive step though it is questionable whether it is done seriously or not.

7.4. Japan and the Present Political Scenario of Myanmar

Understanding Japanese attitude towards Myanmar is imperative for various reasons: Among the industrialised countries, Japan made maximum contribution to the economic development of Myanmar. It is the largest contributor of financial assistance. Seventy per cent of the amount Myanmar receives in the name of Official Development Assistance (ODA) comes from Japan. Japan's Official Development Assistance enabled the country to suffer less during the days of its isolationist policy. On the other hand Japan uses ODA as a principal means of exerting its influence abroad[39]. However, with the massive crackdown of the popular uprising in 1988, an unprecedented strained relation developed between Japan and Myanmar. Like many of the major democracies, Japan suspended its aid allocation to Myanmar just after the bloody crackdown of August 1988. Though it gave formal recognition to SLORC on 17 February 1989 and resumed aid for uncompleted projects yet no major change in the relationship could be seen. It continued giving aids for the incomplete projects based on past agreements. However, no new agreement was further signed. Japan explained that the main reason for the resumption of aid was to convince the SLORC regime towards a peaceful change through friendly persuasion. During this period it followed a policy which lies between policies followed by the US and EU on one side and ASEAN on the other[40]. Though it remained critical of the human rights situation, it refrained from advocating a hard line[41]. However, this middle path did not help in changing the attitude of the junta.

Japan toughened its stand in dealing with the military rulers of Myanmar. It also became more vocal in its demand for a democratic change in the country. Neither could it be pressurised by business groups to resume fresh aid. At certain stages, Japan announced that it would not extend any new investment to Myanmar so long as SLORC was in power. Japan did not make any new commitment or ODA since November 1987. i.e. before the SLORC government was established[42]. Watanabe Michio, the new Foreign Minister, promptly called upon the SLORC to recognise the results of the election of 1990 and allow the elected members to form a parliament[43]. The Japanese government also repeatedly appealed for the release of Aung San Suu Kyi so that it became easier to resume aid without losing face[44]. So, the demand for a democratic reform in Myanmar increased from the

Japanese side taking into consideration its business interest in the long run. This, in turn, indirectly helped those struggling for the restoration of democracy for, Japan was one country which could exercise maximum influence on Myanmar. It also had more access to its top military officials. On the other hand Myanmar considered Japan a role model of Asian success[45]. It never considered Japan posing a military threat. These factors gave favourable ground to Japan for influencing in the affairs of the country. In this backdrop it was the common belief among experts that the opening of a dialogue between Junta and Suu Kyi in 1994 and the consequent release of Suu Kyi in July 1995 was because of Japanese insistence.

While the above developments took place there was an increasing pressure on the Japanese Government from its business circle for resumption of aid. There was a controversy going on between the government policy and the business interests of Japan in its dealing with the Myanmarese affairs which still continues till now. Though the Japanese government followed the policy of the West, particularly that of the United States in suspending economic aid, there was immense pressure from its business groups. Their main argument was based on the apprehension that the sanction would deprive them of the benefits from the rich natural resources and vast business market of Myanmar. As such they wanted the resumption of economic aid to the country. Maximum pressure came from *Keidanren*, the apex umbrella organisation of Japanese companies. It even sent a mission to Myanmar in June 1994 to assess the situation of the country. The members were given a warm welcome by the military rulers. The Japanese government tried to find adequate ground for resuming aid. The point to remember is that Japan, though firm in its demand for the restoration of democracy, strongly desired to resume aid. And, as such when Aung San Suu Kyi was released in July 1995 Japan was quick to resume humanitarian assistance on a project-by-project basis. Actually Japanese government wanted its assistance to resume much beyond humanitarian assistance. However, the situation created by Suu's release alone was not adequate. Besides, it did not want to attract criticism from its Western business partners. It announced that the continuation of its humanitarian assistance to Myanmar did not mean that it would automatically resume its ODA compulsorily. Over and above this Aung San Suu Kyi, immediately after her release requested Japan not to rush in for aid in her country without assessing the actual situation. Her opinion also carried weight.

In the later half of the 90's there was not much improvement in the Japan- Myanmar relations. Japan remained stuck to its emphasis on democratisation and civilian rule in the country. To create the ground for such change in 1996 it attempted to play a mediating role between Myanmar and the West and also between the SLORC and Aung San Suu Kyi[46]. Not only this policy of the government but the "Japanese business groups were also poised to enter Myanmar in a big way but for the moment engaged in 'NATO' (No Action, Talk Only) exercise while waiting for Tokyo to reopen. Overseas Development Assistance, a step that the Foreign Ministry explicitly linked to progress SLORC would have to make in the political front"[47]. The government was strongly against any act of SLORC which ran counter to the democratisation in Myanmar. And, despite strong desire to expand business in Myanmar, many Japanese companies refrained from full-scale investment until the government resumed its ODA. The policy is still maintained. Despite all these, the government still showed its desire to resume aid beyond just humanitarian aid only if the military regime in Myanmar was willing to have a dialogue with the opposition and Suu and also if SLORC changed its political rigidity.

By the late 1990s Japan started giving some non-humanitarian aid under pretext of humanitarian support of Myanmar though it may not be considered as actual ODA. In February 1998 it decided to release Y 2.5 billion for improvement of Yangon's Mingladon airport, which was only a small part of the Y 27 billion originally approved before 1998[48]. However, to repulse criticism from the world community, Japanese government strongly reiterated not to give new aid before democratisation of the country. It also urged the newly formed SPDC to open dialogue with Suu Kyi so that it might move towards gradual normalisation. Despite this the fact remained that fund did start to flow into the country from Japan. Some experts were not ready to consider this fund as nothing less than a form of ODA. Besides, a change could also be seen in dealing with Japan's big business community - the *Keidanren*. The *Keidanren* had already established its office in Yangon after its effort for improvement of relationship with Myanmar started since 1994. And because of this improvement in the business and softening of stand on the part of the Government of Japan towards Myanmar large companies started large investment in the country. For example, Mitsubishi Corporation announced to provide US $ 70 million by the end of July 2000 for building a floating storage off-loading facility for the Yatagon Off shore Oil and Natural Gas Project in Myanmar[49]. Likewise Marubeni and Nissho Iwai financed the operation and construction of S& K Mine at Monywa, Upper Myanmar, for extracting copper, which cost up to US $ 389 million[50]. Since 1998, the softening policy of the country towards Myanmar was also well indicated by the Japanese Premier Keizo Obuchi's meeting with General Than Shwe in ASEAN summit in Manila in November 1998[51]. This was the first meeting in fifteen years between the highest Chief Executives of the two countries, a significant occasion.

Thus, in the whole, there were signs of improvement in the Myanmar Japan relationship though the process of democratisation in Myanmar remained to be realised; and that there was no official resumption of ODA. The chances, however, brightened with improvement of bilateral relationship between the two countries. Japan becomes closer to Myanmar while the West distanced themselves criticising Myanmar for its violation of human rights. Japan, like ASEAN, also started to believe that it could transform Myanmar by dealing with the military regime of the country in a positive and constructive way. Finally, it is the belief among experts that only Japan can play an important role in bringing democratic transformation of the country.

7.5. United Nations Effort for Political Transformation

At the other level it is the desire of the United Nations to end the ongoing conflict between the ruling junta regime and the supporters of democracy and bring a democratic transformation in Myanmar. Soon after the election of May 1990, which was won by the National League for Democracy (NLD) with a landslide majority, it was the demand of the United Nations that power should be transferred to the popularly elected representatives of the people by the country's military regime. Further, the UN criticised the regime for not implementing yet their commitment towards democracy, which it initiated with the holding of elections in 1990. It also reiterated the need for taking up steps towards restoration of democracy fully respecting the will of the people[52]. Various resolutions had been passed from time to time in this direction in the UN General Assembly.

As the involvement of the United Nations became unavoidable in the Myanmarese affairs the international body adopted both persuasive measures and direct or coercive measures. At the same time, for carrying out these measures the UN was involved at two levels , one at the institutional level and the other at the personal or individual level. At the institutional level the main actors were the General Assembly and UN agencies like the United Nations High Commissioner for Refugees (UNHCR), the United Nations Commission on Human Rights (UNCHR), the International Labour Organisation (ILO) and the United Nations Development Programme (UNDP). At the personal or individual level it was the Secretary General and his good offices which was strongly involved in the effort for a transition to democracy. The combined efforts of the two were largely responsible for the release of Aung San Suu Kyi in 1995 from house arrest.

As already mentioned, in the years following the '88 Uprising' UN agencies attempted for bringing a peaceful transition to power. The United Nations Commission on Human Rights (UNCHR), one of the premier agencies concerned with determining human rights condition and safeguarding them all over the world, gave due attention to what was happening in the country. It started sending special rapporteurs to monitor and report the actual happening or condition in Myanmar. Prof. Sadako Ogata, who was appointed UN High Commissioner for Human Rights, was the first UN Rapporteur to be sent to the country- in 1990. She submitted her report in February 1991. " The outcome of the resolution by the UNCHR that expressed concern over the continued detention of a number of politicians, including leaders of the NLD"[53]. However, with the resignation of Sadako Ogata and the increasing incidents of human rights violations in Myanmar the UNCHR in March 1992 adopted yet another strong resolution in this regard. Through this agency the UN again and again pressurised the regime to improve its human rights record, but of no avail. Prof. Yazo Yokota was appointed as the new Special Rapporteur, which in turn was rejected by the SLORC. Despite the rejection he visited the country every year to monitor the human rights condition in the country, till he was relieved from the job. In October1995, he was also able to meet Aung San Suu Kyi. However, he was barred from visiting Myanmar's jails despite repeated requests though numerous accounts of human rights violations and torture could be gathered from former inmates[54]. The effort continued further by the new rapporteur, Rajsoomer Lallah. In November 1997, he pointed out in his report about the continuing extra-judicial activities and the absence of necessary steps towards a democratic transformation[55]. Here, what needs to be observed is that the reports of all these rapporteurs on Myanmar pointed at the government for human rights violations with little sign of improvement. The agency remained undeterred despite many restrictions placed on it by the junta in its work in the country.

The office of the United Nations High Commissioner for Refugees (UNHCR) is also involved in another important aspect i.e., by giving asylum to many student activists and many others, who had fled Myanmar to escape the harassment of the regime . Many were granted refugee status and given protection by the agency. It was also concerned with proper settlement of the displaced groups, including students and ethnic groups like Mons, Karens and Rohingyas. It was only through their negotiations with the junta that these groups were sent back to their original places. In November 1993 a Memorandum of Understanding (MOU) was signed between the SLORC and the UNHCR concerning the repatriation of an estimated 2,50,000 Rohingyas from Bangladesh to Rakhine state[56]. However, this initiative, received strong criticism from the world public as it failed to take into consideration the welfare and safety questions related with the repatriated refugees. It was blamed for short sightedness and also having played a double standard i.e., agreeing to the demands of the junta in the name of taking care for the welfare of the Rohingya refugees. The meaning of 'refugee' as used by UNHCR is also sometimes questionable. All these created policies contradictory in practice and thus affecting the security of the refugees, even though returned to their places. Despite the setbacks, which formed a small part of the routine work of UNHCR, the fact remained that the agency is very much involved in taking care of the thousands of displaced Myanmarese staying in the bordering areas of Myanmar's neighbours, particularly that of Thailand and Bangladesh; to some extent India also. International Labour Organisation (ILO) is another UN agency which was helping the United Nations system in pressurising the Myanmarese government for a change towards democracy and civilian rule. It made all its efforts to safeguard the rights and improve the working conditions of the workers and labourers in the country. It also protested against the use of forced labour which is a gross denial of minimum human rights. It also became an important international forum for Myanmarese democracy groups, particularly NCGUB and FTUB, to transcend the views of the general masses in Myanmar, under the rule of the military. In June 1999, ILO instead of continued protests rejected Myanmar outright[57].

A draft resolution protesting the violation of labour rights in the country was adopted by member states. As a part of it ILO prohibited any further participation by Myanmar in its activities and banned ILO technical assistance[58]. Thus ILO has its own way of pressurising the regime, the present SPDC.

The aforesaid accounts clearly points out the fact that many of the agencies of the UN system worked for restoring normalcy as well as for restoring democracy in the country, though different strategies were adopted by each of them. However, the most important catalytic agent in this direction was the office of the Secretary General. It was because of the effort of the Secretary General and his office that some flexibility could be seen in the existing deadlock between the opposition democracy groups and the regime. Besides continuous demands on the government for a change, the Secretary General also sent emissaries from time to time to bring forth a meaningful negotiation between the two opposite sides through dialogue. In December 1993, after passing the resolution calling for Suu Kyi's release and the creation of a democratic government based on 1990 election results for the third time, the UN General Assembly, for the first time, requested the Secretary General to assist in implementing the resolution[59]. Consequently, in November 1994, Rafeeddin Ahmed, a UN Under Secretary General was sent to Yangon on behalf of the Secretary General Boutros Boutros Ghali, to appeal for the release of Aung San Suu Kyi from house arrest. Ahmed met Myanmarese officials but was not allowed to meet Suu Kyi. Likewise, few years back, in 1998, Alvaro de Soto, the UN Assistant Secretary General for Political Affairs, visited Yangon two times in January and October to convey the desire of the Secretary General for a meaningful dialogue between the junta and Aung San Suu Kyi[60]. In the later visit of October he was able to meet Suu as well as top generals of the SPDC. The present Secretary General Kofi Annan himself also talked with SPDC Chairman Than Shwe in the ASEAN Summit Meet in Kuala Lumpur in 1997. This genuine desire of the UN Secretary General towards the solution of deadlock still continues.

The working style of the United Nations in connection with Myanmar was not, however, without criticism. The foremost problem with the UN was that despite all the positive measures, both persuasive as well as coercive, it failed to realise the concrete goals the UN wanted. Contradictions also came about in its way e.g. funds under the United Nations Development Programmes continued to flow to the junta government at a time when some of its agencies were arbitrarily stopped by the junta government from having free passage to the country thus creating hurdle in free assessment of situation. The denial itself forecast the ulterior motive of the junta not to transfer power. The apprehension of a Chinese veto against any UN resolution also existed among UN policy makers. Above all these, in most cases, it seems that the Myanmar government was not ready to accept any of the recommendation of the UN in real practice though in principle they acted as if they welcome it. But all these setbacks could not deter the massive work carried out by UN and its related agencies for the general masses of Myanmar and the ongoing democracy movement. It continued with its effort for a democratic transition in Myanmar, though a multifaceted approach was followed. The strong action taken against the military government with the first UN Resolution of 1991 that called up on the SLORC (now SPDC) Government "to ensure the foundation of a democratic government", continued every year till today[61]. But still, after all these observations the degrees of success on the part of UN in Myanmar remains a big question; the answer of which would not be easy to give. Its new policy of 'dollar for democracy' also failed to bear much result.

7.6. Problems and Prospects of the Movement in the International Context

The above discussion dealing with reactions to the movement for democracy in Myanmar clearly shows that opinions are divided specially between the West represented by the industrialised democracies on the one hand and the East specially represented by the ASEAN and China on the other. During the last ten years or so one can see changes taking place in relation to the movement for democracy in Myanmar in which industrialised West including the United States were trying to find policies and programme conducive for restoring democracy and normalcy in Myanmar, while many of the major Asian and neighbouring countries of Myanmar tried to improve relations with the ruling junta through diplomatic, strategic and economic ties, the main being China and ASEAN countries. Japan too resumed with its earlier stand of giving aid though under the pretext of humanitarian related programmes. Thus lack of positive action on the part of those countries which have got maximum leverage over Myanmar makes it very difficult for the supporters of the movement to concretise their measures into pragmatic results. Even the United Nations, could not take up direct strong action against the country because of the apprehension of a Chinese veto. Besides, many of the Southeast Asian leaders were not in favour of the western type of democracy as envisaged by Aung San Suu Kyi and her supporters. This may be because of the existence of military based authoritarian political systems in most of the Southeast Asian countries. Not only that, even democratic country like Singapore, for example, looked at Myanmar's problems in a different vision. The senior leader of Singapore, Lee Kuan Yew, even went to the extent of saying that Aung San Suu Kyi is not suitable to lead Myanmar. In this mind-set among leaders of Asian countries with some exception, it became really difficult to incorporate more democratic ideas. Ultimately, the fact in this context of Myanmar remains that two different groups with different interests still work. Countries which could have helped in bringing about democracy have already attached their priority to national interest at the cost of democratic values. In this situation it has become really difficult for those struggling for democracy in Myanmar to make a meaningful impact in the international context. The necessary support from regional powers, most needed for the cause, is not forthcoming. Though some exception from time to time did exist. The fear of Chinese influence is also making ASEAN reluctant to alienate Myanmar though in the name of constructive engagement. And, on the part of the western countries the lack of strategic importance as well as less economic interest in the region has resulted in the adoption of a weak policy.

Added to the above problem, there is no consensus among different international bodies, sub-regional groups and countries dealing with Myanmar. This is evident from the existing frictions between the ASEAN and the European Nations. There are conflicts within the various agencies of the United Nations too. While the UNHCR, UNCHR and ILO tried to pressurise the junta for a change, the UNDP and WHO continued with its humanitarian assistance which in turn helped only the cash scrapped government and its top leaders. Josef Silverstein had rightly said, "If the General Assembly and the UNHRC were moving in one direction, regional organisations and sub-agencies of the United Nations were not always in step"[62]. As a result, it is difficult to create an environment for a meaningful change in the country which in turn give the junta to remain in power.

Then there is the question of a lack of co-ordination and policy differences between the government of countries supporting the democracy movement and their respective business communities. While governments of the United States, the European Union countries, Australia, Canada etc. were concerned with the plight of the people of Myanmar and wanted to bring a democratic change through persuasion and sanctions, most of its companies were concerned only with the economic gain in dealing with the country. And as such, in the initial stage of the outbreak of the movement itself, in the midst of international criticism, the oil companies like Amoco and Unocal (US), Petro Canada (Canada), Total (France), Idemitsu (Japan), BHP (Australia) etc. established business deals with the Myanmar junta. Many other companies dealing with construction, investment, hotels and consumer products followed suit. Up to the mid-90's U.K., France, US and Japan were the main countries whose companies invested most in Myanmar[63]. It was only in the late 90's that the companies withdrew from Myanmar because of condemnation and boycott by their respective countries.

Another main handicap on the part of those struggling for democracy is that it failed to bring out before the international community a strong body or platform representing Myanmarese democratic forces, and which can effectively operate in the international arena as the sole apex body. NCGUB did try but was not wholly successful. And as such despite the recognition given by the Western countries NCGUB failed to make much headway. The continuing cease-fire between the ethnic based insurgent groups and the junta greatly reduced the importance of DAB which, in turn, led to the gradual marginalisation of NCGUB. Therefore, it became really difficult for the international community to decide to whom the help should be extended for the cause of democracy.

The membership given to the junta by ASEAN and its re-entry into the NAM also provided legitimacy to rule. This means a tougher task for the democracy movement. In the circumstances it has become more difficult to convince others about what the present junta is doing while many countries and agencies remain in support of the regime.

From all these setbacks what came out is a clear cut picture that "lack of understanding of the Myanmarese politics has put the movement in a disadvantageous position"[64]. But at the same time it does not mean that the Myanmarese issue was completely grim in the international scenario. On the contrary, changes could be seen in the attitude of the military regime after it became a member of ASEAN. It is also because of increasing pressure that there is some loosening on the part of the junta thus paving ground for starting some meaningful dialogue between the two opposite groups in the country.

In the last few years the movement is receiving massive support from the international NGOs as well as world governments in the form of recognition to the Committee Representing the People's Parliament (CRPP), the committee representing the parliament elected in May 1990, which was formed in September 1998. Formal support and recognition was extended by government bodies including the EU, International Parliamentary Union, Belgium, Denmark, Norway and the United Nations General Assembly also noted it in its resolution on Myanmar[65]. It also got support from 'Free Burma Coalition', an umbrella organisation of more than 100 universities and community groups[66]. The time is also ripe for the supporters of the movement to give more pressure in the international platform as the SPDC, it seems, no longer remains alienated as before. This is very much evident from the European Union brokered dialogue between the SPDC and the NLD under Suu Kyi in February 2001. The Burma Lawyer's Council had rightly described,

"The SLORC, (presently SPDC) have been pursuing a deliberative policy of engagement with the international community and by their action it is evident that they do not want isolation either voluntary or involuntary. It is timely for all the international governments to analyse the current situation regarding the SLORC's engagement policy. That the SLORC do care what the international community thinks, gives leverages to those countries whose foreign policy objective is the restoration of democracy in Burma"[67].

Thus despite certain setbacks in the past and many hurdles at present it is the right time for the Myanmarese dissidents to follow a more pragmatic and active approach in its dealing with international actors. While at the same time there need to be a coherent persuasion, coercion or dialogue whatever means the countries and groups may adopt but as far as possible the efforts must be to have a sort of coherence among them. On the whole, objective approach has to be made in every line of actions aggressively in place of lopsided subjective propaganda and this will go a long way in shaping a future Myanmar Democracy in totality.

NOTES

1. Andrew Selth, "Burma and the Strategic Competition between China and India", John Brandon (ed.) *Burma/ Myanmar Towards the Twenty First Century: Dynamics of*

Continuity and Change (Bangkok: Thai Studies Section, Chulalongkorn University, 1997) p. 149.

2. Far Eastern Economic Review, *Asia 1990 Yearbook* (Hong Kong), p.96.
3. Donald M. Seekins, " Burma –China Relations: Playing with Fire ", *Asian Survey* (Berkeley), vol.37, no.6, June 1997, pp. 529-530.
4. FEER, *Asia 1992 Yearbook*, p.92.
5. FEER, *Asia 1991 Yearbook*, pp.98-99.
6. John Bray, *Burma: The Politics of Constructive Engagement* (London : RIIA, 1995),p.46.
7. FEER, *Asia 2000 Yearbook*, p.92.
8. n.3.
9. In most cases this purchases were exchanged with natural resources of Myanmar.
10. Chi Shad Liang, " Burma's Relations with the People's Republic of China: From Delicate Friendship to Genuine Co-operation", in Peter Carey (ed.), *Burma: The Challenge of Change in a Divided Society*(London: Macmillan , 1997),pp. 84-85.
11. Ibid, p.85.
12. Wayne Bert, "Chinese Policy Towards Democratization Movements: Burma and Philippines", *Asian Survey*, vol.30, no. 11, November 1990, p. 1082.
13. As told to the scholar by Myanmarese students taking asylum in Manipur, India.
14. India's main concern is security, which can be illustrated by the following remark by Mohan Malik of Deakin University, Australia "What worries Indian strategists is the growing military nexus between China and Myanmar and its implication for India's border strategic objective in northern Indian ocean region. New Delhi's desire is for Myanmar to constitute a stable neutral peaceful buffer state between India and China . A tibetization of Myanmar is seen as detrimental to India's security interest because Myanmar also provides the Chinese with invasion route to India." See Mohan Malik, 'Sino-Indian Rivalry in Myanmar: Implications for Regional Security', *Contemporary Southeast Asia*, volume 16, number 2, September 1994, p.144.
15. The major routes from Myanmar to India are from Sagaing

to Tamu to Manipur , and another from Sagaing to Kalay or Tiddim to Mizoram , see Images Asia,KHRG and OSI, *All Quit in Western Front? The Situation in Chin State and Sagaing Division, Burma* (Images Asia:Chiangmai-Thailand,January 1988), p.60.

16. Methamphetamines are derived from ephedrine.
17. By early1992 a string of six new refineries was reported along the Chindwin river, close to the Indian border; north of Sinkaling Kamti, near Tamanthi,Homabis, Moreh , Kalemyo, Tiddim and Paletwa on the western edge of Chin and Arakan states. Resultantly the level of drug addiction and menace of aids increase in a very large scale in the border states of Manipur, Mizoram and Nagaland.and the difficult part of this issue is the believe that those drug lords who run this business are supported by the Myanmarese army ,particularly with the consent of the regional commanders see Bertil Lintner, "Drugs and economic growth in Burma today", Morten B. Pedersen, Emily Rudland and R.J. May(ed.), *Burma / Myanmar : Strong Regime Weak State* (Adelaide: Crawford,2000), pp. 176-177.
18. Ministry of External Affairs, Government of India *Annual Report 1992-1993*,(New Delhi), p.18.
19. Ministry of External Affairs, Government of India, *Annual Report 1993-1994*,(New Delhi), p.4.
20. Ibid, p. 155.
21. *The Telegraph* (Calcutta), 14 November 1999.
22. *The Hindu* (New Delhi), 14 February 2001
23. The road directly links India with Mandalay, the second largest city of Myanmar.
24. J.Mohan Malik, "Sino-Indian Rivalry in Myanmar: Implications for Regional Security", *Contemporary Southeast Asia,* Vol.16, No. 2, September 1994, p.148.
25. Gunter Siemers, "Myanmar 1992; Heading for Guided Democracy", *Southeast Asian Affair* , 1993, p.263.
26. Abu Taher Salahuddin Ahmed, "Myanmar : Road to Democracy or East Asian Model? ", *Bangladesh Institute of International and Strategic Studies Journal* (Dhaka),vol.17,no.1, 1996,pp. 122-143.
27. David H. Demon & Evelyn, "Challenges for the ASEAN", *Pacific Affairs*, vol.71,no.4,Winter 1998-1999, p.506.
28. FEER, *Asia 1993 Year Book*, p.66.

29. Ibid,p.67.
30. FEER, *Asia 1997 Year Book*,p.73.
31. Ibid.
32. Member states here means the countries of the EU. This ban was renewable on a six-month basis.
33. Allen L. Clark, "Myanmar's Present Development and Future Options", *Asian Survey*, vol.39,no.5, September/ October 1999,p.782.
34. Time Maung Maung Than and Mya Than, 'Myanmar : Economic Growth in the Shadow of Political Constraints", *South East Asian Affairs*, 1997, p.214-215.
35. Tin Maung Maung Than , "Myanmar's Golden Anniversary Economic and Political Uncertainty", South East Asian Affairs, 1999,p.221.
36. FEER ,*Asia 2000 Year Book*, p.91.
37. FEER, *Asia 1999 Year Book*, p.87.
38. *Burma Debate*, Fall 2000 7 (3), p. 49. The CRPP is a 10-member committee representing the parliament elected in 27 May 1990 in the country. It was established as a challenge to the regime on 16 September 1998.
39. Donald M. Seekins , " Japan's Aid Relation with Military Regimes in Burma, 1962-1991: The Kokunaika Process", *Asian Survey*, vol.32, no. 3, March 1992, p.246.
40. n.25.
41. Ibid.
42. Minoru Kiryu, "Performance and Prospects of the Myanmar Economy", *Southeast Asian Affairs*, 1992, p251.
43. Josef Silverstein, " Burma in the International Perspective", *Asian Survey*, vol.32, no.10, October 1992, p. 957.
44. n.6, p.52.
45. Morten B.Pedersen, " International Policy on Burma: Coercion, Persuasion, or Cooperation? Assesing the Claims", in Morten B. Pedersen, Emily Rudland and R.J. May(ed.), *Burma / Myanmar: Strong Regime Weak State* (Adelaide: Crawford,2000), p.217.
46. James F. Guyot, "Burma in 1996 : One Economy , Two Politics", *Asian Survey*, vol.38, no.2, February 1998, p.193.
47. Ibid.
48. Donal M.Seekins, " Burma in 1998 : Little to Celebrate", *Asian Survey*, vol.39, no.1, January / February 1999,p.18.

49. *The Irrawaddy* (Chiangmai, Thailand), July 2000,p.6.
50. Ibid.
51. Tom Wingfield, "Myanmar Political Stasis and a Precarious Economy", *South East Asian Affairs,* 2000, p,211.
52. *The Burma Review* (Washington), no.35, August 1992-January 1993.
53. n.4.
54. *The Irrawaddy*, vol.4,no.4-5, 15 February-15 March 1996.
55. *The Irrawaddy*, vol. 5, no.8, 15January 1997.
56. Robert H. Taylor, " Myanmar : New , But Different ?", *Southeast Asian Affairs*, 1995, p,247.
57. n.5,p.209.
58. Ibid.
59. n.56,p.247.
60. n.48,p.18.
61. Jan Donkers and Minka Nijhuis (eds.), *Burma : Behind the Mask* (Amsterdam : Burma Centrum Nederland, 1996),p.93.
62. n.43,p.958.
63. n.54.
64. Emily Rudland and Morten B. Pedersen, " Introduction: Strong Regime, Weak State", in Morten B. Pedersen, Emily Rudland and R.J. May(eds.), *Burma / Myanmar: Strong Regime Weak State* (Adelaide: Crawford,2000), p.16.
65. ALTSEAN, *Burma Special Report : The Committee Representing People's Parliament* (Bangkok: ALTSEAN, September 1999),p.12.
66. Ibid.
67. Burma Lawyers' Council, *Legal Issues on Burma Journal* (Bangkok: Burma Lawyers' Council, Oct. 1997) p. 3.

8

Conclusion

Myanmar opted for parliamentary democracy with its achievement of independence in 1948. However, absence of a well-organised political party, an essential of parliamentary democracy, was largely responsible for it's failure. In addition to this, indecisive and hesitant attitude of the ruling political leadership, communist and ethnic based insurgencies, state religion issue, autonomy demand, deteriorating economic condition and above all intra-party conflict were mainly responsible for the collapse of parliamentary democracy resulting in the ultimate military take over.

Myanmar's military and its leadership was indisputably the only alternative available to rule. Having played a crucial role during critical years of pre-independence struggle for freedom it was able to establish its own credibility when it took over the administration when the civilian government failed. Without much exception the Myanmarese too strongly believed that military under Ne Win's leadership was probably the only hope for their future, national unity and prosperity though it proved otherwise. Ne Win seized political power at a time when the political leadership in the Third World countries were attracted by ideas of socialism. It was a natural process that former colonies would have a desire to be free from exploitation, as they believed that essence of colonialism was economic exploitation. Myanmarese political leadership in this connection was not an exception. Land reform, mass nationalisation of trade and industry were carried out doing away with the earlier policy of privatisation undertaken by U Nu government.

Soon after its seizure of power the Revolutionary Council (RC) formulated a policy known as 'Burmese Way to Socialism' in April 1962. Again another document known as the 'Correlation between Men and His Environment' was issued on 17 January 1963. The Burmese Socialist Programme Party formed in July 1962, the only party allowed to function was to carry out the policy programme so formulated. Land reform, mass nationalisation of trade and industry were carried out. Large industries, foreign trade, domestic wholesale trade and 90 percent of the retail trade were nationalised. The whole banking system was nationalised on 23 February 1963. Mass nationalisation programme reversed the process of privatisation undertaken by U Nu when it didn't work to their expectation. No doubt, Ne Win left only the primary sector to the private hands.

The impact of mass nationalisation was visible immediately after its implementation. Foreign exchange reserves started falling. As a result the budget allocations to different ministries were slashed to 50 percent. Even the Defence Ministry was not spared. Myanmar's historic isolation resulted in the drastic fall in the volume of foreign trade. In actual terms the ratio of foreign trade to GDP which constituted 40 percent in 1950 came down to 26 percent in 1960-70, 13 percent in 1970-77, one of the lowest among the developing countries. Sharp decline in the quantum export of rice was alarming considering great demand for Myanmarese rice in the world market previously. Immediately before the outbreak of mass uprising in 1988 only one third amount of rice of the 1947 level and only half of the 1970-72 was exported. Even in the domestic front Myanmar became a rice-rationed country from a rice exporting country. Not only in the aforesaid fronts but also in others too its economic performance was not impressive. Annual per capita income shrank from $670 in 1960 to $190 in 1987. Official consumer price inflation was around 25 percent. Government's control of 426 consumer items, also to be sold at government shops only, became the source to breed black marketeering and hoarding though later on 34 items were decontrolled. However, almost all the controlled items were sold at 400-500 percent higher than government controlled price. In 1987 foreign debt stood at $5.3 billion, a small amount for others but a big amount for a country like Myanmar where 40 percent of the people survived below poverty line.

Government control of a large number of items resulted in the emergence of black marketeering. Demonetisations of 1964, 1985 and 1987 were basically to check black marketeers and drug runners. However, corrupt bureaucrats, military officers close to government largely contributed to make the basic objective of the demonetisations an unsuccessful attempt. In 1987 acting on the application of the Government of Myanmar the United Nations declared the country as the Least Developed Country in the world which could not be tolerated by its own people.

Myanmar witnessed two kinds of economy running in parallel – official and unofficial. Black Marketeers and drug runners prospered. Accumulation of wealth was in their hands. Three times demonetisations primarily aimed at to flush out hidden wealth were not successful. Heavy reliance on and induction of military officers even including the junior ones without the knowledge of civil administration resulted in incompetence and inefficiency. Ambivalence to foreigners and foreign goods, rigid control and centralisation unduly checked free development and innovations. To cite a small example the State Trading Corporation established to look after the nationalisation sector could not carry out its assigned duties properly. It even failed miserably in the satisfactory distribution of commodities.

Apart from the acute and chronic problems of economy, there was no efficient management of the political issues. Communist and ethnic based insurgencies entailed huge amount of money, material and larger number of man without much success in sight. U Nu's resistance from the Myanmar-Thai border was not insignificant. An armed force which is expected to be a solid and disciplined organisation off and on witnessed signs of discontentment among its ranks and files. Purges meant for *heir apparent* were serious political crisis though not so open. Accumulated discontentment in the military organisation invited assassination plot e.g. in 1975 – a sign of soldier class divided internally. Discontentment and frustration widely prevalent could also easily provoke students, monks and workers who were in the organised sectors. The U Thant burial ceremony of 1975 provoked one such widespread protest against the government. The salary cut, though looks trivial became an aspect to build up anti-government propaganda. Denial of ethnic minority rights in the Constitution of 1974, and the consequent formation of National Democratic Front by the ethnic insurgents was also a sign of strong determination to fight against authoritarian regime. The idea to civilianise the military was not a positive step to change power structure but a tactics to remain in power without changing the basic policies and programmes. The one party rule signifies authoritarianism and intolerance of opposition, meaning no sign of entertaining new ideas and innovations from the opposite side. Above all discontentment prevailed among students, monks, workers, politicians, public leaders and a section of army officers.

Myanmar's deteriorating economy, government's enmity with almost every section of the society, widespread poverty, corruption, black marketeering, inflation, discontentment and frustration needed only a spark. A tea stall incident of 12 March 1988 in the Rangoon Institute of Technology campus where a student Maung Phone Maw was killed became the incident to provoke protests, demonstrations, riots and violence of an unimaginable scale in which people from all walks of life – students, monks, workers, government officials, doctors, nurses, lawyers participated. Started in March 1988 widespread protests demonstrations continued in May, June and July. On 8 August peaceful anti-government demonstrations and processions in all the important major cities and towns throughout the country appeared. In Yangon alone at least 100,000 people marched through streets.

Simultaneous demonstrations could be seen in Mandalay, Yanangyaung, Pegu, Moulmein, Taungyi, Sagaing and Prome. Mass protests covered more than 40 places. The demands were (i) resignation of the BSPP Government; (ii) end of the socialist economy; (iii) establishment of multi-party democracy; (iv) formation of an interim government to conduct multi-party election; and (v) transition to democracy.

Countrywide protests, demonstrations brought down three governments of Ne Win, Sein Lwin and Maung Maung in quick succession. Immediately after that General Saw Maung seized power on 18 September and established a 9-member State Law and Order Restoration Council (SLORC), abolished the People's Assembly, the State Council and the Council of Ministers, banned demonstrations, imposed night curfew, killed not less than 1000 students with brutality; but promised for holding a multi-party democratic election. The SLORC proclaimed Martial Law to bring the situation under control. The proclamation of the martial law was followed by a series of repressive measures. SLORC started a systematic drive to hunt for pro-democracy activists throughout the country. Fear for military atrocities the pro-democracy activists took shelter in the border areas where they established contacts with the ethnic insurgents and the NDF constituents. At least a thousand were killed and many were arrested, tortured or jailed during this post martial law period. Many of them became refugees in three countries - Thailand, Bangladesh and India. They had to face hardships. Food was scarce, there was no medicine no adequate shelter. Above all they were in Malaria prone areas. However, in spite of all these hardships they were able to form a frontal organisation of students – the All Burma Students' Democratic Front (ABSDF) – the most powerful body of the students the presence of which is more felt outside the country today. They also became associated with underground elements.

On the other hand, Government's announcement for holding a multi-party election saw the emergence of political parties allowed under Political Parties Registration Law of

27 September 1988. Newly emerging leaders General Aung Gyi, Aung San Suu Kyi, retired General Tin U formed National United Front for Democracy which later on came to be known as National League for Democracy during the height of widespread agitation. The Burma Socialist Programme Party changed its name into National Unity Party and Tha Kyo as its Chairman. Former Prime Minister U Nu formed the League for Democracy. Following disagreements, Brigadier Aung Gyi formed his own party - the Union National Party. The Government allowed the formation of these political parties after a ban of political parties in 1962.

Though the announcement was made to hold the election on 27 May 1990 martial law was not lifted. Aung San Suu Kyi and Tin U campaigned for the election across the country. Both of them were disqualified by the military junta – Suu Kyi for "having (alleged) links with underground student groups"; and Tin U for inciting public against the military and the creating disunity within the army. He was sentenced with hard labour to a term of three years. U Nu was disqualified to contest the election as he refused the dissolution of his "alternative government" formed earlier. Here, what is to be noted is that the SLORC wanted to use disqualification to check the emergence of political leaders likely to challenge the military rule and the establishment of a political successor.

The promised election was held on 27 May 1990 as scheduled earlier. However, contrary to the expectations of the SLORC, the NLD won a landslide majority i.e., 362 out of 450 seats, the government's party NUP captured only 10 seats while other seats were captured mostly by the NLD allies.

What is now intriguing is why the military did not rig the election in favour of its party, the National Unity Party, so that it could remain in power. It seems the SLORC was overconfident to win the elections though the results came in favour of the opposition which was beyond their expectation.

It was only with the announcement of the election results that the SLORC started giving one excuse or the other to remain in power. Ignoring the results, the SLORC called for a National Convention on 9-10 January 1993 to legitimise armed forces role in politics. It says, " to put it frankly the maintenance of national stability, peace and tranquillity without the participation of the army is extremely risky and dangerous". It indicates that it should take part in executive, legislature and even in judiciary and armed forces should be given free hand in all military matters. Further, the executive should be from the military background having experience in military, political and economic affairs. It spoke highly of the Indonesian model where armed forces had its own quota in the parliament, an unhealthy practice of democracy. It has consistently maintained that (i) it is the government recognised by the United Nations; (ii) it is not bound by any constitution but by martial law; and above all (iii) it works for the prevention of national disintegration. It also maintains that while the unity and integrity was under threat, it could not transfer power. Behind all those pretexts the ultimate reality is that the armed forces want lion's share in the government, a status of military tutelage over any process of political change. It also says that drafting of a new constitution acceptable to all the 135 ethnic groups and races was necessary. National Convention was to lay down the guidelines of the Constitution which was not at all acceptable to the NLD.

Confrontation ensued between pro-democracy activists and the military government. When the troops killed 4 Buddhist monks they announced not to perform religious services of the military personnel and their family members which could not last long. The government passed death sentences against the monks who resisted at the same time there was heavy clampdown. The protest of the monks ended.

The history of post 1988 mass uprising witnessed the emergence of Aung San Suu Kyi as the undisputed leader of the movement for democracy in the country compared with

Nelson Mandela and Mahatma Gandhi. On 30 August 1990 the NLD, on its own initiative, announced to convene the Parliament in September the same year unless the SLORC failed to do so. Forty MPs were imprisoned, 111 MPs were disqualified. Some of them died in jail. This was a big blow to the NLD inside the country.

Mass arrest of NLD MPs, detention, disqualification, death in jail prompted some of the NLD members and student activists to inaugurate a government in exile to seek international support and to internationalise the issue. It was to establish contacts with several governments especially in the West. Intensive lobbying has yielded results. Even though the government is yet to be recognised it has received substantial financial and moral support from most of the Industrialised Western countries for their programmes specially connected with refugee, education, healthcare, and agriculture. Norway has provided funds for running a broadcasting centre in its territory. Under the protective umbrella of NCGUB and NCUB there are a number of organisations working in close coordination and cooperation. They include DAB, CRDB, and Members of Parliament Union (MPU). Most of them are based in the West. However, NCGUB ministers are based in different countries including India and Thailand to keep in touch with Governments of their own neighbouring countries.

The uprising of 1988 was suppressed with a heavy hand. The massacre of the peaceful demonstrators was not without international reaction. Immediate reaction came from many countries. Economic sanctions, boycott of trade, condemnation came from many countries and international agencies. The United States was the first country to officially condemn the carnage followed by economic sanctions, termination of economic assistance and aid soon after the September military coup. The same was followed by Australia, Britain , Canada , Japan , Norway ,Sweden etc. They stopped all bilateral assistance including weapons sale. Among the Southeast Asian countries Philippines joined industrialised West. Among the neighbours India openly supported the pro-democracy activists. International financial institutions – World Bank, IMF, ADB–stopped negotiations on new projects though they continued to disburse funds for previously committed projects.

While the West and Japan continue to impose economic sanctions, suspension of aids and arms embargo, the ASEAN has followed a policy known as "constructive engagement" which avoids involvement in the internal affairs of Myanmar while trying to take economic advantage. Therefore, all the ASEAN countries except Philippines favoured to make economic gains. Now, the ASEAN countries top the list of investors in Myanmar. Many Myanmar watchers feel that member countries of the ASEAN have their own national interest particularly economic in view of the rich natural resources of Myanmar. Moreover, ASEAN leaders fully agree that Myanmar's admission into its fold enhances the image and credibility of Myanmar's military junta. However, they strongly feel to balance the increasing Chinese influence. No doubt, economic gains remain supreme in their considerations. This does not mean that some member countries of the ASEAN do not exercise their own independent view. At the same time ASEAN do not want to hurt the West. In conclusion industrialised West and Japan remain committed to the process of democratisation while India, China and the ASEAN have taken opportunistic stands in view of their own national or group interest.

While discussing reactions to the movement for democracy it is important to highlight the reactions from Japan, People's Republic of China and India. Japan's relations with Myanmar is probably the closest as with any of the industrialised democracies, China's relations is significant considering its economic and strategic relationship while India's relationship is worth watching in view of its sudden change from its earlier stance.

After the '1988 Uprising' it is seen that Industrialised democracies strongly condemned human rights violations, imposed sanctions, suspended economic aid, applied restrictions of Myanmarese Government officials' entry, placed arms embargo etc. While doing so a vacuum was created. This vacuum was filled by China. (i) Frequent exchange of official visits at the highest level; (ii) significant increase in the volume of trade; (iii) Myanmar's heavy dependence on China for arms supply; (iv) expansion of China's economic activities; (v) Chinese protection of junta's interests in world forums like the UN are worth mentioning. In substance after '1988 Uprising' China is the "principal aid donor, arms supplier, source of consumer goods" and the protector of the junta.

India has a dual purpose in improving relations with Myanmar - (i) it wants to balance Chinese influence; and (ii) it wants to pursue a vigorous "Look East Policy" without interfering in the internal affairs of Myanmar. It means India has sacrificed the cause of democracy movement for the sake of an opportunist economic and strategic interest.

Japan's case is unique in a way. It is the largest contributor of ODA to Myanmar. Seventy per cent of the amount Myanmar receives in the name of ODA comes from it. It suspended its aid allocation just after the bloody crackdown of August 1988 and toughened its stand in dealing with the military leaders . It is probably the only country among the industrialised democracies which can pressurise Myanmar. It exercises maximum influence. It is the general belief that a dialogue between junta and Suu Kyi in 1994 and her release was because of Japanese insistence. However, resource poor Japan has shown interest in resuming aid. There is possibility of its companies coming to Myanmar for aid and investment while the government remains aloof which is not unique as it follows a policy of separating economics from politics.

While considering the reactions it is important to note what the United Nations do. It has been consistently demanding that power should be transferred to the popularly elected representatives of the people by the military considering the clear-cut mandate given. U N also played an important role in the release of Aung San Suu Kyi in 1995 from house arrest. ILO acted against military for the use of forced labour and its membership was suspended.

The foregoing concluding remarks clearly show that strong support for the movement for democracy comes mostly from the industrialised democracies while the most needed one is not forthcoming from its important neighbours - China, India and Thailand mainly because of their national interest. The United Nations and one of its agencies the ILO have done to the largest possible extent. The same is true with the ADB, IMF, World Bank, the most important institutions.

Movement for democracy suffers from many disadvantages. Even though Aung San Suu Kyi has established as the undisputed leader her marriage to a foreigner puts her in a disadvantageous position though this kind of view is not acceptable to the champions of democracy movement.

Now what are the prospects of restoration for democracy in Myanmar? Chances are remote. Reasons are many. First of all the military has consolidated its own hold. Secondly, it has succeeded in breaking up the NLD at home. It closed down, destroyed NLD offices, created fear psychosis among the NLD party workers, activists even duly elected People's representatives. It has systematically divided the party, the backbone of Parliamentary Democracy. Some of the party members expressed disillusionment with the leadership i.e., Aung San Suu Kyi. Suu Kyi even admitted the existence of renegade MPs who have become betrayers. At the same time the military government continues to divide the NLD. In November 1999 the country's Election Commission informed that only 92 of the 392 NLD MPs elected in May1990 election remained to be party members. According to it 105 have resigned, 30 have died, 139 have been disqualified or their candidacy has been revoked while 27 have become independents after defections. While there is discrepancy regarding an MP the process of breaking up of the NLD MPs' group is complete now. With it shall we not say that the NLD is weak now at least in the home front. In substance military government has forced the party to remain in disarray. The party is now dislocated. The backbone of Parliamentary Democracy is broken.

Thirdly, the military leadership has successfully negotiated with ethnic based insurgents one by one though with Chinese interference. It has established its own credibility.

Fourthly, establishment of better relationships with ASEAN, China, and India its admission to ASEAN and its re entry into NAM have moreover legitimised the military rule in the country much to the disappointment of the pro-democracy forces. Distant neighbours, industrialised democracies have almost failed in putting pressure as immediate neighbours coming into their places as replacements.

Does the NLD leadership realise it? Of course, yes. Aung San Suu Kyi has urged the government for a dialogue. But dialogues were meaningless in the past. It looks like peaceful means for struggle for the restoration of democracy are now exhausted. However she has expressed her desire once again in August 2002 for a meaningful and productive dialogue and to cooperate with the military rulers in the better interest of the country provided both sides retreat halfway and come to a compromise. The ball is in the court of the junta. In case the junta does not respond, will the pro-democracy activists resort to violence? But it is likely to complicate the movement.

Now even after more than ten years of election victory the military government has failed to honour the election results. Instead, it keeps on accusing the NLD members as "traitors... under the pretext of democracy, Suu Kyi as 'power crazy', an instrument of foreign powers" etc. However, they forget that there is no sign of improvement in its economy and military rule cannot last long in the present global political environment. And, one must be aware that military plays an important role in several of the Southeast Asian countries. But Southeast Asia also has witnessed the fall of

Marcos, Suharto and why not the junta in Myanmar. In spite of all these we cannot rule out a compromise between the pro democracy forces and the military - a compromise in which the military forms a part of the political power structure, an essential of political culture of the region. The fear is that time is running out for pro-democracy forces. Therefore, much will depend on the outlook of the military junta leadership provided they value national interest more than to remain in power.

Epilogue

The beginning of the millennium show three important developments in Myanmar in connection with the movement for democracy: (i) the release of Aung San Suu Kyi in May 2002 and her re-arrest on 30 May the next year; (ii) the death of General Ne Win, the grand old man who dominated Myanmar's political scene for a long time; (iii) the purge of high profile General Khin Nyunt who was considered to be the most powerful political player in the SPDC regime.

After Aung San Suu Kyi's re-arrest, detention[1] and subsequent putting into house arrest in the name of "protective custody" in 2003 she has greatly softened her stand towards the junta. However, the junta, on the other hand, has restricted her from communicating to her supporters outside. There is little or no publicity about her. Foreign diplomats especially those belonging to Western countries were not allowed to meet her. Her health condition, it is believed, is greatly deteriorated. No initiative from the part of the regime was ever taken for a dialogue with her. The junta has completely ignored her if not sidelined.

Secondly, General Ne Win, who was considered to be the man behind the Myanmarese political scene for quite a long time was put under house arrest till he passed away on 5 December 2002. Many people, including the pro-democracy activists even believed that he was the man behind the scene; and therefore, could bring both junta and the pro-democracy leadership together into a negotiating table. However the junta did not even spare his kith and kin and sentenced many of them to prison terms or death penalty[2].

This was followed again by the purging of the high profile Gen Khin Nyunt[3], who was considered to be the most powerful political player in the present SPDC regime. What is the implication? Two men, one is the most powerful one behind scene and another is a powerful one is the present context. Both were removed systematically from the political scene of the country. The implication is the existence of a more powerful force. Whatsoever, in this short period the Myanmarese politics is imbedded with changes. It saw the removal and consolidation of power within the ruling SPDC with more power concentrated in the hands of those generals who go along with Sr.General Than Shwe and Gen. Maung Aye. This development diminishes the initial flicker of hope of democracy supporters for a quick change over to democracy in the country. Political impasse and stalemate coupled with economic deterioration continue. In the situation the restoration of democracy becomes a distant dream.

Since the study deals with finding solution and prospects of a dynamic issue we need to assess the developments and the related background in the last two three years for a clear understanding of the current trend and the environment in which all these are happening. This will give more insight to the implication of each event related with Myanmarese politics. Issues such as Suu Kyi – junta tussle, ceasefire and ethnic aspirations, National Convention, SPDC's Road Map to Democracy, forced labour, working of external forces – manifestation and facets of present Myanmarese body politics – need to be studied. Only then can we form some ideas on the prospects and possibilities of a democratic transition in the country- the effort may be of any one or more party- that is the opposition group led by NLD, the junta, the ethnic groups under UNLD, the pressure groups, or the collective effort of all. In some circle even the idea of a third front has been mooted because of the dislike of SPDC and at the same time lack of confidence on the credibility and ability of NLD.

Currently the main issue is, no doubt, democratic transition of the country which is the foremost concern of every one, both for or against it. And no longer has it remained a purely domestic issue. For the last two years the regime is harping with a seven-point 'Road Map to Democracy'. This has to do with an effort to counter international as well as regional pressure rather than to appease the opposition or with the genuine desire to politically transform the country. Contrary to the expectation of Myanmar watchers soon after the 'Depayin Clash'[4] and subsequent re-arrest of Suu Kyi, there was a reshuffle in the SPDC leading to the appointment of Khin Nyunt as Prime Minister on 25 August[5]. It was in his policy speech of 30 August that he announced, for the first time, the regime's Seven – Point Roadmap for transition to a "disciplined democracy". This includes: (i) reconvening of the National Convention (NC); (ii) step by step implementation of process necessary for the emergence of a democratic system; (iii) drafting a new constitution in accordance with basic principle laid down by the national convention; (iv) holding a National Referendum for the adoption of the constitution; (v) holding free and fair elections for Pyithu Hluttaws; (vi) convening of Hluttaws; and ultimately, (vii) the formation of a new democratic government by the elected leaders.

Pro-democracy groups, however, opposed the Seven-Point Roadmap strongly on the ground that it is a pretext for the SPDC government to remain in power because of the absence of concrete time frame. Supporters both inside and outside the country has strong reservations as to the practicability and genuineness of the idea of the roadmap. For instance the main opposition, the NLD, feels that the map has little or no meaning as it is against the national convention itself which forms an important part of the proposed roadmap. Thus NLD attaches much more importance to dialogue between the SPDC government and the opposition groups for future course of action before taking up any other step. NCGUB, the government in exile, also rejected the roadmap declaring it as nothing more than a political ploy to ease mounting international pressure and extend military rule. Committee Representing the Peoples' Parliament (CRPP) also responded against the proposed roadmap. In between these the newly emerged umbrella organisation of ethnic groups, the Ethnic Nationalities Solidarity and Co-operation Committee (ENSCC) presented its own roadmap with a time frame which was rejected by pro- democracy groups.

Despite the above opinions of the parties and groups the SPDC went ahead with its roadmap. It reconvened the National Convention on 17 May 2004, eight years after it was adjourned in 1996. However, it was adjourned once again on 9 July because of disagreement between the government and the 13 of the participating ceasefire groups. They raised objection to the provisions of the "104 principles and 6 political objectives" put forward by the SPDC[6]. The group was of the opinion that they were detrimental to the interest of the ethnic nationalities as well as to the general purview of the restoration of democracy. They also put forward a 7–Point Proposal demanding self-determination[7]. But despite all these setbacks, loopholes and demands the junta was keen to continue with the convention even with or without the participation of those opposing it. It has once again started from 17 February 2005. And it has remained the only platform for the present junta for national reconciliation despite all the shortcomings and opposition.

The convention received a mixed response. Many more went against it. Delegates from various communities and groups sponsored by SPDC participated. Most of the pro-democracy groups including NLD, UNLD, SNLD, CRPP and the non-ceasefire groups are not ready to accept it. They have reservations on the nature of convention. First they want the release of Aung San Suu Kyi and all the "prisoners of conscience" and start a dialogue between SPDC and the opposition, particularly with NLD, which is very much required for the necessary confidence building atmosphere.

In the present context the roadmap and the national convention are the two main issues linking with the ongoing movement for democracy in Myanmar. The attention of both domestic and international community is drawn towards these issues. Apprehension is also there in some circles because of the sudden removal of General Khin Nyunt as he was considered to be the chief architect of this roadmap. Besides the NLD, the UNLD, a strong umbrella organisation of 25 ethnic based political parties, is against any convention without the participation of the elected representatives of 1990 election. It is in favour of elected representatives forming an interim government for supervising the National Convention and lay down the guidelines and requirements. Likewise the CRPP and the NCGUB are also of the view that the National Convention should be a balanced and an all inclusive one, with representatives from every section of the society.

World community, on its part, has reservations regarding the accomplishment of the National Convention – in the past or at present – unless there is a change in the previous principles, and an unbiased participation of all sections of society. Leaders of many countries are of the view that the National Convention will not be complete without the participation of the democratic forces of the country. And, that it also lacks the required accountability and transparency.

Another aspect of Myanmarese politics which is closely related with the democracy movement is the status of the ethnic groups. Ethnic armed groups entered into a ceasefire, though separately, with the military regime solely because of untiring personal effort of Gen.Khin Nyunt. When he was suddenly purged from SPDC there was a vacuum in communication, uncertainties and apprehensions as to how the hardliners would proceed. This the regime was also well aware of. Thus first step, after taking charge, for the present Prime Minister and the Secretary 1[8] was to fly to the base camps of the ceasefire groups and convince them. Dealing with the ceasefire groups is one of the most delicate issues in Myanmarese politics which cannot be taken lightly. Further, to remove the fear and also to allay international apprehensions Lt.General Thein Sein, Secretary 1, in a public address on 23 November 2004 declared that the policy programmes of the state are not laid down by an individual person but by SPDC as its policy and thus there will be continuity. He further reiterated that government policy does not concern only a single individual – a finger towards the ousted Gen. Khin Nyunt. It was made clear that the ceasefire armed parties had not reached an understanding and agreement with any single individual alone but only with the government as a whole. But incidents and recent happenings bring out the fact that sincerity is lacking on the part of the regime. A glaring example is that, despite the ongoing ceasefire talk between the KNU and the SPDC, more than 200 skirmishes between the two are reported in 2004 alone.

Leaving aside deadlock and stalemate in the domestic front, in the international front also, despite the large scale publicity, less has been done for a meaningful support to the cause of the Myanmarese movement in these few years. With the usual limited sanctions from the side of some western countries including United States the world opinion as such remained divided. National interest, globalisation and liberalisation in the world greatly deterred many of the countries from actually going against the ruling junta. Not only this, but Myanmar, from being a pariah state earlier, has now realised its importance as a geo-strategic player in the region. Since its entry into ASEAN in 1997 the outlook of world countries towards Myanmar has changed considerably. The legitimacy tag has greatly enhanced its own status. Here special emphasis need be given ,as usual ,to those main players in the international scenario including United States, European Union, ASEAN, and the immediate neighbours – India, China and Thailand. But in the whole except for the United States and the European Union the international community is no longer confined to Myanmar bashing. In fact most of the members of ASEAN in general and those in close proximity to the country do not care much about democracy. Rather they are more concerned about finding new mechanisms for a more cordial and 'constructive engagement' relationship.

As usual during the last two three years deadlock and tussle between Myanmar on the one hand and the US and the EU on the other, and subsequent sanctions imposed by them to the former continued. From time to time EU and ASEAN are also at odd over Myanmar' inclusion in any international forum where EU chances of participation is there. However, the degree of verbal attack and pressure from both EU and US has greatly reduced in the last two three years, much to the chagrin of democracy supporters and much below what is actually required. From their side it is mainly verbal support and this has to do with the lack of strategic interest and also the lack of desire to confront China. Members of ASEAN did step up diplomacy to gain the release of Aung San Suu Kyi and a quick democratic transition in the country no doubt.

United Nations continued with its effort of bringing a political transition in the country. Its special envoy, Ismail Razali was sent regularly to check as well as to pursue the generals for a change to democracy. In its 58th Session of the General Assembly in November 2003 it strongly urged the Government of Myanmar (i) to enter immediately into a meaningful dialogue with Aung San Suu Kyi and other leaders of the NLD directed towards democratisation and national reconciliation and, at an early stage; (ii) to include other political leaders in these talks, including representatives of the ethnic groups; and (iii) to restore democracy. Secretary General Kofi Annan also expressed his deep concern over the development in the country and insisted for a meaningful democratic transition in the country. In a recent statement in February this year (2005) he once again reiterated his call on the Myanmarese authorities to take the necessary steps to make the roadmap process more inclusive and credible[9]. Further, the Secretary General also expressed deep concern about the recent detention of several ethnic Shan leaders including the President of the Shan State Peace Council (SSPC) and the Chairman of the SNLD[10].

China on its part went on with its big brotherly attitude keeping in mind the geo-strategic and economic interest it has with Myanmar. Both the countries described their friendship as 'Paukphaw' or fraternal – a form of close brotherhood. One cannot imagine a life style in Myanmar without Chinese influence. Today China supplies the country with virtually every need – from military hardware to household commodities. And obviously the relationship between the two had greatly enhanced in the last two three years with little or no care at all for issue of democracy. Despite efforts of ASEAN and India to reduce China's influence on Myanmar it could not do so in practice. Increase in diplomatic contacts could also be seen. A clear example is the recent visits of China's Deputy Chief of PLA on 1 December, and that of its (China's) Vice Minister of Foreign Affairs on 3 December 2004 simultaneously.

On the regional front ASEAN remains the staunch supporter. As a continuing process it does support the country in the international fora. Of course, it could no longer ignore the mounting pressure for a democratic transition in Myanmar. Some of the member countries were for a genuine change in the country. Since it was ASEAN which had legitimised the military rule by granting entry to its fold the responsibility ultimately fall on it for a change in the political system of Myanmar. Particularly in 2003-2004, Prime Minister Mahatir of Malaysia, the staunchest supporter of Myanmar's entry to ASEAN, before his step-down, took personal initiative of pressurising the junta for a positive change. It is believed that his advice has been taken by the generals, with all seriousness.[11] But despite this, little change could be seen. What really concerned with the group is that the chairmanship of the regional grouping will come to Myanmar in 2006. And by that time if no positive change takes place in the country as such then complication in ASEAN's dealing with EU and US is anticipated. So despite of being a strong deciding factor, and its subsequent efforts, no concrete change towards democratic transition could be observed at present.

There is not much in the Thai - Myanmar relations as to do anything with democracy in the last two three years. Thailand, inspite of being an important member of ASEAN and also one of the immediate neighbours; failed to convince the junta for a political transition in the country. The relation is marked by ups and downs. Even if there is some improvement it is more in the field of trade and commerce. Myanmar acts as the main source of Thailand's natural gas needs. The present Thai Prime Minister Thaksin is also concerned more with expanding trade with Myanmar.

Leaving aside the regional players one country which can really make some difference in the country is Japan, the most important country in modern history of Myanmar. From simply being the largest ODA donor, it failed to bring any positive change in the country in recent times. The usual sanctions imposed on Myanmar remained. It also continues to pressurise SPDC for the release of Aung San Suu Kyi and the participation of the NLD leadership in the ongoing process of convention related with their 'roadmap of democracy'. What is lacking on the part of Japan is that though it took every opportunity to ask the Myanmarese government for a change yet it failed to offer any suggestion or solution for concretising the process of transition to reality.[12] As already mentioned in the beginning, under Japanese policy business affairs is never co-related with political matters. It never bound the Myanmarese generals with any such conditions which link the ODA with anything to do with politics in that country. In this situation nothing is left in hand for Japan to provide a meaningful way out to the country from the stalemate. In fact, its policy towards Myanmar at present is devoid of coherence and strategy[13], though it could have played a very practical role.

In the context of India a move towards more and more closeness to the present Myanmarese regime could be seen in the last two three years. Consideration of national interest makes this country forego its ideological leaning and going for drastic change in foreign policy planning – taking it extremely close to the Yangon government. Its 'Look East Policy'- an all in one policy - with economic, strategic and political implication, has to do with this development. There is an urgency on the part of India in matters of border management, curtailment of insurgency and narco - trade, minimization of China's influence which led to the improvement of relationship between the two. A clear example is the invitation and consequent visit of Head of the SPDC, Sr.General Than Shwe to India on 24 October 2004, and the ensuing commercial and strategic agreements that followed[14]. Besides the security and business concerns India is also more in taking benefits of the unexplored natural resources of the country, particularly the vast reserve of oil and natural gas. In this direction it is very much concerned with the increasing presence of China in Myanmar's growing energy sector. Presently India is trying to bid offshore exploration in the coastline of Rakhine state, in the Bay of Bengal, offered by Myanmar. If it succeeds then it is believed that Myanmar alone can provide 10 to 15 percent of India's energy consumption by 2025[15]. Thus, even if India still provide shelter to the Myanmarese refugees yet the necessary moral as well as diplomatic support to the ongoing movement for democracy is missing.

Finally, in the light of all the above developments, how many more years the movement has to continue before it attains its goal is really questionable at this particular juncture. There was a stage when it seemed the goal was very near. However, the developments in the last two three years as such are not going to take it towards that point. Softening on the part of Aung San Suu Kyi could also be seen. And even if the ongoing military orchestrated political process does succeed it still will take time for a transformation to genuine democracy which could bring all the divisive forces of the Myanmarese society within its fold. Based on the latest developments the world leaders and scholars are of the view that a rational compromise between the two opposing forces is the best solution for a political transition in the country. They further asserted that the main areas of talk between the two should be power sharing in a future democratic government, role of military in Myanmarese politics and the ethnic minorities. When will all these happen is what really concern these Myanmar watchers. The more the gap between the '88 Uprising' and the present, the movement, it seems, become less forceful – with more and more consolidation of power on the part of the ruling junta. But the movement is a continuing process; so it will be too early to concretise and expect the outcome outright. More time and observation is necessary. Hope is there as authoritarian rule can never be a permanent phenomenon in the society.

NOTES

1. She spent nearly four months in detention at a secret location before being put into house arrest.
2. Ardeth Maung Thawnghmung, "Preconditions and Prospects for Democratic Transition in Burma/Myanmar", *Asian Survey*,Vol.43, No.3., May/June 2003, p.455.
3. Gen. Khin Nyunt was arrested on the charge of corruption and was removed from the post of Prime Minister and also from the SPDC on 19 October 2004.
4. Clash between NLD volunteers and SPDC sponsored goons on a relay of NLD headed by Aung San Suu Kyi on 30 May 2003, and subsequent life attempt on her.
5. The post of Secretary 1 which he held till then was relinquished from him. This was perceived by experts as a ploy to remove or degrade his powerful position as intelligence Chief as well as power player within SPDC.
6. The SPDC had laid down 6 objectives and 104 principles in its earlier National Convention of 1996. These same objectives and principles were adopted and pursued in the 2004 National Convention. This the 13 ceasefire groups were not ready accept because they considered the said principles and objectives contradict the very concept of a Union of Burma built on unity, equality and self government which they were hoping for.
7. The 7 Points were as given:

   (i) the right to revise the 6th objective of the convention which is not in accordance with the democratic system and not in keeping with the people's wishes; (ii) the right to revise the principles that donot conform to democratic principles in the stated 104 basic principles of the convention ; (iii) participants should have the right to seek advice and consult any person or association on any relevant issue during the period of the convention; (iv) delegated must have the right to freely consult their respective associations and seek their views during the period of the convention; (v) elected representatives of the people in the 1990 elections must be permitted to attend the convention; (vi) delegates from 'Cease-fire groups' must be genuine; and (vii) Law 5/96 dated 7 June 1996 was intended to protect the 1993-1996 National Convention. It is no longer relevant and should be abolished.

8. Lt.Gen. Soe Win, formerly Secretary 1, is appointed Prime Minister after the removal of Gen. Khin Nyunt. Lt.Gen. Thein Sein, formerly Secretary 2, is elevated to Secretary 1. The latter is also the chief organiser of the National Convention.
9. The *Sangai Express* (Imphal), 20 February 2005.
10. Ibid.,
11. no.2, p.452.
12. Mikio Oishi and Fumitaka Furuoka, "Can Japanese Aid be an Effective Tool of Influence?", *Asian Survey*, Vol. 43, No.6, Nov-Dec 2003, p.902.
13. Ibid.,
14. This is the first Head of State Level interaction between the two countries in 17 years. All together 8 agreements were signed.
15. Şiddharth Varadarajan "India, China vie for Energy, Influence", *The Hindu*, 17 January 2005.

Important Interviews

Name	*Orgn. & Post*	*Place*	*Month & Year*
Kyaw Than	ABSL-Vice President	Imphal	May 1997.
Ramjeet Verma	NLD-Executive	New Delhi	November 1997
Dr.Zaw Win Aung	FTUB-Jt.Secretary	New Delhi	November 1997.
Ko Zin Naing	ABSDF-Foreign Affairs	New Delhi	November 1997.
U Bo Thaung	NLD-MP	Moreh	August 1998.
Ko Than Khe	ABSDF-Executive	Imphal	February 2000.
Dr.Aung Kyaw Oo	ABSDF-Executive	Imphal	February 2000.
Ko Nyo	Radio Free Asia	Imphal	March 2000.
Dr.Tint Swe	NLD-MP	Imphal	November 2000.
Mya Win	NLD-MP	Imphal	November 2000.
Aung Naing	ABSDF-Executive	Chiangmai	February 2001.
Saw Barnabas	NHEC-Program Director	Chiangmai	February 2001.
Saw Wingate	NHEC-Chairperson	Chiangmai	February 2001.
Yee Htun	NHEC	Chiangmai	February 2001.
U Aye Saung	PLF-Chairperson	Chiangmai	February 2001.

Kyaw Hla	MLOB-Chairman	Chiangmai	February 2001.
Keduensai Jaiyen	SHAN	Chiangmai	February 2001.
Aung Thu Nyein	DPNS-Vice President	Chiangmai	February 2001.
Ko Htut	SYCB	Chiangmai	February 2001.
Min Zin	Student Activist & Columnist	Chiangmai	February 2001.
Pornpimol	IAS Chulalongkorn University-Asst.Director	Bangkok	February 2001.
Hla Htay	ABSDF-Secretary 2	Delhi/Bangkok/ Chiangmai	February 2001.
Aung San Myint	FTUB	Delhi/Bangkok	February 2001.

Appendix-I

The Constitution of the Socialist Republic of the Union of Burma, 1974

Preamble

We, the people residing in the Socialist Republic of the Union of Burma have throughout history lived in harmony and unity sharing joys and sorrows in weal or woe.

The people of the land have endeavoured with perseverance and undaunted courage, for the attainment of independence, displaying throughout their struggles for national liberation against imperialism and intense patriotism, spirit of mutual help and sacrifice and have aspired to Democracy and Socialism.

After attaining independence, the power and influence of the feudalists, landlords, and capitalists have increased and consolidated due to the defects in the old Constitution and the ill-effects of capitalistic parliamentary democracy. The cause of Socialism came under near eclipse.

In order to overcome this deterioration and to build Socialism, the Revolutionary Council of the Union of Burma assumed responsibility as a historical mission, adopted the Burmese Way to Socialism, and also formed the Burma socialist Programme Party.

The Burma Socialist Programme Party has drafted the Constitution of the Socialist Republic of the Union of Burma, in accordance with the wishes of the people, after extensive and thorough discussions with them, for the purpose of building a peaceful and prosperous socialist society to which the working people of the national races have long aspired.

We, the working people, firmly resolved that we shall –

- faithfully follow the leadership of the Burma Socialist Programme Party,
- build a socialist system by the Burmese Way to Socialism, for the country to be peaceful and prosperous, opposing all pernicious systems characterized by exploitation of man by man, and of one national race by another, with a view to promoting justice and goodwill among the people, and to freeing them from apathy and callousness, ignorance, backwardness and want of opportunity,
- build a socialist democratic social order which will afford an opportunity to the people to shape their own destiny, by the Burmese Way to Socialism,
- live forever in harmony, unity and racial equality sharing joys and sorrows through weal and woe in the Socialist Republic of the Union of Burma,
- efficiently perform all duties and fulfill all obligations in the interest of the State and for the cause of Socialism while enjoying the democratic rights and personal rights and freedom bestowed by this Constitution,
- constantly strive to promote international peace and friendly relations among the nations, do adopt this Constitution of the Socialist Republic of the Union of Burma by a nationwide referendum this 11th of the waxing of Pyatho of the year 1335 B.E. (the 3rd day of the month of January, 1974 A.D.).

CHAPTER I

THE STATE

Article 1

Burma is a sovereign independent Socialist State of the

working people. The State shall be known as The Socialist Republic of the Union of Burma.

Article 2

The Socialist Republic of the Union of Burma is a State wherein various national races make their homes together.

Article 3

The territory of the State shall be the land, sea and airspace which constitute its territory on the this Constitution is adopted.

Article 4

National sovereignty shall reside in the entire State.

CHAPTER II
BASIC PRINCIPLES

Article 5

A Socialist society is the goal of the State.

Article 6

The economic system of the State is a Socialist economic system.

Article 7

Socialist democracy is the basis of the State structure.

Article 8

There shall be no exploitation of man by man nor of one national race by another in the State.

Article 9

The State safeguards the interest of the working people whose strength is based on peasants and workers.

Article 10

The State shall cultivate and promote the all-round physical, intellectual and moral development of youth.

Article 11

The State shall adopt a single-party system. The Burma Socialist Programme Party is the sole political party and it shall lead the State.

Article 12

The Sovereign powers of the State, legislative, executive and judicial reside in the people, comprising all national races whose strength is based on peasants and workers. The Pyithu Hluttaw, [People's Congress] elected by citizens having the right to vote, exercises the sovereign power invested in it by the people and delegates of Organs of State Power formed under this Constitution.

Article 13

The Pyithu Hluttaw shall exercise the legislative power solely by itself while it may delegate executive and judicial powers to the Central and Local Organs of State Power formed under this Constitution.

Article 14

The Organs of State Power at different levels shall function in accordance with socialist democratic practices which include mutual reporting, mutually offering, accepting and respecting of advice and wishes, collective leadership, collective decision making, abiding by collective decisions, lower organs carrying out the decisions and directives of the higher organs which in turn respect the views submitted by the lower organs.

Article 15

Every citizen has, in accordance with this Constitution and other relevant laws, the right to –

(a) elect, and to be elected as, people's representatives to the Organs of State Power at different levels;

(b) recall elected people's representatives.

Article 16

Every people's representative, elected to any Organ of State Power, shall report back to the electorate on his work and shall also ascertain the wishes of the people.

Article 17

The working people shall have full participation in local matters, so that such matters may be resolved as far as possible, at the local level. They shall be invested with duties and powers.

Article 18

The State –

(a) is the ultimate owner of all natural resources above and below the ground, above and beneath the waters and in the atmosphere, and also of all the lands;

(b) shall develop, extract, exploit and utilize the natural resources in the interest of the working people of all the national races.

Article 19

The State shall nationalize the means of production within the land. Suitable enterprises shall be owned and operated by co-operatives.

Article 20

The State may, in accordance with law, permit such private enterprises which do not undermine the socialist economic system.

Article 21

(a) The State shall be responsible for constantly developing and promoting unity, mutual assistance, amity and mutual respect among the national races.

(b) The national races shall enjoy the freedom to profess their religion, use and develop their language, literature and culture, follow their cherished traditions and customs, provided that the enjoyment of any such freedom does not offend the laws or the public interest.

Article 22

All citizens shall –

(a) be equal before the law, regardless or race, religion, status, or sex;

(b) enjoy equal opportunities;

(c) enjoy the benefits derived from his labour in proportion to his contribution in manual or mental labour;

(d) have the right to inherit according to law.

Article 23

No penal law shall have retrospective effect.

Article 24

Punishments shall not be awarded in violation of human dignity.

Article 25

Laws shall be enacted to enforce the freedom, powers, rights, duties and restrictions prescribed by this Constitution.

Article 26

The State consistently practices an independent foreign policy, aimed at international peace and friendly relations among nations, and upholds the principles of peaceful co-existence of nations.

Article 27

These basic principles constitute the guidelines for interpreting the provisions of this Constitution and of other laws.

CHAPTER III
STATE STRUCTURE

Article 28

Local Autonomy under central leadership is the system of the State.

Article 29

(a) Local areas of the Socialist Republic of the Union of Burma shall be organized as follows :-

(1) villages are organized as village-tracts;

(2) wards are organized as towns;

(3) village-tracts and towns are organized as townships;

(4) townships are organized as stated or divisions;

(5) states and divisions are organized as the State.

(b) The different levels of administrative areas of the Socialist Republic of the Union of Burma shall be as follows :-

(1) wards or village-tracts;

(2) townships;

(3) states or divisions;

(4) the State.

Article 30

(a) Kawthoolei is constituted as Karen State;

(b) Chin Special Division is constituted as Chin State;

(c) Tenasserim Division (1) is constituted as Mon State;

(d) Tenasserim Division (2) is constituted as Tenasserim Division;

(e) Arakan Division is constituted as Arakan State.

Article 31

The States and Divisions of the Socialist Republic of the Union of Burma are as follows :-

(a) Kachin State
(b) Kayah State
(c) Karen State
(d) Chin State
(e) Sagaing Division
(f) Tenasserim Division
(g) Pegu Division
(h) Magwe Division
(i) Mandalay Division
(j) Mon State
(k) Arakan State
(l) Rangoon Division
(m) Iarrawaddy Division

Article 32

The Socialist Republic of the Union of Burma has a unicameral Pyithu Hluttaw.

Article 33

The Council of State shall be formed for the purpose of directing, supervising and co-ordinating the works of the Central and Local Organs of State Power and of the Bodies of Public Services in accordance with the laws, rules and resolutions passed by the Pyithu Hluttaw.

Article 34

The following Central Organs of State Power shall be formed to carry out the tasks laid down by the Pyithu Hluttaw:-

(a) The Council of Ministers;
(b) The Council of People's Justices;
(c) The Council of People's Attorney;
(d) The Council of People's Inspectors.

Article 35

A People's Council shall be formed for each State, Division, Township, Ward and Village-tract.

Article 36

(a) An Executive Committee, a Committee of Judges and an Inspection Committee shall be formed for each State, Division, or Township People's Council.

(b) An Executive Committee and a Committee of Judges shall be formed for each Ward or Village-tract People's Council.

Article 37

Bodies of Public Services, such as bodies of Public Administrative Services, Judicial Services, Law Services and Accounts Services shall be formed where necessary at central and local levels.

Article 38

The Pyithu Hluttaw may, in the interests of the State re-demarcate the territorial limits of the State by a vote of 75 per cent of all the members of the Pyithy Hluttaw.

Article 39

The Pyithu Hluttaw may make laws to –

(a) reconstitute States or Divisions as the need arises, after ascertaining the wishes of the citizens residing in the States or Divisions concerned;

(b) re-demarcate the boundary of any State or Division, as the need arises, after ascertaining the wishes of the citizens residing in the States or Divisions concerned;

(c) change the name of any State or Division, as the need arises, after ascertaining the wishes of citizens residing in the State or Division concerned.

Article 40

The Council of Ministers may constitute or reconstitute villages, village-tracts, wards, towns and townships within a State or Division, as the need arises, in consultation with the People's Councils concerned.

CHAPTER IV

PYITHU HLUTTAW

Article 41

The Pyithu Hluttaw is the highest Organ of state power. It exercises the sovereign powers of the State on behalf of the people.

Article 42

The Pyithu Hluttaw shall be formed with People's representatives elected directly by secret ballot by citizens who have the right to vote under this Constitution and other electoral laws.

Article 43

The regular terms of the Pyithu Hluttaw is four years from the date of its first session.

Article 44

The legislative power of the State is vested solely in the Pyithu Hluttaw.

Article 45

The Pyithu Hluttaw may delegate executive and judicial powers of the State to Central and Local Organs of State Power in accordance with this Constitution.

Article 46

The Pyithu Hluttaw shall have the right to enact laws concerning the culture of a national race only with the consent of more than half of all the members of the Pyithu Hluttaw from the State or Division concerned.

Article 47

The Pyithu Hluttaw shall have exclusive power to enact laws relating to State economic plans, annual budget and taxation.

Article 48

The Pyithu Hluttaw shall decide –

(a) important matters only by a vote of 75 per cent of all of its members;

(b) ordinary matters by a vote of more than half of all its members;

(c) as to whether any matter is important or ordinary by a vote of more than half of the members present.

Article 49

The Pyithu Hluttaw may decide to declare war and to make peace only by a vote of 75 per cent of all its members. The Council of State shall convene an emergency session of the Pyithu Hluttaw should circumstances call for a decision while the Pyithu Hluttaw is not in session.

Article 50

The Pyithu Hluttaw may decide to hold a referendum where necessary.

Article 51

Regular sessions of the Pyithu Hluttaw shall be convened at least twice a year. The interval between two sessions shall not exceed eight months. The Council of State may summon a special or an emergency session of the Pyithu Hluttaw where necessary.

Article 52

The Council of State shall convene a session of the Pyithu

Hluttaw as soon as possible if 34 per cent of all the members of the Pyithu Hluttaw so requisition.

Article 53

(a) A Panel of Chairman shall be elected to preside at each regular session of the Pyithu Hluttaw.

(b) The members of the Pyithu Hluttaw from each State or Division shall elect a chairman from among themselves to the Panel of Chairmen. The Pyithu Hluttaw shall give its approval to the election of the Chairman.

(c) Members of the Panel of Chairmen shall preside over the sessions of the Pyithu Hluttaw by rotation.

(d) A member of the Pyithu Hluttaw who is also a member of the Council of State or of any Central Organ of State Power shall not be a member of the Panel of Chairmen. Should a member of the Panel of Chairmen be elected to the Council of State or to any Central Organ of State Power he shall resign from the Panel.

(e) The Panel of Chairmen shall continue to carry out its duties till a new Panel has been elected at the next regular session of the Pyithu Hluttaw.

(f) The Panel of Chairmen of the Pyithu Hluttaw shall convene a session of the Pyithu Hluttaw if the Council of State fails to comply within 30 days from the date of a requisition made under Article 52.

Article 54

The Pyithu Hluttaw shall –

(a) constitute various Affairs committee of the Pyithu Hluttaw relating to economic, financial, social, public administrative, legislative, foreign, national races and other affairs, with members elected from among those of the Pyithu Hluttaw.

(b) in accordance with law constitute a National

Defence and Security Committee consisting a suitable number of members of the Council of State and of the Council of Ministers.

Article 55

The Pyithu Hluttaw shall enact a law to enable the Council of People's Inspectors to conduct inspections through committees to be formed by it, to determine whether or not the activities and the work of the following bodies are beneficial to the interests of the people :-

(a) Local Organs of State Power;

(b) Ministers;

(c) Bodies of Public Services; and

(d) such other organizations as may be prescribed by law.

Article 56

The Pyithu Hluttaw may form Commissions and Committees as an when necessary and invest them with duties and powers.

Article 57

The Pyithu Hluttaw shall make laws, rules and procedures for itself and for its Affairs Committees.

Article 58

The Council of State and the Central Organs of State Power shall be responsible to the Pyithu Hluttaw.

Article 59

(a) If need should arise to arrest any member of the Pyithu Hluttaw while it is in session, reliable evidence in support of such need shall be produced before the Panel of Chairmen. No such arrest shall be without the prior approval of the Panel of Chairmen.

(b) If need should arise to arrest any member of the Pyithu Hluttaw belongings to any organ of the Pyithu Hluttaw, while such organ is in session, reliable evidence in support of such need shall be produced before the Council of State. No such arrest shall be made without the prior approval of the Council of State.

(c) If any member of the Pyithu Hluttaw is arrested while the Pyithu Hluttaw or any organ of the Assembly to which he belongs is not in session the arrest and reliable evidence in support thereof shall be submitted to the Council of State as soon as possible.

Article 60

All deliberations and actions in sessions of the Pyithu Hluttaw or of the Organs of the Pyithu Hluttaw are absolutely privileged. No member shall be liable or punishable thereof, except under the laws, rules and regulations of the Pyithu Hluttaw.

Article 61

When the Pyithu Hluttaw is not in session, the Central Organs of State Power shall reply to written questions submitted by any member of the Pyithu Hluttaw within three weeks from the date of receipt of the question.

Article 62

The Pyithu Hluttaw may be dissolve if 75 per cent of all its members so resolve.

Article 63

The Pyithu Hluttaw may dissolve any People's Council or People's Councils for any of the following reasons :-

(a) violation of any provision of this Constitution,

(b) actions undermining national unity,

(c) endangering the stability of the State,

(d) contravention of any resolution adopted by the Pyithu Hluttaw,

(e) inefficient discharge of duties.

CHAPTER V
COUNCIL OF STATE

Article 64

The Pyithu Hluttaw shall form the Council of State with the following persons elected from among its members :-

(a) one member each elected by the States and Divisions, from among members of the Pyithu Hluttaw of the State or Division concerned.

(b) members elected by the members of the Pyithu Hluttaw from among themselves, equal in number to the number representatives elected under Clause (a) of this Article, and

(c) The Prime Minister.

Article 65

Members of the Council of State elected under Clauses (a) and (b) of Article 64 shall elect from among themselves the Chairman and the Secretary of the Council of State and shall obtain the approval of the Pyithu Hluttaw for such election.

Article 66

The Chairman and the Council of State shall be the President of the Republic.

Article 67

The term of office of the President is the same as that of the Council of State.

Article 68

The President of the Republic represents the State.

Article 69

If the Chairman of the Council of State is temporarily incapable of performing his duties, the Secretary of the Council of State shall perform the duties of the chairman, in addition to his own.

Article 70

The Council of State shall be responsible for giving effect to the provisions of this Constitution.

Article 71

The Council of State is responsible to the Pyithu Hluttaw. It shall report on its activities to the nearest session of the Pyithu Hluttaw.

Article 72

The term of office of the Council of State is the same as that of the Pyithu Hluttaw. The Council of State shall, on the expiry of the Pyithu Hluttaw, continue to perform its duties and functions till a new Council of State has been duly elected and constituted.

Article 73

The Council of State shall –

(a) convene sessions of the Pyithu Hluttaw in consultation with the Panel of Chairmen of the Pyithu Hluttaw;

(b) interpret the laws than this Constitution for the purpose of uniformity;

(c) promulgate laws enacted and rules made by the Pyithu Hluttaw;

(d) submit lists of candidates from among the members of the Pyithu Hluttaw to enable the Pyithu Hluttaw to elect the Council of Ministers, the Council of People's Justices, the Council of People's Attorneys and the Council of People's Inspectors. [Members of the council of State elected under Clauses (a) and (b) of Article 64 shall collectively submit such lists.];

(e) submit a list of candidates from among the members of the Pyithu Hluttaw to enable the Pyithu Hluttaw to elect Affairs Committees of the Pyithu Hluttaw [Members of the Council of State elected under Clauses (a) and (b), of Article 64 shall collectively submit such lists];

(f) make decisions concerning the establishment of diplomatic relations with foreign countries, severance of such relations and appointment and recall of diplomatic representatives;

(g) make decisions concerning the acceptance of credentials of envoys of foreign States or their recall;

(h) make decisions concerning the entering into, ratification or amendment of international treaties, or the withdrawal from such treaties with the approval of the Pyithu Hluttaw;

(i) make decisions concerning international agreements;

(j) appoint or remove Deputy Ministers;

(k) decide on the temporary suspension from duty or attendance of any session of any member of the Pyithu Hluttaw against whom action for high treason may be called for, provided the approval therefore shall be obtained from the nearest session of the Pyithu Hluttaw;

(l) appoint or dismiss heads of Bodies of Public Services;

(m) abrogate the decisions and orders of the Central and Local Organs of State Power if they are not consistent with the law;

(n) institute, confer or revoke titles, honours and awards;

(o) grant pardons or amnesty;

(p) perform other duties and exercise powers invested under this Consititution and other laws.

Article 74

The Council of State may make, if necessary, ordinances having the force of law, on matters other than those prescribed in Article 47, during the interval between sessions of the Pyithu Hluttaw. Such orders shall be submitted the approval to the nearest session of the Pyithu Hluttaw held within 90 days. If no session of the Pyithu Hluttaw is due within 90 days after the promulgation of such orders, an emergency session of the Pyithu Hluttaw shall be convened and approval obtained. Such orders shall cease to have effect from the date on which they are disapproved by the Pyithu Hluttaw.

Article 75

The Council of State may take suitable military action in the face of aggression against the State and action so taken shall be submitted to an emergency session of the Pyithu Hluttaw. If the situation is such that it is absolutely impossible to convene an emergency session of the Pyithu Hluttaw, the Council of State may continue all necessary military action. Such action shall be submitted for approval to the nearest session of the Pyithu Hluttaw.

Article 76

The Council of State may declare a state of emergency and promulgate martial law in specified areas or in the entire State, if an emergency affecting the defence and security of the State should arise. It may order mobilization in certain areas or in the entire State. Such measures shall be submitted for approval to the nearest session of the Pyithu Hluttaw.

Article 77

The Council of State may propose to the Pyithu Hluttaw the extension of the term of the Pyithu Hluttaw or of the People's Councils at different levels by six months at a time up to three times, if wars of natural disasters or conditions prejudicial to security render elections impossible though the regular term of the Phithu Hluttaw or of the People's councils has expired.

Article 78

If an emergency arises in the entire State, the council of State shall declare a state of emergency and convene an emergency session of the Pyithu Hluttaw. If a sufficient number of Pyithu Hluttaw members necessary to form a quorum fails to attend, the Council of State may take the following measures:-

(a) the Council of State, the Central Organs of State Power, members of the Pyithu Hluttaw belonging to the Organs of the Pyithu Hluttaw and those members who are able to attend the session shall collectively perform the duties and functions of the Pyithu Hluttaw, and

(b) a session of the Pyithu Hluttaw shall be convened as soon as the situation permits and approval obtained on the measures taken on behalf of the Pyithu Hluttaw.

Article 79

The Council of State shall direct, supervise and co-ordinate the work of the Central and Local Organs of State Power and of the Bodies of Public Services in accordance with the laws, rules and resolutions passed by the Pyithu Hluttaw.

Article 80

The Chairman of the Council of State shall sign the laws, rules and resolutions passed by the Pyithu Hluttaw as well as the orders promulgated by the Council of State. These shall be promulgated in the official Gazette.

Article 81

Bodies of Public Services may be constituted only by decision of the Council of State.

CHAPTER VI

COUNCIL OF MINISTERS

Article 82

The Council of Ministers shall be formed as follows :-

(a) The Pyithu Hluttaw elects members of the Council of Ministers from among hose members of the Pyithu Hluttaw whose names are on the list submitted collectively by members of the Council of State elected under Clauses (a) and (b) of Article 64.

(b) The Council of Ministers elects a Prime Minister from among its members.

(c) The Council of Ministers elects Deputy Prime Ministers from among the Ministers nominated by the Prime Minister.

Article 83

The Council of Ministers is the highest executive organ of the State.

Article 84

The Council of Ministers is responsible to the Pyithu Hluttaw when the Pyithu Hluttaw is in session and to the Council of State when the Pyithu Hluttaw is not in season.

Article 85

The Council of Ministers –

(a) shall submit to the Council of State a list of those members of the Pyithu Hluttaw who should be appointed as Deputy Ministers;

(b) may propose to the Council of State the termination of the service of a Deputy Minister, when necessary.

Article 86

(a) The term of office of the Council of Ministers is the same as that of the Pyithu Hluttaw. On the expiry of the term of the Pyithu Hluttaw, the Council of Ministers shall continue to perform its duties until a new Council of Ministers has been elected.

(b) The term of office of Deputy Ministers is the same as that of the Council of Ministers.

Article 87

The Council of Ministers –

(a) is responsible for the management of executive, economic, financial, social, cultural and foreign affairs and national defence on behalf of the Pyithu Hluttaw in accordance with the principle of collective leadership;

(b) implements the socialist system through the economic plans of all the national races;

(c) implements the resolutions of the Pyithu Hluttaw and the orders of the Council of State;

(d) directs and co-ordinates the Ministers, organs of public administration and the Executive Committees of the People's Councils at different levels;

(e) maintains the rule of law and upholds law and order;

(f) performs such other duties as may be laid down by the Pyithu Hluttaw or the Council of State.

Article 88

The Council of Ministers shall draw up, after making necessary adjustments, and submit the following to the Pyithu Hluttaw through the Council of State;-

(a) long-term, short-term and annual economic plans;

(b) annual budgets;

(c) annual reports on the situation of the State;

(d) reports that may be required from time to time.

Article 89

The Council of Ministers shall be solely responsible for the submission of the following bills to the Pyithu Hluttaw through the Council of State for enactment into law:-

(a) bills on economic plans;

(b) bills on budget;

(c) bills on taxation.

Article 90

Each Minister is responsible for the successful performance of the duties of those organs of public administration with which he is charged at their different levels.

Article 91

A Minister is responsible to the Council of Ministers. A Deputy Minister is responsible to the Minister concerned.

Article 92

The Council of Ministers may, with the approval of the Council of State, constitute such Bodies of Public Administrative Services at different levels as may be necessary and may appoint the required personnel to such Services, according to law.

Article 93

The Council of Ministers shall prescribe the duties and powers of organs of public administration at all levels.

Article 94

Organs of public administration at different levels shall be responsible to those of the next higher level as well as to the People's Councils concerned and the be subject to their supervisions and inspection.

CHAPTER VII

COUNCIL OF PEOPLE'S JUSTICES

Article 95

(a) The Pyithu Hluttaw elects members of the Council of People's Justices from among those members of the Pyithu Hluttaw whose names are on the list submitted collectively by members of the Council of State elected under Clauses (a) and (b) of Article 64.

(b) Members of the Council of People's Justices shall elect a Chairman from among themselves.

Article 96

(a) The following Judicial Organs shall be constituted in the State –

(1) the Council of People's Justices;

(2) State Judges' Committee, Divisional Judges' Committee;

(3) Township Judges' Committee;

(4) Ward Judges' Committee, Village-tract Judges' Committee;

(b) The Pyithu Hluttaw shall prescribed, by law, the duties and powers of the Judicial Organs.

Article 97

The term of office of the Council of People's Justices shall be the same as that of the Pyithu Hluttaw. The Council of People's Justices shall, on expiry on the term of the Pyithu Hluttaw, continue to perform its duties and functions till a new Council of People's Justices has been elected.

Article 98

Justices shall be administered collectively by each judicial organ.

Article 99

Military justice for members of the People's Defence Services may be administered according to law by a collective organ or by a single judge.

Article 100

Administrative tribunals may be formed according to law.

Article 101

Administration of justice shall be based on the following principles :-

(a) to protect and safeguard the Socialist system;

(b) to protect and safeguard the interests of the working people;

(c) to administer justice independently according to law;

(d) to educate the public to understand and abide by the law;

(e) to work within the framework of law as far as possible for the settlement of cases between members of the public;

(f) to dispense justice in open court unless otherwise prohibited by law;

(g) to guarantee in all cases right of defence and the right of appeal under law;

(h) to aim at reforming moral character in meeting out punishment to offenders.

Article 102

The Burmese language shall be used in the administration of justice. Languages of the national races concerned may also be used, when necessary, and arrangements shall then be made to make interpreters available.

Article 103

The Council of People's Justices –

(a) is the highest judicial organ of the State and;

(b) shall form the necessary judicial Courts only with its members and administer justice.

Article 104

The Council of People's Justices shall be responsible to the Pyithu Hluttaw and shall report to the Pyithu Hluttaw on the state of administration of justice. When the Pyithu Hluttaw is not in session, the Council of People's Justices shall be responsible to the Council of State.

Article 105

The Council of People's Justices shall supervise all judicial organs and courts within the State.

Article 106

(a) The State People's Councils, the Divisional People's Councils, the Township People's Councils, the Ward People's Councils and the Village-tract People's Councils shall respectively form the State Judges' Committees, the Divisional Judges' Committees, the Township Judges' Committees, the Ward Judges' Committees and the Village-tract Judges' Committees with persons elected from among the members of the respective People's Councils.

(b) Members of the Judges' Committee elected by the People's Councils at different levels under ..... (illegible) shall each elect a Chairman from .... (illegible) members.

Article 107

(a) The Judges' Committees of the People's Councils at different levels shall form with its members, such Courts as may be necessary.

(b) If the number of members of the Judges' Committees is not sufficient to form Courts under Clause (a) above Courts may be formed with members of the People's Councils concerned under the leadership of a member of the Judges' Committee at the respective level. Other suitable citizens may be included in such Courts only if the number of members of the respective People's Council is not sufficient to form such Courts.

Article 108

The term of office of State Judges' Committees, Divisional Judges' Committees, Township Judges' Committees, Ward Judges' Committees and Village-tract Judges' Committees shall be the same as that of the People's Councils concerned at different levels. On expiry of the term of the People's Councils at different levels, the respective Judges' Committee shall continue to perform its duties and functions until a new Judges' Committee has been elected.

Article 109

The Council of People's Justices may, with the approval of the Council of State, form bodies of judicial services at different levels as may be necessary and appoint the required personnel to such services according to law.

Article 110

The State Judges' Committees, the Divisional Judges' Committees, the Township Judges' Committees, the Ward Judges' Committees and the Village-tract Judges' Committees shall supervise the judicial organs and Courts formed by them and such Judges' Committees shall be responsible to the People's Councils concerned.

CHAPTER VIII

COUNCIL OF PEOPLE'S ATTORNEYS

Article 111

(a) The Pyithu Hluttaw elects members of the Council of People's Attorneys from among those members of the Pyithu Hluttaw whose names are on the list submitted collectively by members of the Council of State elected under Clauses (a) and (b) of Article 64.

(b) Members of the Council of People's Attorneys shall elect a Chairman from among themselves.

Article 112

The Council of People's Attorney shall –

(a) protect and safeguard the Socialist system;

(b) protect and safeguard the rights and privileges of the working people;

(c) tender legal advice to the Council of State and to the Council of Ministers;

(d) report to the Council of State any acts of the Central and Local Organs of State Power and of the Bodies of Public Services which infringe the law.

(e) Undertake any other duties prescribed by law.

Article 113

The term of office of the Council of People's Attorneys is the same as that of the Pyithu Hluttaw. On expiry of the term of the Pyithu Hluttaw, the Council of People's Attorneys shall continue to perform its duties and functions till a new Council of People's Attorneys has been elected.

Article 114

The Council of People's Attorneys shall be responsible to the Pyithu Hluttaw . It shall report to the Pyithu Hluttaw on the progress of its work. It shall be responsible so the Council of State when the Pyithu Hluttaw is not in session.

Article 115

The Council of People's Attorney may, with the approval of the Council of State, form as necessary, bodies of law services at different levels and shall also appoint the required law officers in accordance with law.

Article 116

The Council of People's Attorneys shall direct and supervise the Central law officers, State and Divisional law officers and Township law officers.

Article 117

The Pyithu Hluttaw shall be law prescribe the duties and powers of the Council of People's Attorneys, the Central, State and Divisional law officers and Township law officers.

CHAPTER IX

COUNCIL OF PEOPLE'S INSPECTORS

Article 118

(a) The Pyithu Hluttaw elects members of the Council of People's Inspectors from among those members of the Pyithu Hluttaw whose names are on the list submitted collectively by members of the Council of State elected under Clauses (a) and (b) of Article 64.

(b) Members of the Council of People's Inspectors shall elect a Chairman from among themselves.

Article 119

The Council of People's Inspectors is the highest organ of inspection of public undertakings.

Article 120

The Council of People's Inspectors shall be responsible to the Pyithu Hluttaw. It shall submit reports to the Pyithu Hluttaw on the progress of inspection of public undertakings. It shall be responsible to the council of State when the Pyithu Hluttaw is not in session.

Article 121

(a) The Council of People's Inspectors shall conduct inspectors to determine whether the activities of the Local Organs of State Power, Ministers, Bodies of Public Services and such other organizations as may be prescribed by law prove benefited to the interest of the public.

(b) The Council of People's Inspectors shall report on its findings and measures taken by it, to the Pyithu Hluttaw through the Council of State.

Article 122

The term of office of the Council of People's Inspectors is

the same as that of the Pyithu Hluttaw. On expiry of the term of the Pyithu Hluttaw, the Council of People's Inspectors shall continue to perform its duties and functions till a new Council of People's Inspectors has been elected.

Article 123

(a) The State, Divisional and Township People's Councils shall form State, Divisional and Township Inspectorates with members of State, Divisional and Township People's Councils concerned.

(b) Members of each Local Inspectorate shall elect a Chairman from among themselves.

(c) The Pyithu Hluttaw shall by law prescribed the duties and powers of Local Inspectorates.

Article 124

Each Local Inspectorate shall be responsible to the People's Council concerned.

Article 125

The Local Inspectorates shall perform the following duties –

(a) reporting to the People's Council concerned on the activities carried out during the interval between the meetings of the People's Council;

(b) implementing tasks and submitting reports under the guidance of the People's Council concerned and of the organs at higher level.

Article 126

The term of office of the Local Inspectorates is the same as that of the People's Council at different levels. On expiry of the People's Council, the Local Inspectorate shall continue to perform its duties and functions until a new Local Inspectorate has been elected.

Article 127

The Council of People's Inspectors may, with the approval

of the Council of State, form as necessary, Bodies of Accounts Services at different levels and shall also appoint the required accounts officers in accordance with law.

Article 128

The Central Accounts Office shall be responsible to the Council of People's Inspectors and accounts offices at different levels shall be responsible to the Inspectorates concerned and to the accounts offices at the higher level and shall submit to their supervision and inspection.

CHAPTER X

PEOPLE'S COUNCILS

Article 129

The People's Councils at different levels shall be formed in accordance with this Constitution and electoral laws with people's representatives elected directly by secret ballot by citizens having the right to vote in the area concerned.

Article 130

The number of people's representatives constituting the People's Councils at different levels as well as the Organs of the People's Council shall be prescribed by law.

Article 131

The term of office of the People's Councils at different level shall be the same as the regular term of office of the Pyithu Hluttaw.

Article 132

The People's Councils at different levels are Local Organs of State Power and they shall implement the following tasks within the framework of law :-

(a) economic and social affairs and public administration;

(b) administration of justice;

(c) local security, defence, maintenance of rule of law and order;

(d) solidarity of the national races and preservation, protection and promotion of their traditional cultures;

(e) Protection of the rights of the people in the area concerned and organizing and urging them to perform their duties efficiently;

(f) formulation of economic plans and their implementation;

(g) preparation of annual budgets and their co-ordination;

(h) construction, settlement and rural and urban development works;

(i) communications;

(j) directing, supervising and co-ordinating Local Organs of State Power and Bodies of Public Services relating to them;

(k) providing leadership to the people and keeping in close contact with them to obtain their active participation in works of public interest;

(l) preservation, protection and development of natural environment;

(m) co-ordinating the affairs of Local Bodies of Public Services;

(n) performing such other necessary works of public interest as may be prescribed by law.

Article 133

(a) The People's Council at different levels shall hold meetings as prescribed by law;

(b) The Members of the Panel of Chairmen shall be elected from among the members of the People's Councils to preside over the regular meetings of the People's Councils at different levels.

(c) The Members of the Panel of Chairmen shall preside over the meetings by rotation.

(d) A member of a People's Council who is also a member of the Executive Committee, the Judges' Committee or the Inspectorate of such People's Council shall not be a member of the Panel of Chairmen of such Council. Should a member of the Panel of Chairmen be elected to the Executive Committee, the Judges' Committee or the Inspectorate he shall resign from the Panel of Chairmen.

(e) The Panel of Chairmen shall continue to perform its duties till the next regular session of the People's Council is convened and a new Panel of Chairmen has been elected therefore.

(f) The Executive Committee of a People's Council shall convene a meeting of the Council of 34 per cent of all the members of the Council so requisition. If the Executive Committee fails to convene the meeting within 30 days from the date of such a requisition, the Panel of Chairmen shall, as soon as possible, convene the meeting.

Article 134

The State People's Council, Divisional People's Council and Township People's Council shall form People's Council Affairs Committees with members of the People's Council concerned.

Article 135

An Executive Committee shall be elected from among its members by each of the People's Councils at different levels, to implement the tasks decided upon by the People's Council. The members of the Executive Committee shall elect a chairman and a secretary from among themselves. The chairman and the secretary so elected shall concurrently be the Chairman and the Secretary of the People's Council concerned.

Article 136

The Chairman of each of the People's Councils shall concurrently be the Chairman of the State, Division, Township, Ward or Village-tract concerned.

Article 137

The Executive Committee of each of the People's Councils at different levels shall be responsible to the People's Council concerned.

Article 138

The Executive Committees of the People's Councils at different levels shall perform the following duties –

(a) convening meetings of the People's Council in consultation with the Panel of Chairmen;

(b) promulgation and implementation of decisions, orders and directives of the People's Councils;

(c) implementation of the tasks laid down by the Council of Ministers as well as by the People's Councils concerned.

(d) maintaining intercommunications between the Executive Committees at different levels and co-ordinating their activities; directing and supervising of the Executive Committee at the lower level by the one of the higher level;

(e) directing, supervising and co-ordinating the work of Local Bodies of Public Services, co-ordinating the affairs of Public Services;

(f) submitting to the People's Council concerned, reports on the activities carried out during the interval between meetings of the People's Council;

(g) the temporary suspension from duty or attendance of any session of any member of the People's Council against whom action for high treason may be called for, provided that approval therefore shall be obtained from the nearest session of the People's Council.

Article 139

The term of office of the Executive Committees of the People's Councils at different levels is the same as that of the People's Councils. On the expiry of the term of the People's Council, the Executive Committee shall continue to perform its duties and functions till a new Executive Committee has been elected.

Article 140

(a) If need should arise to arrest any member of a People's Council in session, reliable evidence in support of such need shall be produced before the Panel of Chairmen of the People's Council. No arrest shall be made without the prior approval of the Panel of Chairmen of the People's Council concerned.

(b) If need should arise to arrest any member of an organ of a People's Council, while such organ is in session, reliable evidence in support of such need shall be produced before the Executive Committee concerned. No arrest shall be made without the prior approval of the Executive Committee.

(c) If any member of a People's Council is arrested while the People's Council or any of its organs is not in session, reliable evidence in support of such arrest shall be produced before the Executive Committee as soon as possible.

Article 141

All deliberations and actions at the meetings of a People's Council and of any of its organs are absolutely privileged. No member shall liable or punishable therefore except under the laws, rules and bye-laws of the People's council.

Article 142

Members of the People's Councils shall maintain contacts with their electorate and shall report back on their activities and keep them informed from time to time on questions of policy.

Article 143

Members of the People's Councils shall seek, and submit, the wishes, opinions and proposals of the people to the People's Council concerned and work for their realization.

Article 144

The People's Councils may report on local matters of importance and submit advice for the benefit of the public, from the lower to the higher levels of the People's Councils, up to the Council of State.

CHAPTER XI

FUNDAMENTAL RIGHTS AND DUTIES OF CITIZENS

Article 145

(a) All persons born of parents both of whom are nationals of the Socialists Republic of the Union of Burma are citizens of the Union.

(b) Persons who are vested with citizenship according to existing laws on the date this Constitution comes into force are also citizens.

Article 146

Citizenship, naturalization and revocation of citizenship shall be as prescribed by law.

Article 147

All citizens are equal before the law irrespective of race, status, official position, wealth, culture, birth, religion or sex.

Article 148

(a) enjoy the benefits derived from his labour in proportion to his contribution in manual or mental labour and diligence;

(b) freely undertake any vocation permitted by the State within the framework of the Socialist economy;

(c) settle and reside in any place within the State according to the law.

Article 149

Every citizen is sickness shall have the right to medical treatment as arranged by the State.

Article 150

Every working citizen has the right to –

(a) rest and recreation,

(b) fixed working hours and leave as prescribed by law.

Article 151

(a) Every working citizen shall enjoy benefits as prescribed by law or injury due to occupational accidents or when disabled or sick or old.

(b) Heirs to any working citizen shall enjoy benefits as prescribed by law on his death.

Article 152

(a) Every citizen shall have the right to education.

(b) Burmese is the common language. Language or the other national races may also be taught.

(c) Every citizen shall be given basic education which the State prescribes by law as compulsory.

Article 153

(a) Every citizen shall have the right to freely conduct scientific research, work with creativity and initiative to develop the arts, literature and other branches of culture.

(b) Every citizen shall have the right to freely use one's language and literature, follow one's customs, culture and traditions and profess the religion of his choice. The exercise of this right shall not, however, be to the detriment of national solidarity and the socialist social order which are the basic requirements of the entire Union. Any particular action in this respect which might adversely affect the interests of one or several other national races shall be taken only after consulting with and obtaining the consent of those affected.

(c) Notwithstanding the rights enjoyed under Clauses (a) and (b), acts which undermine the unity and solidarity of the national races, national security or the socialist social order are prohibited. Persons who violate this prohibition shall be punished according to law.

Article 154

(a) Women shall enjoy political, economic, social and cultural rights as men.

(b) Mothers, children and expectant mothers shall enjoy those rights prescribed by law.

(c) Children born of citizens shall enjoy equal rights.

(d) Women shall enjoy freedoms and rights guaranteed by law as regards marriage, divorce, partition of property, succession and custody of their children.

Article 155

Every citizen shall have the right –

(a) subject to the provisions of this Constitution, to elect and be elected to the Pyithu Hluttaw and the People's Councils at different levels;

(b) to submit in accordance with law a list of candidates for election as people's representatives to the Pyithu Hluttaw and the People's Councils at different levels;

(c) to recall in accordance with law people's

representatives elected to the Pyithu Hluttaw and the People's Councils at different levels.

Article 156

(a) Every citizen shall have the right to freedom of thought, and of conscience, and to freely profess any religion.

(b) Notwithstanding the rights and freedoms granted under Clause (a), the State may enact laws in the interests either of the working people or of law and order.

(c) Religion and religious organizations shall not be used for political purposes. Laws shall be enacted to this effect.

Article 157

Every citizen shall have freedom of speech, expression and publication to the extent that the enjoyment of such freedom is not contrary to the interests of the working people and of socialism.

Article 158

Every citizen shall have the right freely to take part in political, social, class and mass organizations permitted by law and to enjoy freedom of association, assembly and procession. The State shall provide necessary assistance to the people to enable them to enjoy fully these rights and freedoms.

Article 159

(a) Personal freedom and security of every citizen shall be guaranteed.

(b) No citizen shall be placed in custody for more than 24 hours without the sanction of a competent judicial organ.

(c) The State shall be responsible for the protection, in accordance with law, of citizens of the Socialist Republic of the Union of Burma who are abroad.

Article 160

The privacy and security of the home, property, correspondence and other communications of citizens shall be protected by law subject to the provisions of this Constitution.

Article 161

Every citizen's income, savings, property and residential buildings lawfully earned and acquired by his diligence and manual and mental contribution, instruments of production permitted to be owned within the framework of the socialist economic system, and other lawful possessions shall be protected by law.

Article 162

The right of every citizen to inheritance shall be recognized by law.

Article 163

(a) Every citizen shall fully enjoy the rights provided by this Constitution.

(b) Laws shall be enacted to ensure the most expeditious and effective protection of the rights of citizens, and to prevent their violation.

Article 164

(a) Every citizen shall have the right to lodge complaints concerning their grievances to the competent organ of State power.

(b) The organ of State power shall investigate the complaints expeditiously and take such action as may be necessary.

Article 165

The right to sue for compensation any member of an organ of State power or any of the organs of State power or any public servant or any body of Public Services for abuse of authority entrusted by the people in violation of the rights or interests of any citizen, shall be guaranteed any prescribed by law.

Article 166

Every citizen shall be under a duty in the exercise of his rights and freedom to abstain from undermining any of the following –

(a) the sovereignty and security of the State;

(b) the essence of the socialist system prescribed by this Constitution;

(c) the unity and solidarity of the national races;

(d) public peace and tranquillity;

(e) public morality.

Article 167

(a) Laws may be enacted imposing necessary restriction on the rights and freedoms of citizens to prevent infringements of the sovereignty and security of the State, the essence of the socialist system prescribed by this Constitution, the unity and solidarity of the national races, public and tranquillity or public morality.

(b) Such a preventive law shall provide that the restrictive order shall only be made collectively by a body, and that the order shall be regularly reviewed and modified as necessary, and that the aggrieved person shall have the right of appeal to a higher organ.

Article 168

Every citizen shall be under a duty to abide by the provisions of this Constitution, as well as the laws, work discipline, and local rules made for the building of a socialist society, and discharge efficiency such duties as may be assigned to him by the State.

Article 169

Every citizen shall be under a duty to protect nationalized property, co-operative owned property and public and to a strive to the best of his ability for socialist capital accumulation, for strengthening the defensive capacity of the State and enhancing the standards of living of the people.

Article 170

Every citizen shall be under a duty to protect and safeguard the independence, sovereignty and territorial integrity of the Socialist Republic of the Union of Burma. This is a noble duty.

Article 171

Every citizen shall, in accordance with law –

(a) undergo military training, and

(b) undertake military service for the defence of the State.

Article 172

Every citizen shall be under a duty to pay taxes and duties as prescribed by law.

CHAPTER XII

ELECTORAL SYSTEM

Article 173

The basic aims of the electoral system are as follows –

(a) to elect people's representatives who will truly represent the working people;

(b) to secure a broad participation of citizens in the electoral process;

(c) to elect Organs of the Pyithu Hluttaw and of the People's Councils at different levels that will truly represent the working people.

Article 174

(a) Citizens shall directly elect people's representatives by secret ballot.

(b) Every citizen who has attained the age of eighteen years shall have the right to vote.

(c) All citizens who have the rights to vote shall enjoy equal voting rights.

Article 175

Constituencies for the election of people's representatives to the Pyithu Hluttaw and the People's Councils at different levels shall be formed as follows –

(a) constituency for Ward or Village-tract People's Council;

(b) constituency for Township People's Council;

(c) constituency for State or Divisional People's Council;

(d) constituency for the Pyithu Hluttaw.

Article 176

(a) Constituencies for the Pyithu Hluttaw shall be delimited on township basis.

(b) Each township shall elect one representative to the Pyithu Hluttaw.

(c) Township with large population shall, in addition to the right granted under Clause (b), elect representatives in proportion to population as prescribed by electoral law.

(d) Additional members of the Pyithu Hluttaw shall, by law, be allotted to States or Divisions having less than 10 townships and less than 10 lakhs in population.

Article 177

Persons having the right to vote and possessing the following qualifications are eligible to stand for election as people's representatives to the Pyithu Hluttaw and to the People's Councils at different levels –

(a) being a citizen born of parents both of whom are also citizens;

(b) having attained the age of 20 years to stand for election to Ward, Village-tract and Township People's Councils;

(c) having attained the age of 24 years to stand for election to State and Divisional People's Councils;

(d) having attained the age of 28 years to stand for election to the Pyithu Hluttaw.

Article 178

The following persons shall not have the right to vote or to stand for election –

(a) members of religious orders, and

(b) persons disqualified by electoral law.

Article 179

The Burma Socialist Programme Party, in consultation with mass and class organization formed under its leadership and with the electorate of the constituency concerned, and respecting their wishes, shall submit lists of candidates for election as people's representatives to the Pyithu Hluttaw and to the People's Councils at different levels.

Article 180

A candidate for election as a people's representatives –

(a) shall stand for election to the Pyithu Hluttaw or to the People's Council at one level only and

(b) from only one constituency.

Article 181

(a) The election of people's representatives to the Pyithu Hluttaw and the People's Councils at different levels shall be valid only if more than half of all the persons from the respective constituencies having the right to vote have cast their votes.

(b) A candidate for election as a people's representative shall be duly elected only if he obtains more than half of the votes cast in an election found valid under Clause (a) above.

Article 182

(a) The Pyithu Hluttaw shall form an Election Commission six months before the expiry of the terms of the Pyithu Hluttaw and the People's Councils for the purpose of electing a new Pyithu Hluttaw and new People's Councils at different levels.

(b) The Council of State shall submit to the Pyithu Hluttaw, a list of names of citizens who are qualified by law, other than members of the Council of State and of the Council of Ministers, from among whom the Election Commission may be formed.

(c) The Pyithu Hluttaw which decides to dissolve itself under Article 62, shall form, in accordance with Clause (b), an Election Commission for the election of a new Pyithu Hluttaw.

(d) Elections for the Pyithu Hluttaw and the People's Councils at different levels shall be held as prescribed by law, prior to the expiry of the terms of the Pyithu Hluttaw and the respective People's Councils.

(e) Sessions of the new Pyithu Hluttaw and of the new People's Councils at different levels shall be convened with the newly elected people's representatives on the date of expiry of the term of the old Pyithu Hluttaw and the old People's Councils.

Article 183

(a) If the Pyithu Hluttaw or any People's Council is

dissolved before the expiry of its term elections shall be held as prescribed by law and sessions of the Pyithu Hluttaw or of the People's Council concerned shall be convened.

(b) If any State, Divisional or Township People's Council is dissolved, the Council of State shall form with suitable citizens, an Executive Committee, a Committee of Judges and a Local Inspectorate and temporarily assign duties to them pending the election of the respective new People's Council.

(c) If a Ward or Village-tract People's Council is dissolved, the Council of State shall form with suitable citizens, an Executive Committee and a Committee of Judges and temporarily assign duties to the pending the election of the respective new People's Council.

Article 184

Expenses incurred in the elections of people's representatives to the Pyithu Hluttaw and to the People's Councils at different levels shall be met out of State funds.

Article 185

(a) If the situation is not yet ripe for the election of any State, Divisional or Township People's Council, the Council of State shall form, with suitable citizens, an Executive Committee, a Committee of Judges and a Local Inspectorate and temporarily assign duties to them for the purposes of performing the functions of the People's Council concerned.

(b) If the situation is not yet ripe for election of any Ward or Village-tract People's Council, the Council of State shall form with suitable citizens, an Executive Committee and a Committee of Judges and temporarily assign duties to them for the purpose of performing the functions of the People's Council concerned.

Article 186

The Pyithu Hluttaw shall enact such laws as may be necessary in connection with the election of People's representatives.

CHAPTER XIII
RECALL, RESIGNATION AND REPLACEMENT

Article 187

Any organ of State of the people who have elected and assigned duties to a people's representatives or an organ wishing to recall such representative or organ for any of the following reasons, shall have the right to do so in accordance with law –

(a) violation of any provision of the Constitution;

(b) inefficient discharge of duties or

(c) misbehaviour.

Article 188

Any people's representative who has been elected, or any representative who has been assigned duties in any organ of the Pyithu Hluttaw or of any People's Council, may submit his resignation to the respective organ in accordance with law.

Article 189

A vacancy arising for any reason in the Pyithu Hluttaw or in any People's Council at any level or in an organ of the Pyithu Hluttaw or the Council concerned shall be filled by election in accordance with law.

CHAPTER XIV
STATE FLAG, STATE SEAL, NATIONAL ANTHEM, AND STATE CAPITAL

Article 190

The State Flag shall be as shown below :-

(State Flag not reproduced)

Article 191

The State Seal shall be as shown below :-

(State Seal not reproduced)

Article 192

The Pyithu Hluttaw shall prescribe the National Anthem. Until a new National Anthem is prescribed the present National Anthem shall be used.

Article 193

The capital of the Republic is Rangoon.

CHAPTER XV

AMENDMENT OF THE CONSTITUTION

Article 194

(a) The Preamble of this Constitution, Article 1 and 4 of Chapter I, Article 5, 6, 7, 8, 9, 11, 12, 14, 18 and 21 of Chapter II, Article 28, 29 and 32 of Chapter III, Articles 41, 44 and 46 of Chapter IV and Article 194 of Chapter XV shall be amended with the prior approval of 75 per cent of all the members of the Pyithu Hluttaw, in a nation-wide referendum only with a majority vote of more than half of those who have the right to vote.

(b) Provisions other than those mentioned in Clause (a) shall be amended only with a majority vote of 75 per cent of all the members of the Pyithu Hluttaw.

(c) Members of the Pyithu Hluttaw may submit to the Pyithu Hluttaw motions for amending this Constitution.

(d) If a People's Council wishes to submit a motion for amending this Constitution, such a motion shall be submitted stage by stage from the lower to the higher levels and finally to the Pyithu Hluttaw.

CHAPTER XVI

GENERAL PROVISIONS

Article 195

This Constitution shall come into force throughout the Union after its adoption in a nation-wide referendum by more than half of all the people who have the right to vote.

Article 196

The Revolutionary Council of the Union of Burma shall, continuing to exercise State sovereignty, carry out during the interval between the coming into force of this Constitution and the day the first session of the Pyithu Hluttaw is convened, all the functions of the Pyithu Hluttaw under the Constitution. The work done by the Revolutionary Council to bring the Constitution into force shall be deemed to have been carried out in accordance with this Constitution.

Article 197

Interpretation of the preamble, articles, clauses, words and expressions contained in this Constitution shall be based only on the Burmese text.

Article 198

Burmese shall be used as the official language for the purpose of uniformity and clarity in communications between the higher and lower level organs of the State and between such organs at the same level. If necessary the language of the national race concerned may be used.

Article 199

All policy guidelines laws, rules, regulations, notifications, proclamations, measures, responsibilities and rights of the Revolutionary Council of the Union of Burma shall devolve on the Socialist Republic of the Union of Burma.

Article 200

(a) In interpreting the expressions contained in this Constitution, reference shall be made to the Interpretation Law promulgated by the Revolutionary Council of the Union of Burma.

(b) Amendments to and further interpretation of expressions contained in the Law mentioned in Clause (a), shall only be made by the Pyithu Hluttaw.

(c) The validity of the acts of the Council of State, or of the Central or Local Organs of State Power under this Constitution shall only be determined by the Pyithu Hluttaw.

Article 201

The Pyithu Hluttaw may publish interpretation of this Constitution from time to time as may be necessary.

Article 202

(a) This Constitution is the basic law of all laws of the State.

(b) Existing laws and rules shall remain in force in so far as they are not contrary to this Constitution until and unless they are repealed or amended by the Pyithu Hluttaw.

(c) Existing regulations, bye-laws, notifications, orders, directives and procedures shall remain in force in so far as they are not contrary to this Constitution until and unless they are repealed or amended by the Council of State.

(d) Existing laws and rules shall be repealed or amended by the Pyithu Hluttaw to bring them into consonance with this Constitution.

(e) Existing regulations, bye-laws, notifications, orders, directives and procedures shall be repealed or amended by the Council of State to bring them into consonance with this Constitution.

(f) Existing laws, rules, regulations, bye-laws, notifications, orders, directives, and procedures shall, pending their repeal or amendment, be interpreted and acted upon by the Central and Local organs of State Power in the spirit of this Constitution.

(g) The Bodies of Public Services shall perform their duties in the spirit of this Constitution.

(h) All functioning organs and all public servants and workers, serving under the Revolutionary Council of the Union of Burma on the day this Constitution comes into force shall continue in their functions unless otherwise prescribed by the Council of State.

Article 202

(a) The Council of State and the Central Organs of State Power may, subject to this Constitution and to laws, rules and resolutions passed by the Pyithu Hluttaw, promulgate such regulations, bye-laws, orders, directives and procedures as may be necessary.

(b) The Local Organs of State Power may, subject to this Constitution and to laws, rules and resolutions passed by the Pyithu Hluttaw and to regulations, bye-laws, orders, directives and procedures promulgated by the respective Central Organs of State Power, promulgate such orders, directives and procedures for the respective local areas as may be necessary.

Article 204

(a) Members of the Pyithu Hluttaw, the Council of State, the Council of People's Justices, the Council of People's Attorneys and the Council of People's Inspectors shall have the right to submit to the Pyithu Hluttaw draft legislation on matters other than those mentioned in Article 89.

(b) The Council of Ministers shall have the right to submit to the Pyithu Hluttaw draft legislation on matters mentioned in Article 89 as well as on other matters.

(c) The People's Councils at different levels may submit draft legislation on matters other than those mentioned in Article 89, stage by stage from the lower to the higher levels of the People's Councils and finally to the Pyithu Hluttaw.

Article 205

The Burma Socialist Programme Party, mass and class organizations formed under its leadership, and the working people may submit suggestions and advice to the organs of State power at different levels, on legal matters, economic planning, the annual budget and other matters.

Article 206

(a) Members of the Council of State, and of the Council of Ministers shall not serve on any other Organ of State Power other than the organ to which they belong, except in cases provided for in Clause (b) of Article 54 and in Clause (c) of Article 64.

(b) Members of the Council of People's Justices, of the Council of People's Attorneys and of the Council of People's Inspectors shall not serve on any Organ of State Power other than the organ to which they belong or on any other Organ of the Pyithu Hluttaw.

(c) Members on the Executive Committee and of the Inspectorates of the People's Council at the State, Divisional and Township levels shall not serve on any Local Organ of State Power other than the organ to which they belong or on any Affairs Committee.

Article 207

The number of people's representatives which shall

constitute the quorum at meetings of the Pyithu Hluttaw and the People's Councils at different levels shall be 75 per cent of all the people's representatives.

Article 208

The Council of State or an Affairs Committee of the Pyithu Hluttaw may invite any Central Organ of State Power to attend and answer questions, and such organ shall be under a duty to respond.

Article 209

(a) Should the Pyithu Hluttaw or any People's Council at any level be dissolved before the expiry of its regular term, the term of office of the newly elected Pyithu Hluttaw or People's Council shall be for the remaining period of the term of the dissolved Pyithu Hluttaw or People's Council.

(b) Should any People's Council be formed after the formation of the Pyithu Hluttaw, the term of such People's Council shall be the same as the regular term of the Pyithu Hluttaw.

Appendix-II

Pyithu Hluttaw Election Law, 31 May 1989

THE STATE LAW AND ORDER RESTORATION COUNCIL LAW NO.14/89, 13TH WANING DAY OF KASON

1351 B.E., 31ST MAY, 1989

In order to hold a free and fair Multi-Party Democracy General Election and to elect the representatives of the *Pyithu Hluttaw*, the State Law and Order Restoration Council hereby enacts the following Law :-

CHAPTER I

TITLE AND DEFINITION

1. This Law shall be called the *Pyithu Hluttaw* Election Law.

2. The following expressions contained in this Law shall have the meanings give here under :-

(a) *Hluttaw* means the Pyithu Hluttaw;

(b) *Commission* means the Multi-Party Democracy General Election Commission;

(c) *Sub-commission* means the State, Division or Zone or Township or Ward or Village-tract Sub-commissions formed by the Commission. The expression also includes Sub-commission formed by the Commission with members of the State or Division Sub-commission to act as Zone Sub-commission;

(d) *Election* means the Multi-Party Democracy General Election;

(e) *Constituency* means the Hluttaw Constituency/

(f) *Hluttaw representative* means a person who has been elected to the Hluttaw;

(g) *Member of religious order* means the following individuals:-

(i) in the case of Buddhists, monks, novices, religious laymen, nuns, hermits and hermitesses serving the Buddhist religious order;

Explanation : The expression member of religious order applies to a religious monk or a member of the religious order while he is serving temporarily as such;

(ii) in the case of Christian, persons who have been recognized and ordained or assigned duties by the relevant Churches as an individual who has dedicated himself mainly to serving the Christian religious order, persons included in the group of individuals or organization which of their own volition have submitted to the control of the respective head according to the religion professed as organized by religious discipline or vow;

(iii) in the case of Hindus, Sanvazi, Mahant or Hindu priests;

(h) *Electoral Roll* means the roll of persons entitled to vote within the constitutions prescribed for the Hluttaw Election;

(i) *Convicts* means persons terms of imprisonment

under sentence passed by any court. The expression also includes persons who are serving prison terms by the order of the court and pending appeal against the sentence of imprisonment of the Court concerned.

(j) *Polling Booth Team* means team which is assigned by the Township Sub-commission concerned the duty of taking collective responsibilities in connection with voting at a polling booth within a constituency;

(k) Polling *Booth Officer* means the person who is in charge of the Polling Booth Team;

(l) *Electoral Right* means the right of a person to stand or not to stand as a Hluttaw candidate or to withdraw from being a Hluttaw candidate or to vote or refrain from voting at the election;

(m) *Corrupt Practice* means any practice mentioned in Chapter XIII of this Law.

CHAPTER II

FORMATION OF THE HLUTTAW

3. The Hluttaw shall be formed with the Hluttaw representatives who have been elected in accordance with this Law from the Hluttaw constituencies.

CHAPTER III

SPECIFICATION OF CONSTITUENCIES

4. The constituencies from which Hluttaw representatives are to be elected are as specified in the Appended Schedule. Provided that, prior to the declaration of the date for holding the election, if the Government prescribes certain new areas within a township or an amalgamation of areas within contagious townships as a Township, the Commission may prescribe as appropriate, in order to form at least one constituency in the original township or in the newly-formed

township, although the number of constituencies contained in the Appended Schedule has been exceeded.

5. One representative each shall be elected from one constituency.

CHAPTER IV

PERSONS ENTITLED TO VOTE

6. Persons with the following qualifications are entitled to vote at the election irrespective of sex and religion:-

(a) citizen, associate citizen and naturalized citizen who have completed the age of eighteen years in the day of commencement of election and who do not contravene the provisions of this Law;

(b) persons whose names have been included on the electoral roll of the respective constituency.

7. The following person shall not be entitled to vote at the election:-

(a) members of religious orders;

(b) persons who have been adjudged to be of unsound mind as provided for in the relevant law;

(c) persons serving prison terms, having been convicted under sentence of a court for any offence;

(d) foreigners.

CHAPTER V

PERSONS ENTITLED TO STAND FOR ELECTION

8. Citizens possessing the following qualifications shall be eligible to stand for election irrespective of sex or religion :-

(a) At the time of filing the nomination paper for the purpose of election:-

(i) persons who have completed the age of twenty-one and who are not contrary to the provisions of this Law;

(ii) persons both of whom parents are already citizens or even if both parents have died they would have the right to acquire automatic citizenship under the Union Citizenship Act, 1948 if they were alive or at the time of death of the said both parents they were already citizenships or if one of the parents was a national and the other parent who died before the promulgation of the Burma Citizenship Law, had at the time of death been eligible to apply for naturalization;

(b) persons residing in the Union of Burma;

(c) persons included in the electoral roll;

9. A person having the right to stand for election is eligible to contest the election either individually or as a member of a political party.

10. The following persons shall not be entitled to stand for election:-

(a) members of religious orders;

(b) persons adjudged to be of unsound mind as provided for in the relevant law;

(c) persons serving prison terms, having been convicted under sentence of a court for any offence;

(d) citizens who are not born of parents mentioned in Section 8 Sub-section (a) clause (2);

(e) persons who are under any acknowledgement of allegiance or adherence to a foreign Power, or are subjects or citizens or entitled to the rights and privileges of a subject or a citizen of a foreign Power;

(f) associate citizens, naturalized citizens and foreigners;

(g) members of organization declared as unlawful association according to any existing law;

(h) members of organization in armed revolt against

the State; persons against who there is sufficient grounds of having links with the said organizations or with its members to revolt;

(i) individuals or members of organization who obtain and make use of State fund, building, vehicle, property directly or indirectly;

(1) The expression State fund does not included pension or the official monetary support given by the State for the services rendered for the benefit of the State;

(2) The expression building, vehicle, property, property belonging to the State does not include buildings and apartments belonging to the Housing Department, other buildings and apartments belonging to the State which have been used under any existing law or rented from the State; aircraft, train, steamers and motor-cars belongings to the State which have been hired on charges from the State;

(j) individual or members of organization who obtain and make use of money, property, other assistance from the Government or religious organization or any other organization of a foreign country directly or indirectly;

(k) individuals or members of an organization who, for political purposes, use religion as an excuse, and utter, deliver speeches and make declarations to vote or not to vote and who encourage and incite such acts;

(l) members of defence forces such as Armed Forces, People's Police Force, public servants from various public service bodies and various State-owned economic organizations and other public servants enjoying salary from the State fund.

Note. Retired persons are not included among such public servants.

11. After being elected a *Hluttaw* representative shall have no right to continue to be a Hluttaw representative on infringement of any of the following:-

(a) permanently becoming a member of a religious order;

(b) being adjudged to be of unsound mind as provided for in the relevant law;

(c) being declared to cease to be a citizen in accordance with the respective law;

(d) being declared by the Election Tribunal to be under any allegiance to foreign Power or is a subject or citizen or entitled to the rights and privileges of a subject or citizen of foreign Power;

(e) being permitted by the Commission or by the authority concerned to resign as a *Hluttaw* representative;

(f) being declared by the authorities concerned as a citizen not born of parents provided in Section 8 Sub-section (a) clause (2).

(g) Being decided by a court as a person or a member of an organization provided for in Section 10 Sub-section (g) or (h);

(h) Being decided by the Election Tribunal to be a person or a member of an organization as provided for in Section 10 Sub-section (i), (j) or (k);

(i) Being informed by the respective head of public services body to be a public servant as provided for in Section 10 Sub-section (l).

CHAPTER VI

PREPARATION OF ELECTORAL ROLL

12. (a) The Commission shall prepare the electoral roll for those who are entitled to vote in the election of *Hluttaw* representatives in various constituencies;

(b) In connection with the preparation of the electoral roll the Commission may assign duty to Sub-commission.

13. (a)The Ward and Village-tract Sub-commission shall include in the electoral roll every citizen, associate citizen, naturalized citizen not being contrary to the provision of this Law, and residing in the constituency and having completed the age of eighteen years on the day, commencement of election;

(b) The Ward or Village-tract Sub-commission shall include in the respective electoral roll as prescribed, the Armed Forces personnel; diplomats of the Union of Burma and members of their household, embassy staff and members of their household, State scholars and members of their household, delegates and members of their household who are outside the country; and those who are outside the country with the permission of the Government and members of their household.

14. (a)Every citizen, associate citizen, naturalized citizen whose name is included in the electoral roll of a constituency shall have the right to vote only in that constituency;

(b) a person who has the right to vote and wishes to transfer from the electoral roll of one constituency to the electoral roll of another constituency showing sufficient grounds may apply to the respective Sub-commission as prescribed;

(c) Whoever has the right to vote in any *Hluttaw* constituency shall not be on the electoral roll of any constituency other than that of the constituency concerned at the same time.

15. A list of the names of those persons who have the right to vote shall be declared in advance as prescribed before the election is held in the respective constituency.

16. (a)A person who has the right to vote under this Law, but is not included in the respective electoral roll may apply

to the respective Ward or Village-tract Sub-commission in the manner prescribed to be included in the electoral roll;

(b) If the Ward or Village-tract Sub-commission concerned does not insert the name there is a right of appeal to the Township Sub-commission as prescribed. The decision of that Sub-commission, subject to the provisions of Section 45, shall be final and conclusive.

17. (a)If any person whose name is in the electoral roll objects to the inclusion of any person who is not entitled to vote in the electoral roll of the constituency, objection may be submitted to the Ward or Village-tract Sub-commission in the manner prescribed;

(b) If that name is not cancelled from the electoral roll by the respective Ward or Village-tract Sub-commission, there is a right of appeal to the Township Sub-commission in the manner prescribed. The decision of such Sub-commission shall be final and conclusive, subject to the provisions of Section 45;

(c) A person whose name is already included in the electoral roll shall not be debarred from voting during the pendency of the appeal with the Township Sub-commission. A vote cast under such a right shall be valid.

18. The Commission and the Sub-commission at different levels shall add, in the supplementary electoral roll, the names which are not included, although eligible, or shall cancel the names not eligible from the electoral roll.

CHAPTER VII

NOMINATION OF *HLUTTAW* CANDIDATES AND APPOINTMENT OF ELECTION AGENT

19. A person desirous of contesting the election shall file nomination of candidate with the respective Zone Sub-commission in the manner prescribed.

20. A candidate shall not have the right to file a nomination for the candidature at the same time in more than one constituency.

21. The Zone Sub-commission concerned shall scrutinize in the manner prescribed nomination of a person or the Hluttaw candidature as to whether it is in conformity with the stipulations or not, and whether it should be accepted or not.

22. A person who has filed nomination for Hluttaw candidature has the right to withdraw the nomination as prescribed.

23. At the time of scrutinisation by the Zone-Sub-commission concerned under Section 21:-

(a) the person concerned having filed nomination for candidature shall have the right to produce the evidence as desired by him;

(b) any eligible voter producing sufficient evidence may object is prescribed manner that the person concerned who has filed his nomination for Hluttaw candidature is not eligible or qualified for the election.

24. The Zone Election Sub-commission concerned may, after scrutinisation as prescribed, order one of the following:-

(a) declaring the respective person having filed his nomination for *Hluttaw* candidature as eligible;

(b) declaring the person who has filed the nomination for *Hluttaw* candidature as not eligible.

25. A person dissatisfied with the order made under Section 24 has the right to appeal to the respective State or Division Election Sub-commission in the prescribed manner. The decision of that State or Division Election Sub-commission is final and conclusive subject to the provisions of Section 45.

26. A person having filed nomination for the election shall appoint himself or another person as his election agent in the prescribed manner.

27. (a)Only a person who is qualified to be a candidate under

this Law shall be appointed as an election agent. Such appointment shall be made only with the consent of that person;

(b) In that event of resignation or death or revocation of election agency of the election agent appointed under Sub-section (a), the candidate may again appoint another person as his election agent.

CHAPTER VIII

VOTING

28. The Commission shall :-

(a) hold the election simultaneously on the same day as far as possible;

(b) hold the elections on public holiday as far as possible;

(c) determine and declare the date of election in advance.

29. *Hluttaw* representatives shall be elected by the eligible voters residing in the respective constituencies directly by secret ballot.

30. The Commission may allocate the number of the polling booths for the Wards and Village-tracts on the basis of the number of eligible voters and the conditions of the locality or may delegate such powers to the State or Division Sub-commissions. The Township Sub-commissions may be assigned the duty of locating the venue for the polling booths.

31. Arrangements shall be made for the polling booths to be secure and not detrimental to the secret ballot at the place easily accessible to the public. The venue of the polling booths shall be notified to the public in advance.

32. In order to supervise the polling booths at various *Hluttaw* constituencies, the Township Sub-commission concerned shall:-

(a) appoint suitable persons from amongst the public servants as polling booth officers;

(b) form polling booth teams consisting of public servants, citizens, associate citizens and naturalized citizens who are trusted and respected by the local public, and assign duties as prescribed;

(c) prescribe by Rules the duties and powers of the polling booth teams and polling booth officers.

33. On the day of election, each *Hluttaw* candidate may appoint a polling booth agent and an assistant who are to act on his behalf at the respective polling booth in the constituency where he is contesting. Such agent and assistant shall be eligible voters.

34. (a)If there is only a single candidate in a constituency, election for such constituency shall not be held, and the Commission shall declare such candidate to be the *Hluttaw* representative;

(b) If there are more than one candidate in a constituency, voting shall be arranged with the ballot boxes and ballot papers as prescribed by Rules.

35. On the day of the election, polling booths shall be kept open from 6 a.m. to 4 p.m. However, polling booth may be closed earlier than 4 p.m. if all eligible voters have cast their votes.

36. Eligible voters shall personally draw the ballot papers from the respective polling booths. Such ballot papers shall be cast personally into the respective ballot boxes and not by proxy.

37. Any eligible voter in an election shall :-

(a) have the right only to a single vote;

(b) not have the right to vote more than once.

38. (a)The respective Township Sub-commission shall arrange for the Armed Forces personnel, students, trainers, public servants, detainees and inpatients at the hospitals who are away from their constituencies, to vote with advance ballot paper in the respective constituency;

(b) The Ward or Village tract Sub-commission concerned shall arrange for an eligible voter who is on the electoral roll land who will be away from his constituency on the day of election, to vote with advance ballot paper;

(c) If persons residing in the constituency who are unable to come to the polling booth to vote in person due to any of the following reasons wish to vote, the Ward or Village-tract Sub-commission concerned shall arrange for them to vote with advance ballot papers as prescribed :-

(i) having contracted leprosy;

(ii) being seriously ill;

(iii) being of old age;

(iv) giving birth at home;

(v) being detained in a police custody or in prison;

(vi) taking medical treatment as an in-patient in hospital;

(vii) public servants, Armed Forces personnel and members of the Public Force who are on duty, away from the area in which they have their electoral roll;

(d) Rules shall be prescribed as regards the manner of voting by persons having difficulties in making entries on the advance ballot paper or ballot paper on their own.

39. (a)The Commission shall make arrangements to enable the diplomats and members of their household of the Union of Burma, embassy staff and members of their household, State scholars and members of their household, delegates and member sof their household who are outside the country at the time of holding election and those who are outside the country with the permission of the Government and members of their household at the time of holding election to vote in advance for their respective constituency;

(b) The Ministry of Foreign Affairs of the Government of the Union of Burma shall take the responsibility of communicating with those who are outside the country and who have the right to vote so as to enable them to vote in advance.

CHAPTER IX

COUNTING OF VOTES AND DECLARING CONFIRMATION

40. (a)The Ward or Village-tract Sub-commission shall hand over the advance ballot papers already cast under Section 38, Sub-section (b) and (c) and the list of those who have voted with advance ballot papers in connection with the various polling booths to the respective polling booth officer before the opening of the polling booths on election day;

(b) Immediately after the ballot papers are cast in each constituency, the polling booth officer or a member of the polling booth team assigned by him shall count the votes in the polling booth in the presence of the members of the polling booth team, the public and the polling booth agents. In counting, valid votes and invalid votes are to be differentiated in accordance with the Schedule List of votes shall be sent to the Township Sub-commission. A copy shall be sent to the Ward or Village-tract Sub-commission;

(c) The Ward or Village-tract Election Sub-commission shall supervise the dispatch of the voting list schedules compiled by polling booths officers in its area in prescribed manner to the Township Election Sub-commission as fast as possible to reach it in time;

(d) The Township Election Sub-commission shall, before 4 p.m. on election day, count all advance ballot papers already cast under Section 38 Sub-section (a) and Section Sub-section (a) in the presence of Hluttaw candidates or election agents and the public and shall combine the voting-list schedule for each Hluttaw constituency in the manner prescribed.

41.(a) Should there be more than one candidate in a constituency, the Township Sub-commission shall announce the number of votes each candidate has received. To enable the Commission to declare the candidate with the highest number of votes to be the elected candidate and to enable the election to be held again in case of a tie of votes, the Township Sub-commission shall submit it to the Zone Sub-commission as soon as possible.

(b) On receiving the report of the Township Sub-commission under Sub-section (a), the Zone Sub-commission shall submit it to the Commission together with remarks and opinion. A copy shall be forwarded to the State or Division Sub-commission;

(c) The Commission shall declare the elected candidate as per the lists submitted by the Zone Sub-commission under Sub-section (b). On submission under Sub-section (a) that there is a tie of votes the Zone Sub-commission shall proceed in accordance with the Rules as instructed by the Commission in connection with holding a new election. If an election is to be held afresh on account of the tie of highest votes, only the candidates whose votes are so equal are eligible to stand for election.

CHAPTER X

POWERS OF COMMISSION

42. The Commission

(a) may postpone the election in certain constituencies in which elections could not be held due to natural disasters till such a time as the disaster is over;

(b) may postpone the election in a constituency where preparation of list of voters or balloting is not possible due to lack of security;

(c) may decide to hold election in some areas within the constituency where the situation permits and may decide not to hold election in some areas within the constituency where the situation does not permit. It may also decide to transfer the polling booth to secure places. However, if 51 per cent of voters have cast votes, a valid election shall be deemed to have been held. Should it be the opinion of the Commission that fire and fair election cannot be held, it may postpone the decision in the entire constituency.

43. The Commission may delegate to Sub-commission the powers to postpone election and to transfer the venue or polling booths to secure places.

44. In a constituency where there is only a single candidate if, before the election is held, that candidate dies or is found that he is not entitled to stand for election, the election for that constituency shall start afresh from the stage of the nomination of the candidate.

45. In election matters the Commission has the power to call for the proceedings and documents *suo moto* of each sub-commission as it deems fit and study and decide accordingly. This decision shall be final and conclusive.

46. The Commission may take measures as necessary for the successful holding of free and fair election.

CHAPTER XI

ELECTION AGENTS AND EXPENSES

47. The election agent shall keep accounts of the expenses of the elections concerned systematically as prescribed. He shall submit the account of the expenses as prescribed to the Zone Sub-commission concerned.

48. The maximum scale of expenses and the number of persons employed for payment for the *Hluttaw* candidate shall be as prescribed by Rule.

CHAPTER XII

ELECTION OFFENCES AND PENALTIES

49. (a)A person's right to stand for election and to vote shall not be violated by force, threat, undue influence, cheating, taking or giving of bribes to any person;

(b) Whoever sits in contravention of Sub-section (a) shall be punishable with imprisonment for a term which may extend to one year or with fine which may extend to two thousand kyats or with both.

50. No person shall contravene any of the following prohibitions. Whoever contravenes shall be punishable with imprisonment for a term which may extend to one year or with fine which may extend to two thousand kyats or with both :-

(a) obtaining the electoral right by unlawful means or after obtaining such right committing, giving and taking bribes by way of money, goods, foodstuff, position or service transfer;

(b) threatening a Hluttaw candidate or a voter to prevent him from freely exercising his electoral right;

(c) making speeches, making declarations and instigating to vote or not to vote on grounds of race and religion or by abetment of such;

(d) instigating, making speeches at meeting, writing, distributing, using posters to disrupt the voting.

51. No person shall contravene or cause another to contravene any of the following prohibitions. Whoever contravenes or abet such contravention, if convicted, shall be punishable with imprisonment for a term which may extend to six months or with the fine which may extend to one thousand *kyats* or with both:-

(a) dishonestly making illegible or destroying list, notices and documents published by the Commissions and Sub-commissions;

(b) dishonestly destroying list of votes or ballot papers or making the envelope or pouch sent by post containing such illegible;

(c) giving the ballot paper to some other person in an improper manner;

(d) inserting into the ballot box an article other than a ballot paper;

(e) opening or destroying without authorization the ballot box or ballot paper which is in use;

(f) voting in an election at more than one constituency;

(g) voting more than once in an election of one constituency;

(h) impersonating another person to obtain and cast a ballot paper;

(i) entering the polling booth without permission while the election is in progress;

(j) putting one counterfeit ballot paper or more into the ballot box.

52. Whoever is found guilty of disturbing any eligible voter so as to prevent him from casting the vote on the election day or whoever is found guilty of abetting such act shall be punishable with imprisonment for a term which may extend to six months or with fine which may extend to one thousand *kyats* or with both.

53. (a)No person shall commit any of the following acts inside the polling booth or within the radius of one hundred yards from the polling booth on the election day:-

(i) canvassing;

(ii) soliciting a voter to vote for a certain candidate for the Hluttaw;

(iii) persuading a voter not to vote for a certain Pyithu Hluttaw candidate or persuading a voter to vote or not to vote at an election;

Explanation : This section does not apply to sticking or

fixing campaign poster etc. regarding the election in any places other than the polling booth.

(b) Whoever is found guilty of contravening any provisions of Sub-sections (a) shall be punishable with imprisonment for a term which may extend to six months or with the which may extend to one thousand *kyats* or with both.

54. Any person discharging duties in connection with the election including different levels of Sub-commission shall abide by the following provisions. Whoever is guilty of contravening any provision shall be punishable with imprisonment for a term which may extend to six months or with fine which may extend to one thousand *kyats* or with both:-

(a) to accurately prepare and maintain the lists, schedules and records regarding elections;

(b) to help and safeguarding secret voting;

(c) all matters, with the exception of those permitted to be published by the Commission, shall be kept confidential;

(d) acting rightfully, not canvassing votes and not showing partially, in favour of any Hluttaw candidate, during the election.

55. (a)No person shall convene a public meeting within a constituency on the election day other than for a religious purpose and no person shall attend such a meeting;

(b) Any person found guilty of contravening the prohibitions mentioned in Sub-section (a) shall be punishable with imprisonment for a term which may extend to six months or with fine which may extend to one thousand kyats or with both.

56. (a)No person shall cause disturbance to the voters or the polling booth officer and members of the polling booth team on duty by using loud speakers or by such equipment which amplify the human voice or by other undisciplined acts, inside the polling booth or within five hundred yards radius from the polling booth;

(b) Any person found guilty of contravening the prohibitions mentioned in Sub-section (a) shall be punishable with imprisonment for a term which may extend to six months or with fine which may extend to one thousand kyats or with both.

57. (a)Whoever acts in an improper manner inside the polling booth, during polling hours or who disobeys the lawful orders of the polling booth officer shall be evicted from the polling booth by a member of the People's Police Force on duty, or by any security personnel on duty under the order by the polling booth office or by the member of the polling booth team authorized by the polling booth officer;

(b) Any person who is evicted from the polling booth and who returns to the polling booth without the permission of the polling booth officer, and if found guilty, shall be punishable with imprisonment for a term which may extend to six months or with fine which may extend to one thousand kyats or with both.

58. Any person who commits an offence punishable under Section 54 shall be prosecuted with the permission of the Commission, or with the permission of the Government when the Commission is dissolved or with the permission of the person who is appointed for this purpose by the Government.

59. Whoever dishonestly and fraudulently lodges any criminal proceedings against any person regarding offences relating to elections, if found guilty, shall be punishable with imprisonment for a term which may extend to six months or with fine which may extend to one thousand kyats or with both.

60. If the polling booth officer finds any person who commits or is committing any officers under this Law, he may order a member of the People's Police Force on duty, or any security personnel on duty to arrest that person.

61. Regarding offences relating to election, any voter of the constituency concerned, or any Hluttaw candidate, or any elected member of the *Hluttaw* or a member of a Sub-

commission concerned or any member of the polling booth team having sufficient proof may field a complaint in the Township Court before the election or during the election or within fifteen days from the election.

CHAPTER XIII

CORRUPT PRACTICES

62. The following practices are deemed to be corrupt practices:

(a) *Hluttaw* candidate either by himself or by his election agent or any person with the approval of one of them commits the following offences :-

(i) giving or taking bribes;

(ii) interfering with the electoral right;

(iii) impersonation;

(iv) making verbal or written false declaration;

(v) signing false statement;

(b) casting of vote more than once in one constituency or in more than one constituency when elections are simultaneously held, which will be to the advantage of a candidate he favours;

(c) a *Hluttaw* candidate or his election agent has incurred contrary to the stipulation more than the authorized expenditure or consented to incur more than authorized amount during the election;

(d) failure to account for the election expenses on the part of the election agent;

(e) any person who takes away the ballot paper from the polling booth, with the consent of the *Hluttaw* candidate or his election agent;

(f) with the permission or consent of the *Hluttaw* candidate or his election agent committing the following :-

(i) whoever accepts bribe or agrees to accept bribe, with the intention of participating or not as a candidate in the *Hluttaw* election or resigning from the membership of Hluttaw, in return;

(ii) whoever accepts bribe for himself or for other person or agrees to accept such bribe, with the intention of inducing or trying to induce a voter to vote for a particular candidate or to abstain from voting;

(g) submission of false accounts of the election expenses or declaring the false accounts to be true or failure to submit the election expenses as prescribed;

(h) any person who is not a *Hluttaw* candidate or not an election agent of that *Hluttaw* candidate, without the permission of such candidate, convenes a meeting, or distributes papers and documents or incurs or consents to incur expenses in any other way, with a view to making him win election as a *Hluttaw* candidate or abets or such purpose;

(i) publishing an distributing announcements, posters and bills without mentioning names and addresses of printers and publishes for the benefit of the *Hluttaw* candidate, whom he favours;

(j) any *Hluttaw* candidate, or his election agent or any person with the consent of one of them, obtain help from a public servant, or abets or attempts in obtaining help from such public servant so that a Hluttaw candidate may be elected;

(k) using of religious emblem in the election campaign, or making use of nationality or religion or the purpose of inducing to vote or not to vote with a view to getting a *Hluttaw* candidate elected;

(l) resorting to violence, making and writing false accusation and creating public disorder to a person or a party, with a view to getting a *Hluttaw* candidate elected.

CHAPTER XIV

DECISIONS ON OBJECTIONS CONCERNING ELECTIONS

63. If objection is desired to be made as regards being elected, it shall be made in forms prescribed in accordance with the provision in this Chapter.

64. (a)Objections to being elected a *Pyithu Hluttaw* representative may be made as prescribed by any Hluttaw candidate or any voter for reasons of his own other than matters which have been decided by the Commission under Section 45 to such person as may be appointed by the Government for this purpose;

(b) The applicant may file objection against an elected *Hluttaw* member. If he intends to seek a declaration that only he has obtained the majority votes and should he be elected, he is to base his objections on one of the following:-

(i) the reason that only the applicant did in fact obtain the maximum valid votes;

(ii) the reason that if votes obtained by the elected *Hluttaw* representative did not include votes obtained by corrupt practices, the applicant could obtain the maximum valid votes.

65. . (a)The Government shall form three-member Election Tribunals each consisting of legal experts and suitable .... (illegible) for enquiry into objections regarding the election;

(b) Remuneration for members of the Election Tribunals shall be as prescribed by the Government;

(c) Expenses incurred by the Election Tribunals shall be borne by the Supreme Court;

(d) The accommodation for the Election Tribunals and staff required for performance of their function shall be provided by the Supreme Court;

(e) All matters concerning election objections shall be taken up by the Election Tribunals;

(f) In respect of the election held for one constituency, if more than one objection are raised, the person appointed by the Government shall assign the objections to only one Election Tribunal. Such tribunal may inquire into the objections separately or collectively;

(g) If an appointed member of Election Tribunal cannot carry out his duties as a member of the tribunal or is unable to carry them out during an inquiry, the Government shall appoint a substitute member. The reconstituted Election Tribunal may make fresh inquiry of the pending objections, if it so desires.

66. While the objections in connection with elections are being hear, the tribunal, if necessary, may invite the Attorney-General and seek legal advice. If the Attorney-General is unable to come to the tribunal, he may depute a suitable person not below the rank of a Law Officer Grade I from the Attorney-General's Office to act on his behalf.

67. The Election Tribunal may decide the election of the *Hluttaw* representative to be void if it finds that the elected *Hluttaw* representative has infringed any of the following:-

(a) that it is apparent the elected *Hluttaw* representative received the majority votes by corrupt practice; or by inducement or the success or failure of the election is due to corrupt practice;

(b) that is apparent corrupt practice has been committed for the benefit of the elected Hluttaw representative;

(c) that is apparent the election is not free and fair,

(d) that it is apparent the election is not free and fair because of bribery and interference with the exercise of electoral rights, or that the success in the election is due to such acts;

(e) that it is apparent he is an individual or a member of any association in Section 10, Sub-section (e), (i), (j) or (k).

68. After objec5tions have been exercised, the Election Tribunal shall report to the Government where the question arises as to whether or not the person elected as the *Hluttaw* representative or the person who objects and states that he himself should be declared elected, should be elected.

70. All members of the Election Tribunal shall sign and submit the report of their decision to the Government as early as possible. The Government shall issue order as reported and shall publish that report in the Burma Gazette. The order of the Government shall be final and conclusive.

71. If there is any difference of opinion among members of the Election Tribunal on the report or on any other matter concerning objections in connection with the election, the opinion of the majority shall prevail.

72. The Election Tribunal shall have all the powers of the Court in which power under the Code of Civil Procedure are vested. It may on its own motion summon and examine any person who is in a position to give important material evidence.

73. Not contrary to the provisions of this Law, the provisions of the Evidence Act shall be deemed to apply in all respects to all matters under inquiry,

74. Any document not duly stamped or not duly registered as prescribed shall not be inadmissible as evidence.

75. In an inquiry the witness shall answer the questions in respect of the relevant issues. However,

- (a) the voter shall not be questioned to reveal for whom he has voted;
- (b) no witness who is compelled to answer a question shall be arrested or prosecuted or his statement be used as evidence in any criminal proceedings except for perjury.

76. The person himself or his representative or a lawyer acting on his behalf may appear before the Election Tribunal. Nevertheless, should the Election Tribunal direct him to appear to person, he shall do so accordingly.

CHAPTER XV
MISCELLANEOUS

77. The Commission and Sub-commission may obtain necessary assistance from Government organizations or other organizations and individuals.

78. Whoever carries out the duties of a member of the commission or Sub-commission, or carries out the said duties of the Election in any capacity shall be deemed to be carrying out the duties of the State.

79. No Court has jurisdiction on the acts and decisions made by the Commission and Sub-commissions at various levels and the Election Tribunals, other than by the provisions of this Law.

80. No civil or criminal action shall be taken against the Commission and members of the Commission, Sub-commissions at various levels and their members, Election Tribunals, members of the Election Tribunals, members of the polling booth teams including polling booth officers who discharge their duties according to law in good faith and to the best of their ability.

81. The Commission is empowered to make rules, procedures, orders and directives for the successful implementation of the provisions of this Law.

82. The following Laws and Rules are repeated by this Law:-

(a) *Pyithu Hluttaw* and People's Councils at Different Levels Election Law (*Pyithu Hluttaw* Law no. 8 of 1976).

(b) *Pyithu Hluttaw* and People's Councils at Different Levels Elections Rules (*Pyithu Hluttaw* Rules No.7 of 1976).

Sd/- Saw Maung

General, Chairman, The State Law and Order Restoration Council.

Select Bibliography

PRIMARY SOURCES

DOCUMENTS & REPORTS

British Burma Gazetteer (Rangoon : Government Printing Press, 1880).

BSPP, *The System of Correlation of Man and His Environment : The Philosophy of the Burma Socialist Programme Party* (Rangoon, January, 1963).

Burma Communist Party's Conspiracy to Take Over State Power (Rangoon : Ministry of Information, 1989).

Director of Information, *Is trust vindicated ? A Chronicle of a Trust, Striving and Triumph. Being an Account of the Accomplishments of the Government of the Union of Burma, November 1, 1958 – February 1, 1960* (Rangoon, 1960).

Frontier Areas Committee of Enquiry, *Report Presented to Her Majesty's Government in the United Kingdom and the Government of Burma* (Rangoon, 1947).

Ministry of External Affairs,Government of India, *Annual Report 1987-88*(New Delhi).

Ministry of External Affairs, Government of India,*Annual Report 1988-89*(New Delhi).

Ministry of External Affairs, Government of India,*Annual Report 1989-90*(New Delhi).

Ministry of ExternalAffairs, Government of India, *Annual Report 1990-91* (New Delhi).

Ministry of External Affairs, Government of India, *Annual Report 1991-92* (New Delhi).

Ministry of External Affairs,Government of India, *Annual Report1992-93* (New Delhi).

Ministry of External Affairs,Government of India, *Annual Report1993-94* (New Delhi).

Ministry of External Affairs,Government of India, *Annual Report1994-95* (New Delhi).

Ministry of External Affairs, Governmentof India, *Annual Report 1995-96* (New Delhi).

Ministry of External Affairs,Government of India, *Annual Report1996-97* (New Delhi).

Ministry of External Affairs,Government of India, *Annual Report 1997-98* (New Delhi).

National League for Democracy: Statements, Letters and CRPP Notifications 1999 (New Delhi: Burma Info., 1999).

National League for Democracy: Statements, Speeches and Letters, 1998 (New Delhi: Burma Info., 1998).

NCUB, Political Progress Report (Chiangmai: NCUB Information Committee, Nov./Dec. 1995).

United States, *Department of State Bulletin* (Washington, May 1989).

United States, *Department of State release* (Washington, March 1995).

Weller, Mark (ed.), *Democracy and Politics in Burma : A Collection of Documents* (Manerplaw : NCGUB, 1993).

SECONDARY SOURCES

YEAR BOOKS & ENCYCLOPAEDIAS

Encyclopaedia Britannica (Chicago : Encyclopaedia Britannia Inc., 1980), 18th Edition.

Far East and Australasia, 1996 (London : Europa Publications, 1995), 28th Edition.

Far East and Australasia, 2000 (London : Europa Publications, 1999), 32nd Edition.

FEER, *Asia 1988 Year Book* (Hong Kong, 1987)

FEER, *Asia 1989 Year Book* (Hong Kong, 1988)

FEER, *Asia 1990 Year Book* (Hong Kong, 1989)

FEER, *Asia 1991 Year Book* (Hong Kong, 1990)

FEER, *Asia 1992 Year Book* (Hong Kong, 1991)

FEER, *Asia 1993 Year Book* (Hong Kong, 1992)

FEER, *Asia 1994 Year Book* (Hong Kong, 1993)

FEER, *Asia 1995 Year Book* (Hong Kong, 1994)

FEER, *Asia 1996 Year Book* (Hong Kong, 1995)

FEER, *Asia 1997 Year Book* (Hong Kong, 1996)

FEER, *Asia 1998 Year Book* (Hong Kong, 1997)

FEER, *Asia 1999 Year Book* (Hong Kong, 1998)

FEER, *Asia 2000 Year Book* (Hong Kong, 1999)

Keesing's Record of World Events, vol.34, October 1988.

National Coalition Government of the Union of Burma, *Human Rights Yearbook 1998-99: Burma* (Nonthaburi, Thailand, 1999).

SIPRI Yearbook, 1995: Armament, Disarmament and International Security (NY: Oxford University Press, 1995).

The Statesman Yearbook 1995-96 (London : Macmillan Press Ltd., 1995).

BOOKS

ABSDF, *Burma and the Role of Women* (Bangkok: Documentation and Research Centre-ABSDF, 1997).

ABSDF, *Tortured Voices: Personal Accounts of Burma's Interrogation Centres* (Bangkok: All Burma Students' Democratic Front, July 1998).

ALTSEAN Burma, *Ten Years On: A Parliament Denied* (Bangkok : ALTSEAN, 1999).

ALTSEAN, Burma Special Report : The Committee for Restoration of People's Parliament *(Bangkok : ALTSEAN Burma , September 1999).*

Amnesty International, Myanmar : Renewed Repression *(London: Amnesty International Publications, July 1996).*

Amnesty International, *Myanmar* (London: Amnesty International Publications, November 1990).

Amnesty International, *Myanmar, No Law at all: Human Rights Violations under Military Rule* (London: Amnesty International Publications, October 1992).

Amnesty International, *Myanmar: Intimidation and Imprisonment, Sept.-Dec. 1996* (London : Amnesty International Publications, February 1997).

Amnesty International, *Union Of Myanmar : Arrest and Trial of Political Prisoners January to July 1991* (London: Amnesty International Publications, 1991).

Aung San Suu Kyi and Clements, Alan, *The Voice of Hope* (Harmondsworth: Penguin, 1997).

Aung San Suu Kyi, *Aung San of Burma* (Delhi: Rupa and Co., 1992).

Aung San Suu Kyi, *Letters from Burma* (New Delhi: Irrawadi Publications, 1997).

Aye Saung, *Burma in the Back Row* (Hong Kong: Asia 2000 Ltd., 1989).

Bachoe, Ralph and Stothard, Debbie, *From Consensus to Controversy : ASEAN's Relationship with Burma's SLORC* (Bangkok : ALTSEAN-Burma, July 1997).

Ball, Desmond, *Burma's Military Secrets : Signal Intelligence (SIGINT) from 1941 to Cyber Warfare* (Bangkok : White Lotus Press, 1998).

Bixler, Norma, *Burma : A Profile* (New York, Washington and London : Praeger, 1971).

Boucaud, Andre and Lois, *Burma's Golden Triangle: On the*

Trial of the Opium Worlords (Bangkok: Asia Books Co. Ltd., 1992).

Brandon , John (ed.), *Burma / Myanmar in the Twenty First Century : Dynamic of Continuity and Change* (Bangkok: Thai Studies Section, Thammasat University, 1997).

Bray, John, *Burma : The Politics of Constructive Engagement* (London : Royal Institute of International Affairs, 1995).

Brig. Khin Nyunt, *BCP's Conspiracy to Take over State Power* (Rangoon, 1989).

Bunge, Frederica M. (ed.), *Burma: A Country Study* (Washington D.C., American University, 1983)

Burma Action Group, *Burma: The Alternative Guide* (London: BAG, 1996).

Burma Ethnic Research Group, *Conflict and Displacement in Karenni : The Need for Considered Responses* (Chiangmai : Burma Ethnic Research Group, May 2000).

Burma Lawyers' Council, *Legal Issues on Burma Journal* (Bangkok : Burma Lawyers' Council , October 1997).

Burma Project, *Burma: Country in Crisis* (New York, 1998).

Butwell, Richard, *U Nu of Burma* (Stanford: Stanford University Press, 1969).

Cady, John F., *The United States and Burma* (Cambridge, Mass.: Harvard University Press, 1976).

Carey, Peter (ed.), *Burma : The Challenge of Change in a Divided Society* (London: Macmillan Press Ltd., 1997).

Chakravati, N.R., *The Indian Minority in Burma* (Oxford University Press, 1971).

Clements, Alan and Kean, Leslie, *Burma's Revolution of the Spirit : The Struggle for Democratic Freedom and Dignity* (New York : Aperture Foundation, 1994).

Clements, Alan, *Burma: The Next Killing Fields* (Berkeley: Odonian Press, 1992).

Donkers, Jan and Nijhuis, Minka (eds.), *Burma: Behind the Mask* (Amsterdam: Burma Centrum Nederland, 1996).

Donnison, F.S.V., *Burma* (New York: Praeger, 1970).

Dr. Maung Maung, *The 1988 Uprising in Burma* (New Haven: Yale University – Southeast Asian Studies, 1999).

Earth Right International and Southeast Asian Information Network, *Total Denial: A Report on the Yadana Pipeline Project in Burma* (Bangkok: ERI and SAIN, 1996).

Falla, Jonathan, *True Love and Bartholomew: Rebels in the Burmese Border* (Cambridge: Cambridge University Press, 1991).

Ghosh, Amitav, *Dancing in Cambodia, At Large in Burma* (Delhi: Ravi Dayal Publisher, 1998).

Ghosh, Anjali, *Burma: A Case of Aborted Development* (Calcutta: Papyrus, 1989).

Ghosh, Lipi, *Burma: Myth of French Intrigue* (Calcutta: Maya Udyog, 1994).

Gravers, Mikael, *Nationalism as Political Paranoia in Burma: An Essay on the Historical Practice of Power* (Copenhagen: Nordic Institute of Asian Studies, 1993).

Hall, D.G.E., *A History of South East Asia* (London: Macmillan, 1968).

Hippler, Jochen, *The Democratisation of Disempowerment: The Problem of Democracy in the Third World* (Amsterdam: Pluto Press and Transnational Institute, 1998).

Images Asia, Karen Human Rights Group and the Open Society Institute-Burma Project, *All Quiet on the Western Front? The Situation in Chin State and Sagaing Division, Burma* (Chiangmai: Images Asia, Feb. 1998).

Images Asia, *No Childhood At All: Child Soldier in Burma* (Chiangmai: Images Asia, 1997).

Institute for Asian Democracy, *Towards Democracy in Burma* (Washington: Institute of Asian Democracy, 1992).

Khin Maung Nyunt, *Foreign Loans and Aid in the Economic Development of Burma – 1974/75 to 1985/86* (Bangkok:

Institute of Asian Studies Chulalongkorn University, 1990).

Kin Oung, *Who Killed Aung San?* (Bangkok and Cheney : White Lotus, 1996), 2nd Edition.

Lawyers' Committee for Human Rights, *Summary Injustice: Military Tribunals in Burma* (New York, 1991).

Lehman , F.K. (ed.), *Military Rule in Burma Since 1962* (Singapore : Maruzen Asia, 1981).

Lintner, Bertil, *Burma in Revolt: Opium and Insurgency Since 1948* (Bangkok : White Lotus, 1994).

Lintner, Bertil, *Land of Jade: A Journey Through Insurgent Burma* (Edinburgh and Bangkok : Kiscadale and White Lotus, 1990).

Lintner, Bertil, *Outrage : Burma's Struggle for Democracy* (Bangkok:White Lotus, 1990), 2nd Edition.

Lissak, Moshe, *Military Role in Modernization: Civil Military Relation in Thailand and Burma* (California and London : Sage Publications, 1976).

Macdonald, Martin, *Kawthoolei Dreams, Malaria Nights: Burma's Civil War* (Bangkok: White Lotus Press, 1999).

Maung Maung Gyi, *Burmese Political Values : The Socio – Political Roots of Authoritarianism* (New York : Praeger, !983).

Maung Maung, *Burma and General Ne Win* (Bombay: Asia Publishing House, 1969).

McCloud, Donald G., *Southeast Asia : Tradition and Modernity in the Contemporary World* (Colorado : Westview Press, 1995).

Minoru Kiryu (ed), *Industrial Development and Reforms in Myanmar: ASEAN and Japanese Perspectives* (Bangkok: White Lotus Press, 1999).

Mirante, Edith T., *Burmese Looking Glass: A Human Rights Adventure and A Jungle Revolution* (New York : Grover Press, 1993).

O'Brien, Harriet, *Forgotten Land: A Rediscovery of Burma* (London: Michael Joseph, 1991).

Pedersen, Morten B., Rudland, Emily and May, Ronald J. (eds), *Burma Myanmar: Strong Regime Weak State* (Adelaide: Crawford House Publishing, 2000).

Pye, Lucian W., *Politics, Personality and Nation Building: Burma's Search for Identity* (New Haven and London: Yale University Press, 1969).

Sardesai, D.R., *Southeast Asia: Past and Present* (New Delhi: Vikas Publishing House, 1983).

Sharan, P., *Government and Politics in Burma* (Delhi: Metropolitan Books Co., 1983).

Sharp, Gene, *From Dictatorship to Democracy: A Conceptual Framework for Liberation* (Committee for the Restoration of Democracy in Burma, 1994).

Silverstein, Josef, *Burma: Military Rule and Politics of Stagnation* (Ithaca, New York : Cornell University Press, 1997).

Silverstein, Josef (ed.), *Independent Burma at Forty Years: An Assessment* (Ithaca: Cornell University Southeast Asia program, 1989).

Silverstein, Josef (ed), *The Political Legacy of Aung San* (Ithaca: Southeast Asia Program, Cornell University, 1993).

Singer, Noel F. and Strachan, Paul, *Old Rangoon: City of the Shwedagon* (Scotland: Kiscadle, 1995).

Smith, Martin, *Burma: Insurgency and Politics of Ethnicity* (London: Zed, 1991).

Steinberg, David I., *Burma's Road Towards Development: Growth and Ideology Under Military Rule* (Boulder: West View Press, 1981).

Steinberg, David, I., *Crisis in Burma: Stasis and Change in a Political Economy in Turmoil* (Bangkok: Institute of Security and International Studies, Chulalongkorn University, 1989).

Taylor, Robert H., *The State in Burma* (London: C Hurst & Company, 1987).

Trager, Frank N., *Burma – From Kingdom to Republic: A Historical and Political Analysis* (New York: Praeger, 1966).

Trevor Ling (ed), *Buddhist trends in Southeast Asia* (Singapore: ISES, 1993).

Tucker, Shelby, *Among Insurgents: Walking through Burma* (Bangkok: White Lotus Press, 2000).

ARTICLES

Ahmed, Abu Taher Salahuddin, " Myanmar : Road to Democracy or East Asian Model?", *Bangladesh Institute of International and Strategic Studies Journal* (Dhaka), vol.17, no.1, 1966, pp.122-143.

Alamgir, Jalal, "Against the Current: The Survival of Authoritarianism in Burma", *Pacific Affairs* (Vancouver), vol.70, 1997, pp.333-350.

Badgley, John, "The Burmese Way to Capitalism", *Southeast Asian Affairs* (Singapore), 1990, pp.229-254.

Bert, Wayne, "Chinese Policy Towards Democratization Movements: Burma and Philippines", *Asian Survey* (Berkeley), vol.30, no.11, November 1990, pp.1066-1083.

Bhattacharya, S.S., "Political Crisis in Myanmar", *Strategic Analysis* (New Delhi), vol.12, no.10, January 1991, pp.1129-1146.

Brown, Marc I., and Valencia, Mark J., "Thailand's Resource Diplomacy in Indo-China and Myanmar", *Contemporary Southeast Asia* (Singapore), vol.14, no.4, March 1993, pp.332-351.

Burma Watcher, "Burma in 1988 : There came a whirlwind", *Asian Survey*, vol.29, no.2, February, 1989, pp.174-180.

Burton, Sandra, " Commotion in the Compound", *Time* (New York),10 November 1997.

Butwell, Richard, "The Burmese Way of Change", *Current*

History (Philadelphia), vol.71, no.422, December 1976, pp.205-208, 224.

Callahan, Mary P., "Building an Army: The Early Years of the Tatmadaw", *Burma Debate* (Washington), vol.4, no.3, July/August 1997.

Callahan, Mary P., "Burma in 1995 : Looking Beyond the Release of Aung San Suu Kyi", *Asian Survey*, vol.36, no.2, February 1996, pp.158-164.

Callahan, Mary P., "Junta Dreams or Nightmares ? Observations of Burma's Military Since 1988", *Bulletin of Concerned Asian Scholars* (Oakland, California), vol.31, no.3, 1999, pp.52-58.

Callahan, Mary P., "Myanmar in 1994 : New Dragon or Still Dragging ?", *Asian Survey*, vol.35, no.2, February 1995, pp.201-208.

Choudhury, Nilufar, "Burma's Foreign Policy : Continuity and Change", *Bangladesh Institute of International and Strategic Studies Journal*, vol.7, no.2, April 1986, pp.168-196.

Clark, Allen L., "Myanmar's Present Development and Future Options", *Asian Survey*, vol.39, no.5, Sept./Oct. 1999, pp.772-791.

Demon, David H. and Colbert, Evelyn, "Challenges for the Association of South East Asian Nations (ASEAN)", *Pacific Affairs*, vol. 71, no.4, Winter 1998-99, pp.505-523.

Diller, Janelle M., "Constitutional Reform in a Repressive State : The Case of Burma", *Asian Survey*, vol.33, no.4, April 1993, pp.393-407.

Dr Thaung Htein, "Student Activism in Burma: A Historical Perspective", *Burma Debate*, April/May 1995, pp.4-10.

Fox, Martin Stuart, "Whither Burma?", *World Review*, vol.30, no.4, December 1991, pp.34-35.

Guyot, James F. and Badgley, John, "Myanmar in 1989: Tamadaw V", *Asian Survey*, vol.30, no.2, Feb. 1990, pp.187-195.

Guyot, James F., "Burma in 1996: One Economy, Two Politics", *Asian Survey*, vol.37, no.2, Feb. 1997, pp.188-193.

Guyot, James F., "Burma in 1997: From Empire to ASEAN", *Asian Survey*, vol.38, no.2, Feb. 1998, pp.190-195.

Haseman, John B., "Burma in 1987", *Asian Survey*, vol.28, no.2, Feb. 1988, pp.223-228.

Haseman, John B., "The Destruction of Democracy: The Tragic Case of Burma", *Asian Affairs* (New York), vol.20, no.1, Spring 1993, pp.15-25.

Holmes, Robert A., " Burmese Domestic Policy: The Politics of Burmanization", *Asian Survey*, vol.7, no.3, March 1967, pp. 188-197.

Jayanth, V., " The Struggle for Democracy", *The Hindu* (New Delhi), 24 March 1996.

Jayasurya, S.K., " Technical Change and Revival of the Burmese Rice Industry", *The Development Economics*, vol. 22, no.2, June 1984, pp. 137-153.

Levin , Burton, " Reminiscences and Reflections on 8.8.88", *Burma Debate*, vol.5,no.3, Summer 1998, pp.4-13.

MacDougall, Hugh C., and Wiant, Jan A., " Burma in 1985", *Asian Survey*, vol.26,no.2, Feb.1996.

Malik, J. Mohan, " Sino-Indian Rivalry in Myanmar : Implications for Regional Security", *Contemporary Southeast Asia*, vol.16,no.2, September 1994,pp. 137-155.

Malik, J.Mohan, " Myanmar's Role in Regional Security : Pawn or Pivot?", *Contemporary Southeast Asia*, vol.19,no.1, June 1997,pp. 52-73.

Mathew, Bruce, "Myanmar's Agony : The Struggle for Democracy", *The Round Table* (London), vol.325, pp.37-49.

Mathew, Bruce, "The Present Fortune of Tradition Bound Authoritarianism in Myanmar", *Pacific Affairs*, vol.71, no.1, Spring 1998, pp.7-23.

Mathews, Bruce, " Buddhism under a Military Regime : The

Iron Heel in Burma", *Asian Survey*, vol. 32, no. 4, April 1993, pp.408-423.

Maureen Aung Thwin, "Burmese Days", *Foreign Affairs* (New York), Spring 1989, pp.143-161.

Minoru Kiryu, "Performance and Prospects of the Myanmar Economy", *Southeast Asian Affairs*, 1992, pp.238-253.

Mohan, C.Raja, " Myanmar – Isolation or Engagement", *The Hindu*, 21 December 1996.

Moksha Yitri, "The Crisis in Burma", *Asian Survey*, vol.29, no.6, June 1989.

Mya Maung, "Burma's Economic Performance under Military Rule : An Assessment", *Asian Survey*, vol.37, no.6, June 1997, pp.503-524.

Mya Maung, "Burmese Road to the Past", *Asian Survey*, vol.39, no.2, March/April 1999, pp.265-286.

Mya Maung, "The Burma Road from the Union of Burma to Myanmar", *Asian Survey*, vol.30, no.6, June 1990, pp.602-624.

Naidu, G.V.C., "Burma : A Nation in Turmoil", *Strategic Analysis* (New Delhi), October 1988, pp.795-807.

Naidu, G.V.C., "Burma at crossroads", *Economic and Political Weekly* (New Delhi), 8 October 1988, pp.2099-2102.

Neher, Clark D., "Democratization in Southeast Asia", *Asian Affairs*, vol.18, no.3, Fall of 1991, pp.139-152.

Oishi, Mikio and Furuoka, Fumitaka, "Can Japanese Aid be an Effective Tool of Influence?", *Asian Survey*, vol. 43, no. 6, Nov.-Dec. 2003, pp. 890-907.

Seekins, Donald M., "Burma in 1998 : Little to Celebrate", *Asian Survey,* vol.39, no.1, January/February 1999, pp.12-19.

Seekins, Donald M., "Burma-China Relations : Playing with Fire", *Asian Survey*, vol.37, no.6, June 1997, pp.525-539.

Seekins, Donald M., "Japan's Aid Relation with Military

Regimes in Burma, 1962-1991 : The Kokunaika Process", *Asian Survey*, vol.32, no.3, March 1992, pp.246-262.

Selth, Andrew, "Burma's Military Expansion Program : Plans and Perceptions", *Journal of Contemporary Asia* (Manila), vol.26, no.4, 1996, pp.466-481.

Shakoor, Farzana, "Burma : An Overview", *Pakistan Horizon* (Islamabad), vol.44, no.2, April 1991, pp.55-74.

Siemer, Gunter, "Myanmar 1992 : Heading For Guided Democracy ?" *Southeast Asian Affairs*, 1993, pp.245-266.

Silverstein, Josef, "Burma : A Time for Decision", *Current History*, Dec. 1984, pp.422-425, 32, 44.

Silverstein, Josef, "Burma in 1981 : The Changing of the Guardians Begins", *Asian Survey*, vol.22, no.2, Feb. 1982, pp.180-189.

Silverstein, Josef, "Burma in an International Perspective", *Asian Survey*, vol.32, no.10, October 1992, pp.951-963.

Silverstein, Josef, "Change in Burma", *Current History*, Dec.1995, pp.440-443.

Silverstein, Josef, "The Idea of Freedom in Burma and the Political Thought of Daw Aung San Suu Kyi", *Pacific Affairs*, vol.69, no.2, 1996, pp.211-228.

Steinberg, David I., "Crisis in Burma", *Current History*, April 1989, pp.185-188, 196-198.

Steinberg, David I., "International Rivalries in Burma : The Rise of Economic Competition", *Asian Survey*, vol.30, no.6, June 1990, pp.587-601.

Steinberg, David I., "Myanmar : Regional Relationship and Internal Concerns", *Southeast Asian Affairs*, 1998, pp.179-195.

Steinberg, David I., "Myanmar in 1991 : Military Intransigence", *Southeast Asian Affairs*, 1992, pp.221-237.

Steinberg, David I., "Myanmar in 1992: Plus Ca Change

..........?", *Asian Survey*, vol.33, no.2, Feb. 1993, pp.175-183.

Stifel, Lawrence D., "Burmese Socialism : Economic Problems of the First Decade", *Pacific Affairs*, vol.45, Spring 1972, pp.60-74.

Suryanarayana, P.S., " A Trade-Off for Myanmar", *The Hindu*, 13 December 1998.

Thawnghmung, Ardeth Maung, "Preconditions and Prospects for Democratic Transition in Burma/Myanmar", *Asian Survey*, vol. 43, no. 3, May/June 2003, pp. 443-460.

Taylor, Robert H., "Burma's National Unity Problem and the 1974 Constitution", *Contemporary Southeast Asia*, vol.1, no.3, December 1979, pp.232-247.

Taylor, Robert H., "Change in Burma : Political Demands and Military Power", *Asian Affairs* , vol.22, no.2, June 1991, pp.131-141.

Taylor, Robert H., "Myanmar : New, but Different ?", *Southeast Asian Affairs,* 1995, pp.3-19.

Thayer, Carlyle A., "Southeast Asia : Challenges to Unity and Regime Legitimacy", *Southeast Asian Affairs*,1999, pp.3-19.

Tilman, Robert O., "Burma in 1986", *Asian Survey*, vol.27, no.2, February 1987.

Tin Maung Maung Than and Mya Than, "Myanmar : Economic Growth in the Shadow of Political Constraints", *Southeast Asian Affairs*, 1997, pp.205-230.

Tin Maung Maung Than, "Myanmar's Golden Anniversary : Economic and Political Uncertainty", *Southeast Asian Affairs*, 1999, pp.207-233.

Trager, Frank N. and Scully, William L., "The Third Congress of the Burma Socialist Programme Party : The Need to Create Continuity and Dynamism of Leadership", *Asian Survey*, vol.17, no.9, September 1997, pp.830-838.

Trager, Frank, N., "Burma : 1967 : A Better Ending then

Beginning", *Asian Survey*, vol.8, no.2, February 1968, pp.110-119.

Wiant, John A., "Burma : Loosening up on the Tiger's Tail", *Asian Survey*, vol.13, no.2, Feb. 1973, pp.129-186.

Wingfield, Tom, "Myanmar : Political Stasis and a Precarious Economy", *Southeast Asian Affairs*, 2000, pp.203-238.

PERIODICALS AND WEEKLIES

Asia Week : Hong Kong.

Burma Issues : Bangkok, Thailand.

Burma Links : Ottawa, Canada.

Burma News : London, England.

Burma Prospect : Imphal, India.

Burma Update : Bangkok, Thailand.

Far Eastern Economic Review : Hong Kong.

Fist : New Delhi, India.

Green Wind : Chiangmai, Thailand.

Independence : Chiangmai, Thailand.

Newsweek : New York, United States.

The Arakan Forum : Dhaka, Bangladesh.

The Burma Review : New York, United States.

The Burmese Relief Centre : Chiangmai, Thailand.

The Irrawaddy : Chiangmai, Thailand.

The New Era Journal : Bangkok, Thailand.

The Young Monk Journal : Chiangmai, Thailand.

Times : New York, United States.

UN Newsletter : New Delhi, India.

NEWSPAPERS AND DAILIES

Bangkok Post.

Deccan Herald (Banglore).

Desert News (Utah).

Hindustan Times (New Delhi).

International Herald Tribune (Paris).

New Strait Times (Kuala Lumpur).

New York Times.

The Statesman (Calcutta).

The Asian Age (Calcutta).

The Hindu (New Delhi).

The Indian Express (New Delhi).

The Nation (Bangkok).

The Sun News (California).

The Telegraph (Calcutta).

Times of India (New Delhi).

Washington Post.

Working People's Daily (Yangon).

Index

C

N

O

P